The Demise of
COMMUNIST
EAST EUROPE

The Demise of
COMMUNIST
EAST EUROPE
1989 in Context

ROBIN OKEY
University of Warwick

A member of the Hodder Headline Group
LONDON

Distributed in the United States of America by Oxford University Press Inc., New York

First published in Great Britain in 2004 by
Hodder Arnold, a member of the Hodder Headline Group,
338 Euston Road, London NW1 3BH

http://www.arnoldpublishers.com

Distributed in the United States of America by
Oxford University Press Inc.
198 Madison Avenue, New York, NY10016

British Library Cataloguing in Publication Data
A catalogue record for this book is available from the British Library

Library of Congress Cataloging-in-Publication Data
A catalog record for this book is available from the Library of Congress

ISBN 0 340 74056 6 (hb)
ISBN 0 340 74057 4 (pb)

1 2 3 4 5 6 7 8 9 10

Typeset in 10/12 Sabon by Servis Filmsetting Ltd, Manchester
Printed and bound in Malta.

What do you think about this book? Or any other Arnold title?
Please send your comments to feedback.arnold@hodder.co.uk

Contents

Preface

The events of 1989 in east-central Europe will surely rank with other dramatic turning points of modern history, like those of 1789, 1848 and 1917. As in these, the tumultuousness of the initial mass action spurred participants and observers to list them among those rare assertions of moral clarity in the flux of human life. 'Bliss was it in those days to be alive,' wrote Wordsworth of the storming of the Bastille, and the demise of east European communism evoked similar euphoria. The elapse of little more than a decade has sufficed to show how 1989 resembles previous red-letter years in its ambiguities as well as its drama. Just as the grand narrative of feudal absolutism's overthrow by bourgeois democracy in 1789 breaks up in the hands of modern historians, so in hindsight do ideas of a communist totalitarian model suddenly hitting the buffers in 1989. The communism which collapsed in 1989 was a protean beast bearing the marks already of a long process of dissolution and decay; on the other hand, it has left its mark. It becomes increasingly apparent that the demise of communism was not an event but a process, with roots deep in the past and offshoots reaching into the present. Only when its three aspects are studied together, in their causes, course and consequence, can the nature of the phenomenon be fully grasped. To attempt this is the challenge of this book.

All three phases of communism's demise pose distinctive problems. Was the communist system fundamentally flawed and, if it was, why did it last until 1989 and what specifically caused its collapse? As evidence accumulates of its terminal incoherence by the later 1980s, why did this collapse take so many by surprise? The ease with which communism gave up the ghost over much (not all) of the region raises the question of whether we are dealing with revolutions at all in the conventional sense. Or were these those rare events in human affairs where the chief revolution is one of the spirit? Certainly the way in which participants in the great demonstrations of that autumn came to endorse notions of a liberal utopia which bore little relation to the region's history or, arguably, their own interests requires explanation. Why, in the aftermath, did ex-communist parties return so quickly to power in much of the region? Does their electoral success merely highlight communism's disastrous legacy in reinforcing an authoritarian mindset, or does it also reflect elements of genuine modernization brought about by the communists which benefited mass parties of the left, shorn of their pretensions to absolute power? Placing 1989 in context turns out to involve a judgement on the role of the communist epoch in the long struggle of the region's peoples for ethnic and social emancipation, and integration as equal members in the European comity of nations. It thereby suggests a wider context still, since the starting point of these emancipatory struggles both in the east and the west of the continent had been 1789, with its famous revolutionary triad: liberty, equality, fraternity. The symbolism 1789–1989 may be too glib but there are many aspects of the recent east European experience which prompt speculation about the shifting roles played since the fall of the Bastille by liberalism, socialism and nationalism, the three most powerful ideologies of the modern world.

Not surprisingly, such recent phenomena as east European communism and its demise have been more studied by social scientists than historians. The field of comparative communism was an important branch of political science, opening up debates between the 'totalitarian' and the 'comparative political development' approaches to communist societies which historians can follow with profit. The former school stressed the distinctiveness of these societies, by dint of their 'totalitarian' ideology; the political development school, increasingly influential from the 1960s, saw many parallels between them and other 'modernizing' regimes in Latin America, Africa or Asia. Ironically, as it seems to a historian, the more the study of communist political systems was integrated with wider concepts of political science, in an autonomous discipline unbeholden to history or sociology, the less useful it became as a guide to what was happening. Not only was 1989 not predicted but the discipline responded by generalizing the topic of 'democratization', subsuming east European events into a 'wave' of democratization starting in the Iberian peninsula and Latin America from the mid-1970s. The transition period became a field of study for itself, so that a political scientist could remind colleagues that they should not forget the communist era in seeking to explain the forms transition took.[1] Such narrowing of focus and the pressure to build 'theory' on the shifting sands of rapidly evolving situations have made much of the work of political scientists on the 1990s of less interest to the historian.

Sociologists' concern with issues of social structure has yielded important insights into the nature of communist society. Not only western sociologists but also east European-based observers, both official (Jan Szczepański, Zsuzsa Ferge) and dissident (György Konrád, Iván Szelényi, Sylviu Brucan), asked how far a new kind of society had actually come into being, how it was stratified and whether this meant a move towards the more egalitarian future Marxism posited or to new forms of class domination. Polish and Hungarian sociology in particular has thrown much light on trends in the immediate run-up to and aftermath of 1989 (Jadwiga Staniszkis, Elemér Hankiss). Powerful critiques of communist economic systems, including their ostensibly reformed versions, were developed (Włodimierz Brus, János Kornai), while since 1989 a bevy of international economists have concerned themselves with the problems of transition from command economies to market economies in the region. The ideological impasse into which east European Marxism fell has been dissected by natives in emigration like the Polish philosopher Leszek Kołakowski and the Hungarians Ferenc Fehér and Agnes Heller, but also by writers remaining in the region, swelling into the dissident schools of Poland and Czechoslovakia: Adam Michnik and Václav Havel became the leading figures here.

Historians' contributions have not had a comparable concentration of focus. Alongside general surveys of the region under communism (Richard Crampton, Joseph Rothschild) or of particular communist countries, case studies have been few. Timothy Garton Ash has been the most consistent commentator on events of the 1980s and 1990s from a historian's longer-term perspective. The bulk of many works on 1989 itself and on following crises like the Yugoslav wars have come from journalists or journalists turned historians, Misha Glenny being a distinguished example. In the plethora of material which has appeared from a variety of disciplines, however, there are none which attempt quite the task of the present work, namely to give roughly equal attention to the antecedents, course and aftermath of the fall of communism and to appraise its significance in the modern development of the region. In the immediate wake of eastern Europe's emancipation, the view was often expressed or implied that her peoples had shaken off an unnatural yoke which had been a merely superficial interruption of their national existence. This is surely an oversimplification. If historians are to contribute to the study of so modern a period they must compensate for their lack of social scientific rigour by sensitivity to patterns of continuity and discontinuity over time. The hypothesis behind this book is that communism was a historical force powerful enough to remould east European society to an extent that ruled out its removal by a single, initial crisis. Communism passed through various phases, falling eventually as a result of a cumulative exhaustion of its credibility, a fig tree able to leaf no more. But its legacy has dogged many of its successor regimes and helped prevent until now their integration into the 'normality' of the 'Europe' of their dreams.

Understandably, as a map shows, citizens of Prague, Warsaw or Budapest see themselves as central rather than east Europeans. Since Germany might be considered the classic land of *Mitteleuropa*, however, it is justified historically to use the term east-central Europe for the lands on her eastern borders. If eastern Europe is often used in this book, it is not to negate the self-perception of (east)-central Europeans but as a term which was generalized in the period under discussion and is less cumbersome.

My thanks are due, finally, to my publishers and to my colleagues, Iain Smith and Roger Magraw, for their much appreciated comments on the manuscript.

I

CAUSES

Failure of an experiment

1

A flawed legacy

Visionaries speak of the future, but of necessity draw legitimacy mainly from a view of the past. The revolutionaries of 1989 looked back on 40 years of a failed utopia, yet the communist era they rejected had itself been shaped by men and women who beheld a past they found equally discredited: by centuries of injustice and humiliation followed by the collapse of the independent eastern Europe created in 1918. It was with visions of regeneration that east European communists sought to legitimize regimes for which no majority had voted and in which vast numbers merely acquiesced. The story of communist eastern Europe is the story of the successive erosion of legitimacy and the ultimate withdrawal of acquiescence.

A legacy of lost causes

The historic peripherality of our area, which visionaries sought to overcome, can be traced to its status as hinterland of the classical empires. Ranke, the father of modern European historical study, saw this as a discourse of the Latin and Germanic peoples, implicitly excluding the Slavs, Hungarians and Turks who successively migrated into the wedge of territory between modern Germany and Russia. The flat European plain in the north provided space for the largest of many small and medium-sized nations in the zone, the Poles. South of them the Danube basin, together with its flanking Carpathians and Alps and the lowish, mountain-rimmed plateau of Bohemia-Moravia to the north-west, made a home for Hungarians, Romanians, Slovaks, Czechs and Austro-Germans. To the south in the Balkans lived Albanians, Bulgarians and the peoples of the former Yugoslavia, including Slovenes, Croats and Serbs. Except for the Hungarians (Magyars) and the pre-migration autochthonous Albanians and Romanians, the latter admixed with Roman colonists, all these were Slav peoples, whose languages were closely akin.

Despite Ranke's disregard, Poles, Czechs, Hungarians, Serbs, Croats and Bulgarians all created kingdoms in the Middle Ages. The Turkish invasions from the fourteenth to the sixteenth centuries, however, destroyed all but the first two of these, and only an imperial dynasty, the Austrian Habsburgs, was able to stem the Muslim onslaught. Early modern eastern Europe was a zone of empires, in which economically backward elites, by-passed by the Age of Discovery, ruled over a medley of peoples reduced to peasant status. The long-ramshackle Polish state was the last to fall, to the Russian-led partitions of 1772–95. Most of these peoples lost with their independence their own landlord class and none of them entered the modern era with a significant native bourgeosie. The religious subordination of Christians in the Balkans, non-Catholics in the Habsburg Monarchy and non-Orthodox in the Tsarist empire completed a pattern of multiple layers of subjection which made the majority of the region's population become hewers of wood and drawers of water for alien masters. Some nineteenth-century figures disclose the heritage against which modern eastern Europe has had to fight. Illiteracy stood at 93 per cent in Serbia in 1874 and Slovenes, Slovaks and Ukrainians had not a single secondary school in their mother tongue between them for some time after this. Sofia was a town of just 6000 inhabitants when it became the capital of reborn Bulgaria in 1878.

The beginnings of the attempt at regeneration reach back to the national movements of the nineteenth century, which initially had to concentrate on the very reconstitution of national consciousness and literary languages that could be used to spread enlightenment and patriotic goals. The self-image of modern east European intelligentsias as leaders of the nation goes back to this period. The slow emergence of the masses from torpor, beginning with the abolition of serfdom (Habsburg empire 1848; Russian Poland 1861; Romania 1864), the expansion of primary education and by *c.*1890 the start of cooperative movements in the countryside gave nationalist leaders a following with which to press political claims. In 1914 the reckless plunge of the dominant empires into war provided a platform for the insertion of ideas of national self-determination into international politics. At the Paris peace settlement of 1919 the creation of the so-called Succession States to the fallen realms of Habsburgs and Hohenzollerns, Ottomans and Romanovs seemingly ratified a century of patriotic endeavour.

It is the failure of independent eastern Europe between the wars which more than anything legitimized the communist era in the eyes of its supporters. The peace terms reflected the bankruptcy of the old order rather than the maturity of the new national states. Actually they were not nation states. On grounds of economic and military viability the new states incorporated numerous minorities; moreover, Croats were lumped together with Serbs and Czechs with Slovaks because nationality was glibly assumed to go together with language and national self-determination was still implicitly assumed to require a certain scale. Thus Czechs made up just 50 per cent of Czechoslovakia, Poles and Romanians roughly two-thirds of their titular states and Serbs some 40 per cent of Yugoslavia. Ethnic complexity, as reflected in a multiplicity of ethnic political parties, made it difficult to operate the parliamentary systems of the new states.

Parliamentarism was a key aspect of the liberal democracy independent eastern Europe ostensibly operated, in line with its British and French sponsors at Versailles. Yet the tension between the liberal values of civil rights and the more nationalist overtones of mass democracy, which had only gradually been eased in western Europe, was never overcome in the east. As the old elite liberals of the nineteenth century disappeared, they were replaced by strongly nationalist or populist parties, like the Polish National Democrats, the Czech National Socialists or the Serbian Radicals. These parties of a nationally minded middle class had a plausible programme, of democratic institutions, land reform and industrialization, but they had too narrow a social base to carry it out alone. Whereas in Britain Gladstone's Liberals had been able to win the tenantry of England and even more of the Celtic fringe to their values, the east European bourgeoisie could not hegemonize the peasant majority, which everywhere had its own political parties. Only in Czechoslovakia did a literate and prosperous peasantry share enough interests with urban professionals for the Agrarian Party to form the basis of stable multi-party coalitions, which gave the interwar Czechoslovak state its powerful reputation as the only successful democracy in the region. The reputation can be qualified. Czechoslovak democracy had habits like the appointment of governments of civil servants to tide over awkward crises which would seem unparliamentary in the west, and the coalition system afforded a core of Czech parties permanent ultimate control over the half of the population which was not Czech. But this was a world away from Poland, where disagreements between peasants and landowners over land reform contributed to the instability which led to Piłsudski's *coup d'état* in 1926, or 80 per cent peasant Bulgaria, where the Agrarian Union rode roughshod over the bourgeois parties until its leader was assassinated in a military coup in 1923. National animosities between the two largest parties in Yugoslavia, the Serbian Radicals and the Croatian Peasant Party, spurred King Alexander's proclamation of a royal dictatorship in 1929.

The blows suffered by democracy in 1923, 1926 and 1929 came before the slump crippled the already fragile east European economy. By the 1930s democratically orientated opposition movements did emerge in Poland and Yugoslavia, building on bourgeois–peasant cooperation, but they remained untested. The debilitating experience in power (1928–30) of the Romanian National Peasant Party, which had fused peasantists and bourgeois nationalists, moderates optimism about the potential effectiveness of such combinations. A major problem was the sheer difficulty of solving the peasant problem, due to poor credit and marketing facilities, and inadequate infrastructure and education. Basically, there were too many peasants. Premodern birth rates swelled rural populations far beyond what feebly industrializing societies could absorb, so that hidden unemployment and real deprivation were rife in the countryside. Peasant parties, with their worthy programmes of credit, consumer and producer cooperatives, ultimately served the interests of a minority of better-off peasants. This lent a logic to peasantist–bourgeois cooperation, since part of the solution to rural overpopulation would have come from the bourgeois dream of industrialization. Yet given the poverty of the home market and unlikelihood of breaking into western ones, the prospect of anything more than a few inefficient, state-subsidized plants was minimal.

If liberal democratic and peasantist solutions had flaws, still less could be said for the social democratic option. Eastern Europe's undeveloped industry set limits to the working class that was its natural recruiting ground. The Czech lands and Poland had significant socialist traditions, but Polish socialists represented a working-class enclave substantially more developed than the society as a whole. Elsewhere in the region socialists were content with muted roles in return for modest trades union rights; the irony of non-industrial societies like the Balkans was that peasant revolutionary traditions fed into a communist movement detached from the reformist drift of the few, mainly artisanal-type social democratic organizations. Throughout the region the socialist/communist split was a factor in weakening the impact of the left.

The purpose of these details is to illustrate the barriers in the way of 'progressive' solutions to the region's problems between the wars. Of course, by the later 1930s many were seeking solutions on the right, in the authoritarian royal regimes of Kings Boris and Carol in Bulgaria and Romania, the convergence of post-Piłsudski regime stalwarts and fascist-influenced National Democrats in Poland and of the 'radical right' and the fascist Arrow Cross movement in Hungary. Anti-Semitic legislation was also being pressed in Hungary and Poland. The whole zone, with the exception of pre-Munich Czechoslovakia, was slipping as along a fault-line into the orbit of Nazi Germany with governing groups agreed on the repudiation of the liberal democratic baggage of 1918.

The shock of the Second World War did little to induce a reassessment of these dispiriting trends. Romania, Hungary and Bulgaria experienced the war as Hitler's allies, not forgetting Monsignor Tiso's 'clerico-fascist' Slovakia, which had become an independent one-party state with the extinction of Czechoslovakia in 1939. The traditionalist gentry regime in Hungary could not prevent the murder of more than half Hungary's Jews or its replacement by the Arrow Cross in the last months of the war. King Boris's Bulgaria did somewhat better, resisting pressure to join the war against the Soviet Union and saving its Jews. The puppet government of the

Protectorate of Bohemia-Moravia in the Czech lands attempted a double game of collaboration with the Nazis at home and secret contacts with Edvard Beneš's exiled government in London; but by 1942 it had been reduced to a hapless cipher. Czech opinion seems to have been leaning to repudiation of the Czechoslovak interwar political system which it felt had failed. Indeed, for all the resilience and heroism shown in the face of adversity, some caution is necessary in judging accounts of wartime resistance. The Polish government in exile in London was an uneasy mixture of pro- and anti-Piłsudski elements and its inflexible public posture on Poland's eastern territories where Belorussians and Ukrainians formed the large majority, though arousing sympathy insofar as the man demanding them was Stalin, was based on the historic dominance there of a Polish landlord class feeding values quite at odds with modern democracy; interwar attempts to impose a Polish identity on the region had been met with a mixture of sullenness and insurgency by non-Poles. The Warsaw rising of 1944 was heroic but poorly organized and largely led by traditionalists of the old school. In the case of Yugoslavia the exiled London government was riven by internal polemics over massacres of Serbs by the Nazi-sponsored Croatian ustasha state, only part of internecine strife involving Serbs, Bosnian Muslims and Albanians. It takes a sanguine eye to perceive the germs of a revivified liberal democracy in the traumatized world of eastern Europe in the Second World War, followed by Red Army occupation of most of the region.

The communist vision

Except in the case of Yugoslavia and Albania, communism in postwar eastern Europe was the result of the conquest of the region by the Red Army and the de facto division of Europe which emerged as the wartime allies fell out from 1945. But against the backdrop described above, east European communists saw the Red Army differently: not as an instrument of force but of providential succour, enabling history to fulfil its progressive purpose. In 1945 classical western capitalism seemed to many, and not just Marxists, as discredited as revolutionary socialism after 1989. 'The shortcomings of Europe's prewar liberal democracy contributed greatly to the rise of the prewar dictatorships – first the development of Fascism, then of Nazism,' wrote the Czechoslovak President Beneš in 1946.[1] Young intellectuals were particularly susceptible to the new message. Having thirstily imbibed creed after vapid creed in the heady atmosphere of 1930s Europe, only to be led into a disastrous war, many of them, in the words of the Hungarians Aczel and Meray, had discovered Marxism 'within themselves' long before encountering its literature, drawn by the hope of a rational alternative and finding in it 'an exact and perfect method to explain and change the world'.[2] The young Polish poet Tadeusz Różewicz, briefly a 'fellow-traveller' sympathizer with the Marxist alternative, showed the willingness to embrace new values in the secular humanist twist he gave the Eden story:

> in the garden I see an apple tree
> the apple tree blossoms
> the fruit takes form
> they ripen my father is picking up an apple
> that man who is picking up an apple
> is my father[3]

Here the emphasis is not on the sin, punishment and female frailty of traditional Christianity but on fruitfulness and maturation, and the father figure himself picks up the apple. If non-communists could feel this mood, communists' vehemence about the coming of a new order can be appreciated. In the Polish leader Władysław Gomułka's view of history, while the first Polish republic had perished in the throes of dying feudalism, the second had been born in 1918 at a point where the capitalist system was already beginning to crumble, in a period of developed class struggles and revolutions of social liberation which had now come to fruition.[4] The wartime events from which academic accounts of communist regimes tend to start were thus well past the formative period for such men and were interpreted by them in terms of their ingrained ideology. Thus Gomułka saw the Warsaw rising as an anti-Soviet plot led by men who preferred to 'hand over the heroes of fighting Warsaw to the filthy hands of the Hitlerites' rather than join forces with Polish troops advancing under the Red Army's command.[5] The partisanship in such interpretations may seem extraordinary until one recalls the Labour politician Aneurin Bevan's contemporary dismissal of British Conservatives as vermin.

The dismissal of an 'outdated' past was reinforced by evocations of the new and youthful. In Tito's words to young Yugoslav construction workers in 1946, their labours were 'hammering out new people, people with a high consciousness, people with a new zeal'.[6] For communists their ideas were a compendium of scientific answers to mankind's problems, whose truth would win any mind uncontaminated by class interest: a planned economy utilizing resources for the common good rather than the boom-and-bust capitalist cycle; universal, free medical care so that people's life chances should not depend on others' profit; mass education reoriented from elite dead languages to society's real developmental needs and a network of 'people's universities' for life-time learning; the emancipation of women and youth, and the mobilization of their enthusiasm for national reconstruction; the replacement of unaccountable bureaucracies by elected bodies in all fields of public life; the multiplication of public libraries, parks and playing fields, and of opportunities to appreciate art and theatre and enjoy sponsored annual holidays for the masses who had known nothing but toil. In addition, in a region where most neighbours heartily disliked each other, internationalism was proclaimed, and various forms of (nominal) territorial autonomy or cultural infrastructure were offered to minorities like Hungarians in Romania and Albanians in Yugoslavia. Attractive as this rational vision was to many liberal-minded people across the world, in eastern Europe it was embraced with a zeal that went beyond the rational. The refrain of the New Man, the New Woman and the happy future they would create together bespoke a chiliastic outlook that now that evil had been vanquished, only good would reign. As often happens when relatively backward communities adopt radical ideas – the anarcho-syndicalist farm workers of prewar Spain are another case – conventional religion was replaced by a secular version which retained the religious conviction of infallibility, but without orthodox religion's sense of the frailty of human nature.

As Marxist rationalists, communists would have decried a secularized religious inspiration and pointed to the concrete example of the Soviet Union. Never had Soviet prestige stood higher. Vowing that Czechoslovakia would implement cooperation with the Soviet Union in all spheres, the 1945 programme of the multi-party Czechoslovak National Front paid tribute to 'the matchless military skill, unexampled self-sacrifice and measureless heroism' of the Red Army.[7] Its performance in the world war validated for communists the Soviet version of democracy which did not stress the rights of individuals or procedural issues of the rule of law but, as the Hungarian leader Rákosi put it in 1946, 'the decisive influence of workers, peasants and the progressive intelligentsia over the government and administration of a country'.[8] The Soviet Union offered the guarantee that a state could survive and flourish without the hegemony of traditional elites.

Though it was the inspiration, the Soviet Union was not at first an exact model for east European communists. The ostensible goal in 1945, conditioned by Stalin's nervousness about western intentions towards communism, was 'people's democracy' as opposed to the bourgeois democracy of the west. Politically, this meant the absence of opposition to the left-wing, communist-dominated national fronts now in power. Economically, it stood for a three-fold pattern of state, cooperative and private enterprise in place of the Five Year Plans and collectivization of the Soviet Union. In the immediate aftermath of the upheavals of 1989 some circles, ex-communist or socialist or even peasantist, looked back to the 1945–47/8 years as a potential model for the emerging new order. Yet the parallel was specious. On no side, except perhaps for some social democrats, was the people's democratic set-up of 1945–47/8 seen as a permanent settlement. Non-Marxists thought it would have to revert to conventional democracy, at least of the British Labour type. Communists saw it in terms of the Marxist stages theory of history, as a tactical episode along the 'national road to socialism' which Stalin urged upon them. In the last analysis the excitement of the communist vision overshadowed qualifications about national roads that appealed to national pride or reflected common practicality. When Stalin decided to overthrow these reservations in 1948 – the occasion was Yugoslavia's defiance of his suzerainty – east European communists identified without much difficulty with the Soviet model he then imposed.

Thus the founding pattern that east European communism was to live with became the centralized dictatorship, command economy and rigidly controlled propaganda state of Stalin's Soviet Union. Whether or not a nominal National Front remained, with ghostlike other parties as transmission belts of communist policies (East Germany, Poland, Czechoslovakia), the system presupposed that citizens did not need protection from a people's regime through an independent judiciary or the intermediary bodies of classical liberal theory. Party organs paralleled state ones and took precedence over them, reserving the right to appoint to a vast range of posts – the origins of the 'nomenklatura' or party-controlled bureaucracy. Parliaments were reduced to ciphers that met for a few days a year. The 'indicative planning' of the postwar years was replaced by Soviet-style five-year plans, while collectivization was imposed upon the countryside. All news publications had to reflect the party line and artistic output was to adopt the criteria of Soviet socialist realism. Of crucial importance was the forfeiture of full national independence, objectified by the stationing of Soviet troops in Poland, East Germany, Hungary and (until 1958) Romania. Yet this was the classic zone of European nationalism. Only Soviet force could impose an artificial uniformity on peoples differing so widely. Poles and Hungarians had strong gentry traditions; Czech democracy had arisen from a peasant and artisanal base; Balkan societies were still overwhelmingly peasant, but Serb and Bulgarian political culture was still egalitarian in style, while elite–peasant differences in Romania were profound. Religiously, the region contained a Catholic west and an Orthodox east, not to speak of majority Muslim Albanians, secular-minded Czechs and part-Protestant Hungarians. Temperamentally, Czechs and Slovaks, Serbs and Croats were far apart.

The utopian vision had two roots: a quasi-patriotic idealization of the progressive forces in one's own society and idealization of the Soviet Union as the fatherland of socialism. The balance between these two inspirations varied between individuals. Idealism, of course, could be mixed. The Soviet Union inspired because it was socialist and also because it was powerful. Stalinists interviewed in later life have spoken of seeing the Soviet purges as the regrettable by-products of great events, nothing that the individual activist could do anything about.[9] What was common to all such activists was the sense, in the Czech novelist Milan Kundera's words, of being 'at the helm of history', of participating in events of permanent significance. Beyond any concrete policy, and ultimately for many beyond any moral commitment, the defining feature of the communist vision was the conviction of an irreversible historical process from the old bourgeois order towards a new kind of society. While communism's developmental and egalitarian goals had an enduring appeal, the means by which they were to be realized, through intense commitment to an abstract model of total social harmony drawn from the Soviet Union, proved disastrous. This misfit between ends and means was to be the basic flaw in the system that resulted.

Stalinism and the loss of moral legitimacy

Recognition that communism's flaws were indeed basic and irremediable only came gradually to erode the commitment of its devotees. The hypothesis suggested here is that legitimacy was lost in stages, with the stripping away in turn of moral, political and economic rationales for what originated as a utopian social experiment. The separating out of these stages is inevitably somewhat artificial, in that moral, political and economic dimensions were present together throughout communist regimes, as in all others. Nonetheless, it seems helpful to highlight the way successive crises, in 1956, 1968 and again in the 1980s, undermined successive emphases in the claims of the proponents of the communist project.

The fascination of European communism's last act was to watch reform communists defying Alexis de Tocqueville's shrewd axiom (based on the French *ancien régime*) that a bad regime is never in so much danger as when it attempts to improve. Mikhail Gorbachev looked back to a principled Leninism for inspiration. But how could this constantly invoked inheritance be regained without reminding people of what lay between: the Stalinist quagmire in which so many dreams had died? This work argues that Stalinism bequeathed communist regimes a kind of original sin that might be overlooked, even forgotten in subsequent periods, but which told powerfully against them in the events of 1989. Gorbachev's stress of socialism's superior potential over capitalism as a means to the just society only evoked memories of the way in which revolutionary utopianism had violated basic moral standards in the Stalinist period.

As social rebels in a relatively undeveloped area, most east European communists were not sophisticates and inclined naturally to simple polarizations of right and wrong. The presence of intellectuals in the movement's upper echelon and the appeal of Marxism to many student youth disguise the unprecedented isolation of the new rulers from traditional educated elites. None of the 102 full and associate professors of Berlin University surviving denazification in 1946 was a communist and only 3.7 per cent of Polish professors and 4 per cent of students two years later. A mere 7 per cent of Czech university students before 1948 were of worker origin.[10] By contrast, communist apparatchiks emphasized the primitivism of their natural constituency, who needed to be mobilized through simple slogans of traitor, spy or agent. Ex-peasants and workers filled all but the top ranks of communist security services; the Hungarian Paloczi-Horvath found that his interrogator did not know Istanbul and Constantinople were one and the same.[11] The 'Stalin revolution' from the late 1920s had destroyed the power of the Old Bolshevik intelligentsia, bringing to the fore 'new men' from what had been the most backward country in Europe. That Russia was different was a commonplace even among east European communists: that 'immense Byzantine empire where the manners of the former great lords are strangely mixed with revolutionary traditions', as Imre Nagy called it, adding, 'Leningrad is Europe'.[12] Yet this society now set the tone. 'Love of the Soviet Union does not tolerate the slightest reservation,' wrote the Czechoslovak communist organ in 1952.[13]

Politically, this meant a most extreme centralization and uniformity in a region marked historically by the diversity of its often antagonistic peoples. As in Stalin's Russia, even communist party dominance yielded to the dictatorship of the party general secretary, sometimes flanked by an inner coterie. Brutal suppression of opposition had started immediately after the war; tens of thousands so deemed were killed both in Bulgaria and in Yugoslavia. Next came the elimination of former allies, like the execution of the Bulgarian peasantist leader Nikola Petkov, and the pressurized fusion of the social democrats with the communists. From the second half of 1948 began the hunt for communist 'Titoists', which in targeting patently some of the most dedicated of communists – the Hungarian ex-interior minister Rajk being the best example – put great strain on activists' loyalties. In fact the period of purges (1949–53) roped in large numbers of smaller fry: 178 executed on State Council indictment in Czechoslovakia and 150 000 imprisoned in Hungary. The extraction of confessions followed Soviet models and was coordinated by Soviet security police, including, as in Rajk's case, the presentation of confession as the last service to the party. The imprisonment or internment of the Catholic primates of Hungary, Czechoslovakia and Poland were other measures of unprecedented severity. Rothschild has plausibly suggested that it was not so much the communists' monopolization of power which shocked east European populations, for all parties had done that, but the exceeding of all previous bounds and for the benefit of another state, the Soviet Union.[14]

Much of the persecution resulted from the need to find scapegoats for socio-economic dislocation. The Soviet 'command economy' model allowed no role for market supply and demand and real costs, but set prices to reflect the state's priorities and then struggled to calculate (in a pre-computer age) input and output requirements for many thousands of products. In 1952, for example, 472 changes were made to the Hungarian quinquennial plan and 1113 changes to the current annual plan.[15] Hungary's doubling of already illusory national income growth targets because of the Korean War (1951) was another example of utopian irrationalism which contributed to a fall in workers' real wages of 16 per cent between 1949 and 1953. In this period the share of household expenditure going on food went up from 46 per cent to 59 per cent. Conditions were worsened everywhere by the inflow of people from the countryside where enforced collectivization was bitterly resented and resisted: three to three and a half million hectares of Hungarian arable land were uncultivated by 1953 and 400 000 peasants had been fined. Even draconic state policies could not eliminate signs of discontent, from open insurrection (Potsdam workers in 1953, Poznań workers in 1956) to what has been called infra-political or hidden resistance.[16] 'We've really screwed up: everybody hates us', the young Budapest police chief Kopacsi was told by an older comrade on return to his home town.[17]

The attack on tradition was most sensitive in the sphere of culture. Eastern Europe was flooded with Soviet advisers, whose arrogance combined a knowing sense of the brute reality naïve east Europeans were now in for with an oppressive conceit in the superiority of the Soviet system. Yet the confrontation of east Europeans and Soviet people during the Second World War had confirmed the formers' prejudices about Russian backwardness. 'Give me your watch!' became a standard refrain for the encounter of Soviet troops with a higher standard of living. A Soviet culture impoverished by the dictates of socialist realism (odes to the Great Leader, tractors in sunlit cornfields) aroused the consternation of east European communist intellectuals. Pinpricks like the adoption of Soviet-style army uniforms or examination grading schemes could be as psychologically irritating as compulsory school Russian and a surfeit of Russian films and books for societies whose dominant ideology since the nineteenth century had been nationalism.

Tocqueville's adage about the danger faced by improving regimes found a limited application after Stalin's death. The 'Thaw' of 1953–56 was the context for political eruptions in Poland and Hungary in 1956, which in Hungary became revolution. Improved living standards under Imre Nagy's 'New Course' in Hungary (1953 to early 1955) did not restore the communists' popularity with workers but the stories of released purge prisoners shook Marxist intellectuals' faith. The Hungarian insurrection of October 1956 received most active support from strata the communists particularly wanted on their side: students and youth in general, urban workers and the creative intelligentsia. The whole episode anticipated the narrow bounds within which subsequent attempts at reform communism had to operate, between popular resentment and communist reservations. For the Soviet invasion of Hungary was ordered by Nikita Khrushchev, who had condemned Stalin's crimes, and approved by Hungarian liberal communists' chief hope in 1956, Josip Broz Tito, who secretly arranged the betrayal of their leader, Imre Nagy.

The Hungarian revolutionaries fought against Soviet domination and Stalinist excess; no doubt many, by extension or social background, fought against socialism too. But they did not yet fight, for the most part, with the intellectual tools of 1989, in the name of civil society, the free market and the unviability of the socialist project. Workers' councils played an important role in the popular movement in both Hungary and Poland, while Poles exuberantly cheered the coming to power of a national communist leader, Władysław Gomułka, who had succeeded in averting Soviet military action. The immediate cause of these events was a revulsion at the sheer brutality and inefficiency of Stalinist utopianism turned sour. The most striking feature of this utopianism was its exponents' moral contortions, making it difficult to distinguish between pure cynicism and a socialist version of antinomianism, the religious doctrine whereby the elect, certain of salvation, can commit any kind of sin irrespective. Thus the first great breach in communist legitimacy was the exposure of the communist claim to represent the superior morality of a new and better world.

There is much evidence that contemporaries felt the deepest ground of their criticism of Stalinism to be moral. Imre Nagy himself wrote that socialism could only come about when 'we ourselves have become new socialist beings' influenced above all 'by the new and loftier socialist ethics and morals'; it was precisely this vision which was being rocked by 'the violent contrast between words and deeds' in Stalinist Hungary.[18] One of the spurs in Czech communist Zdeněk Mlynář's path to reformism was his revulsion at the thought of party leader Novotný sleeping between the sheets of his executed former colleague, foreign minister Clementis, whose bed linen Mrs Novotný appropriated.[19] Likewise the decisive article in the disgrace of the Yugoslav communist leader, and later famous dissident Milovan Djilas in 1954 was a short story about vindictive jealousies among high-ranking communists' wives.[20] Unfortunately, under Stalinist antinomianism a higher communist ethos could take the warped form of one of Paloczi-Horvath's senior interrogators: communists should be 'above' the 'ugly realities'; they had 'different rules', which could mean achieving heroism by accepting the party's demand to die the death of a criminal.[21]

Ironically, Stalinism's very moral crudeness stopped it from destroying the faith of most communists at the time. Though Khrushchev's denunciation of Stalin's crimes in 1956 ended blind faith in the party, it seemed plausible to them to believe that the socialist system could recover from such self-inflicted setbacks by intellectual means and a dose of common humanity. The real effect was on the masses. It may be said that the great bulk of them had never believed in communism anyway, but this is not quite the point. Through its flagrant violation of basic norms of humanity and decency Stalinism not only reinforced negative assumptions about communism bequeathed through faith, class, family or patriotism but scuppered for an indefinite future communists' chances of eventually turning a system based on force into one based on conviction. For all its Machiavellianism, it was a stupid as well as malignant creed which thought it pointful to inscribe wartime bombs against Nazi Germany 'for Katyn', when over-whelmingly – and rightly – Poles ascribed the 1940 Katyn massacre of Polish officers to the Soviets. East European communist regimes were never to escape the bind of their Stalinist birth.

1968 and the loss of ideological legitimacy

The decade or so following 1956 appears, in hindsight, the most successful of the communist experiment. Initiatives to overhaul the Stalinist order proceeded apace. Living standards rose, repression slackened and events outside the region improved the climate for communism. The Soviet Union's prestige increased as it put the first sputnik into earth orbit, then launched Yuri Gagarin into space (1957–60). The accelerating anti-colonial movement provided natural allies, while in the west the French and Italian communist parties regularly won about a quarter of the votes. Heading the last paragraph of a book on Russia 'Will Russia conquer the world in thirty years?' the weighty American international commentator John Gunther answered: 'Perhaps. It is possible', though less likely than that she might simply 'make very strong advances'.[22]

Khrushchev, undisputed Soviet leader from 1955 to 1964, sought to strengthen Soviet power by institutional means rather than terror. The idea was of some sort of commonwealth of socialist states, with the Soviet Union *primus inter pares* by virtue of the leading role of its communist party. International conferences of communist parties were held in Moscow in 1957 and 1960. Comecon, the economic organ of communist states, founded in 1949, took on a more significant role, trade between its formally equal members rising five-fold between 1950 and 1964. The Soviets' economic exploitation of their satellites largely ceased with the winding up of joint companies (1954) and was replaced by a regime of effective subsidy, through supply of energy at below world prices and acceptance of east European products unlikely to find a market in the west. A military parallel to NATO was called into being by the Warsaw Pact (1955). Personal contact at many levels reinforced this framework, from the thousands of foreign students funded to study in Russia to the constant meetings of senior functionaries.

These circumstances of 'liberalization' or 'destalinization' allowed for the sprouting of varieties of what scholars have dubbed reform communism. Theoretically speaking, reform communism spawned a school of assertions that Marxism should not be schematized, that it provided a creative method rather than rigid formulae, that everything was to be questioned and so on, exemplified in the essays of the Polish philosopher Kołakowski in 1956.[23] Kołakowski's career showed, however, the problems of this position. He had been attracted to Marxism both by its apparently rational explanation of history and by its utopian strain – you could only achieve anything by setting your sights beyond the immediately possible. But he could not believe that matters of human moral consciousness, which made philosophy eternally relevant, were reduceable to purely class terms and he believed that when the utopian impulse was lost, communist parties could become as conservative as 'the right' they had displaced. He was expelled from the Polish communist party in 1966 for a speech criticizing lack of democracy and free speech. The multi-facetedness of Marx's revolutionary philosophy, a help before victory, played against it later. It had combined an explicit rationalist critique of society with an implicit moral utopianism which came apart in government, exposing both facets to criticism. Thus Marxism as a tool for analysing power relations and social inequities was turned against communist regimes first by Milovan Djilas (*The New Class*, 1957), then the Polish researchers Jacek Kuroń and Modzelewski ('Open Letter to the Party', 1964), all of whom argued that the party bureaucracy had engrossed to itself the control of ownership allegedly vested in the people's state. All three received prison terms.

Reform communism was more acceptable to the authorities where it could present itself as a pragmatic response to practical problems. In economics it was strong enough to become formally adopted by 1965 in Hungary, Czechoslovakia, Yugoslavia and the Soviet Union. The case against the command economy was easily made: too many plan targets drowned the system in bureaucracy, encouraged concentration on the easiest targets and led to sub-standard work because the plan was based on quantity, not quality. Reliance on physical targets stimulated managers to minimize their declared capacity and covertly maximize their hoarding of raw materials. Solutions proposed nearly all included introducing elements of a profit motive, incentives to reduce costs and decentralization from central industrial ministries to regional industrial trusts. The difficulty of the profit motive was that managers' efficiency could not be judged fairly as long as prices were state-fixed, and freeing them was a complicated matter, usually seen as a rolling process involving different pricing categories, with many staples remaining fixed at artificially low levels. Hence the potential difficulty of economic reform was that, faced with inevitable teething troubles, proponents either had to recentralize or go on to further bouts of liberalization. However, the principle of reform was not in itself questioned in the mid-1960s since it could be justified practically in terms of existing waste (less economic use of energy than in the west, worsening capital–output ratios) and more theoretically by claims that socialism had nothing against combining plan and market. Moreover, reform economists were no Jeremiahs but forcefully asserted that their proposals were made in an overall context of successful growth.

Political sociologists also had a positive contribution to make, particularly Yugoslavs and Czechoslovaks. This was a time when the Yugoslav system of socialist self-management had an enthusiastic following on the western left, and less overtly in eastern Europe. It represented an extension of the workers' control principle so that not just factories but schools, health centres, indeed all bodies except the army, democratically allotted wages and housing among themselves, debated the annual plan and decided the balance beween wages and reinvestment for their enterprise. In Czechoslovakia, where economic slowdown by 1963 lent legitimacy to reform ideas, the most interesting figure was the Central Committee secretary Zdeněk Mlynář, a student friend of Mikhail Gorbachev in Moscow in the brief post-Stalin thaw. Realizing that his private preference for a two-party system (both parties being socialist) was unacceptable to the communist mainstream, Mlynář publicly advocated 'socialist pluralism', whereby the communist party adjudicated between the different interest groups in the society, a view whose parallels with western interest group theory he recognized. Indeed, the 1960s heard much talk of growing convergence between the two great systems, with Stalinism apparently discarded in the east and western public opinion challenging social taboos and protesting against American intervention in Vietnam. Both halves of Europe were influenced by the academic exploration of 'the young Marx', whose stress of man's alienation from his true nature under capitalism was felt to vindicate a humanistic Marxism speaking the language of individual fulfilment rather than faceless class. In a related key, reform communist economists saw a revolution in science and technology in the west which the communist world had to match if its competitiveness was to be maintained.

This is the background to the Prague Spring of 1968, with which the reform communist period in eastern Europe culminated. Beginning with the appointment of Alexander Dubček as Czechoslovak communist party secretary in January, it endured the armed intervention of half a million Warsaw pact troops on the night of 20–21 August and finally petered out with Dubček's fall in April 1969. Dubček and the Action Programme of the party issued in April 1968 are perhaps the most quintessential expression of the post-Stalinist spirit. For Dubček, it was axiomatic that communism was the best form of society and all that was necessary was for party members of good will to demonstrate 'socialism with a human face'. The Action Programme therefore echoed reformist buzz words about the 'scientific-technological revolution', 'democratization', respect for 'freedom of different views' and the 'various needs and interests of individual people and social groups' but declared that the leading role of the communist party and Marxism-Leninism was the essential basis for building socialism. The key statement 'The Communist Party enjoys the voluntary support of the people' breathed the conviction that communist policies were so self-evidently right that consensus around them was natural.[24] Though Dubček's regime allowed unprecedented media freedom, it rejected calls by ex-Social Democrats for the re-legalization of their party, and on the strength of such stances denied Warsaw pact charges that socialism was under threat in Czechoslovakia. Hence Dubček's reproachful cry when the

Soviets and four Warsaw pact allies invaded in August, 'So they did it after all – and to *me*.'[25]

The collapse of the Prague Spring was a key event in the erosion of the legitimacy of socialist regimes. At the time Czechoslovak reform communists argued – with much support from western sympathizers – that the Soviets had invaded to prevent a rival model of democratic socialism from showing up their own system, thereby suppressing the only inspirational hope for a socialist future in the longer term. The failure of Gorbachev, an admirer of the Prague Spring, and the rapid passage of east European states to fully fledged capitalism after 1989 have poured much cold water on this perspective. Many arguments can indeed be adduced against the long-term viability of the Dubček regime, even if left alone. Polls showing 90 per cent support for the Czechoslovak communist party leadership during the crisis need not mean that they would have retained that support in more mundane times. Almost equal numbers of East Germans supported the continuation of a 'reformed' East German state in autumn 1989 but within a few months the same people demanded union with capitalist West Germany. The Prague Spring's fate would have depended on the success of its economic reform which, by analogy with later Hungarian and Yugoslav experience of reform economics, would have been unlikely. The naïve arrogance of assuming the people's voluntary support for a party which did not allow free competition would surely have been exposed as real politics developed. The counter-claim that Czechoslovaks would have voluntarily reined in demands threatening the party's privileged position, for fear of provoking a similar fate to Hungary's in 1956, seems undermined by the willingness of their media during the Prague Spring to raise sensitive issues like alleged Soviet economic exploitation. Intellectuals like Iván Sviták and Václav Havel in 1968 barely veiled their suspicions of all communism, publicly arguing, in Havel's case, that only the formalized right of an opposition party to exist could guarantee that concessions offered, like a free press, would not subsequently be withdrawn. From a Soviet perspective, perhaps the strongest argument might be that even if the Prague Spring could have given communism national legitimacy in Czechoslovakia, similar freedom would have had the opposite effect in the multi-national Soviet Union, threatening the unity of the state, as was to happen in 1991. On the basis of these arguments it was not the Soviets who were naïve about their true interests in 1968, but the Czechoslovak reform communists who mistook temporary popularity for a sign that they really had created a viable new socialist order.

Recently published documents on Soviet–Czechoslovak relations tend to point up the weaknesses of both sides. Brezhnev huffing and puffing about right-wing 'scoundrels' and their 'second centre' in the Czechoslovak communist party, against whom Dubček should turn to the 'healthy' elements, reveals a damning identification of politics with personnel and socialism with a system of total control: the ossification of imagination which Gorbachev later pinned on Brezhnev's 'era of stagnation'. Yet Dubček not once tried to defend his policies to the Soviets in terms of a socialism rooted in popular consent. His evasive uninformativeness on the implementation of agreements for personnel changes and media control which Brezhnev claimed they had reached in pre-invasion meetings make the Soviet leader's charges of deceit quite understandable.[26] It is difficult not to agree with Mlynář that the Prague Spring's leader had no real understanding of what a democratic process might be, other than the assumption that the people would fall in with the party's good intentions if asked nicely enough.

Yet reform communism need not be dismissed as readily as Dubček's statesmanship. The failure of Gorbachev's path does not necessarily imply that the Prague Spring could not have worked in a far more developed society than the Soviet Union, before a further generation of socialist stagnation had piled up economic problems and the international climate had taken on the conservative stamp of the 1980s. But Dubček did exemplify a key weakness of the reform communist position which points towards scepticism. While its exponents recognized that Old Stalinist calls for heightened class consciousness were not enough, and that expertise and flexibility were now needed, when it came to dealing with the clashes of interest which flexibility would bring they still invoked the old utopian faith in a moral consensus round the socialist ideal. In Marxist language, differences of interest would be 'non-antagonistic', unlike in capitalism; hence they could be contained within a one-party system. More probing thinkers like Mlynář were in a minority. Unthinking attachment to the single party could be encouraged by evocation of the humanist values of the young Marx, which tended to preserve a cosy sense of idealism compatible with a subjective 'socialist' commitment. This socialism's relation to the communist party was not worked out, a confusion encouraged by the fact that Marxist–Leninist rhetoric often used socialism and communism as synonyms. The empty bombast of which reform communism was capable is demonstrated by its Czech spokesman in British exile, Eduard Goldstücker, who drew from 1968 no doubts about the communist party monopoly, but the conclusion that 'the only revolutionary thing in the world is the truth'.[27] Whether such phraseological Marxism had the potential for systemic renewal or not, the most succinct lesson of 1968 was that this would not be permitted. Communism's political legitimacy, the belief in its potential for reform once the Stalinist legacy had been shuffled off, never recovered.

The 1970s and the wager on economic legitimacy

After 1968 Marxism's stock in eastern Europe was exhausted, to the dismay of western socialists who accused ex-reform communists of throwing the baby out with the bathwater.[28] Remaining pockets of relatively independent

Marxist thought, the Lukács school in Hungary and the *Praxis* school in Yugoslavia, were suppressed in their respective countries in 1975, the leaders of the former beating a retreat to Australia, an unexpected host for the last spokespersons of the great central European Marxist tradition. Thereafter, Marxist ideology transmuted into 'Eurocommunism' in most western communist parties (an unacknowledged shift towards social democracy) or became a vanity act of communist hierarchs. Brezhnev linked his name to the slogan of 'really existing socialism'; the Romanian Ceauşescu proclaimed 'multi-lateral developed socialism'; Enver Hoxha of Albania categorized world socialism into various revisionist heresies: Soviet social imperialism, Chinese 'third worldism', Yugoslav 'non-alignment' – and the Party of Labour of Albania.

But these formulations were a façade. The actual energy of communist politics in the 1970s was expended on winning people for a society whose material well-being compensated for its politics. Socialism was now to come consumer-style. Roots of this pragmatic approach can be traced back to Kádár's famous remark of 1961 that 'he who is not against us is for us'. In 1968 Hungary introduced a far-reaching version of economic reformism known as the New Economic Mechanism (NEM) which largely survived the post Prague Spring backlash against such schemes elsewhere. Technocrats played a bigger role in communist leadership. An example was the Silesian boss and ex-miner Eduard Gierek, who replaced the austere Gomułka in 1970 after Polish shipyard workers' protests were suppressed with several dozen deaths. Gierek's strategy was to modernize the economy not through economic reforms now seen as dangerous but by using foreign loans and technology, to be paid for by the new manufactures Poland was to export. The first five years of his rule saw real wages, which had stagnated in the 1960s, go up by 40 per cent. Under Dubček's successor, Gustáv Husák, Czechoslovakia was to be 'normalized' (read: depoliticized) by prosperity and the security police. Czechs who could set off in family cars for long weekends in summer homes in the countryside would, it was hoped, worry less about the absence of political liberties. Other aspects of life could be exploited, like sporting pride – Olympic successes undoubtedly raised East Germans' level of identification with their state – or the national sentiment played on by Ceauşescu, or by Kádár when he secured the return of the Holy Crown of St Stephen from the New York vault where anti-communist emigrés had deposited it. The main pitch of communist pragmatism remained, however, the economy. Comecon's 1971 Comprehensive Programme for Socialist Economic Integration was a renewed attempt to coordinate development, frustrated by Romanian opposition in the 1960s. Projects like the 4000-kilometre Friendship pipeline supplied Soviet oil to Hungary, Czechoslovakia and Germany; the 1700-kilometre Orenburg pipeline did the same for gas. Increased attention to chemicals, petro-chemicals and electronics marked a further stage in industrial progress, reflected also in the growing share of manufactured products in bloc exports. Consumer items like washing machines and televisions became quite general acquisitions in the 1970s, and cars and foreign holidays were no longer vanishingly rare if still very much a minority matter. On the whole, real wages by the end of the 1970s were three to four times their level of 1950. These processes, which will be examined more thoroughly in the next chapter, permit one to speak almost of a rebranding of communism in the decade following the Prague Spring. Of course, consumerism came socialist-style – advertisements played no part, for example – and the growing attention to material incentives was intended to smooth the way for the assimilation of socialist values which the mere passage of time would make more familiar and unquestioned. Society, said a Polish sociologist in 1979 in words expressing no doubt what the regime wished to think was happening, was prepared to accept the communist state into the family.[29]

Western scholarship and east European society

To a fair extent such projections of communism in developmental terms were taken over by western scholarship in these years. There were two main reasons for this. One was the need felt by many western students of communism for an alternative approach to the analyses in terms of 'totalitarianism' of the 1950s and early 1960s, which it was felt failed to allow for the 'polycentrism' and 'liberalization' increasingly perceived in the communist world after Stalin's death.[30] The other was the wish of many east European specialists to enter the mainstream of political science and escape the charge of seeking to isolate their subject behind a smoke-screen of historical and linguistic expertise. The search for a more conceptual, overarching approach, leading to a theory of east European political structures, came to centre round current notions of 'modernization' as applied to the emerging regimes in the post-colonial world. The prestigious political scientist Samuel Huntington's notion that all modern government was about the management of change was also an important influence in changing perceptions, as was his tenet that the real distinction in modern politics was not between communist and non-communist systems, but between efficient and inefficient ones. Developmental paradigms like Huntington's presented ideology and charismatic leadership as features of the initial 'transformative' stage, which yielded to professionalization as 'consolidation' advanced.[31] 'I view the East European states as not essentially different from other countries facing the crisis and problems associated with modernization and development,' wrote A. Korbonski in 1974.[32]

An interesting aspect of much discussion of communism as modernization was the implication that communist regimes could not be wholly denied legitimacy. While one wing of the approach predicted that communist authoritarianism lacked the flexibility to respond to the growing complexity of modern society, this judgement too was criticized by some scholars as overly deterministic: political science lacked the means to prove or predict interrelationships between social and political variables of change.[33] Three comments may be made on the debates. First, the desire to fit east European reality into wider political science paradigms could at times patently miscue that reality. Studies of 'participation', for example, abound in almost comical remarks like this one on Romanian elections: 'Unfortunately, the number of votes received by each candidate remains confidential.'[34] Second, assumptions that political 'development' would nonetheless advance were implicitly plotted against a posited economic development, which turned out to be problematic. Third, the treatment of Marxist ideology as no longer very significant subsumed it, as a brand of social egalitarianism, into a rather general doctrine of societal development permitting much leeway for scholarly debate. What this overlooked was the revolutionary origins of the communist regimes and the violence of the Stalinist phase, which meant these regimes could only feel secure through maintaining the dictatorship of the communist party. Justification through an extreme utopian ideology, much stronger than ameliorist welfarism, was structurally essential to the whole set-up. As east Europeans like Kołakowski commented in response to gradualist images of an east European future, scholarly debate there would inevitably run up against limits; communist apparatchiks' fears of democracy were not just paranoid but based on realistic observation.[35] Much western political science comment on eastern Europe in the 1970s ignored the element of 'original sin' which this chapter has set at the heart of the evolving story.

There was another angle to study of eastern Europe in the 1970s, a sociological one more concerned with social than political structures. Works by the Hungarian dissidents György Konrád and Iván Szelényi challenged the optimistic assumption of some western scholars that as communist countries developed, so the party bureaucrats would be challenged by the new technocratic specialists. The authors argued that technocrats feared the bureaucrats less than they did the workers, while the bureaucrats aped the lifestyle of the traditionally admired 'creative' circles of writers and artists. These three groups, bureaucrats, technocrats and cultural workers, made up an intelligentsia which in eastern Europe, in the absence of a strong western-style bourgeoisie, had always led the modernizing process in the region. Now it was making its bid for 'class power', not on the basis of its ownership of the means of production but its control of the means of information. Any future upheaval in eastern Europe would not therefore come from reform communist intellectuals, whose weakness had been exposed in 1968, but from workers under the regime's thumb, with the likely assistance of 'marginal intellectuals' whom the system had not squared.[36] Meanwhile, the idea that workers might be the malcontents of the future was statistically developed by the American sociologist W.D. Connor. Connor showed that the upward social mobility which had turned peasants into urban workers in communism's first generation could hardly be duplicated in its second; now that so many peasants had made the switch, further mobility would mainly be a matter of workers pressing against the rigidifying bureaucratic and managerial circles.[37]

Indeed, time-span in its various aspects is a very important factor in the origins of 1989. Just as the leaders of communist eastern Europe had been moulded by the failures of interwar democracy, so in the 1970s anyone over 30 had vividly experienced the establishment of communist power or its early abuses. A human lifetime remains a potent framework for analysis of core values. Samuel Huntington knew this when he stressed the importance of generational change in eastern Europe, when a new set of politicians should take the helm. Precisely because the communists had put such stress on youth, however, the difficulty of replacing the cadres of 1945, revolutionary but ill-qualified, was being noted from the 1960s until the system's end. The strength of Marxist ideology was to combine economic, social, political and, least averred but perhaps most important, moral elements in a singularly powerful synthesis. Any one of them might motivate and inspire. As it happened, in a kind of historical striptease they were tested one by one. By the end of the 1970s, the moral idealism and ideological utility of Marxism as a blueprint for a superior kind of democracy had been drained, and the system was hanging by two threads – internally, on its success in delivering the economic goods; externally, on the international structures of the cold war. The 1980s were to bring unforeseen stresses for each of these.

2

The 1980s
A flawed society

At the start of the 1980s hardly anyone predicted that east European communism would be finished by the end of the decade. The strides communist societies had made towards the creation of a modern infrastructure provided much evidence for the developmental approach to their study outlined at the end of the previous chapter. But the Polish Solidarity movement of 1980–81 quickly confirmed the sociological prediction that the next east European outburst would be worker-based. Was the Polish crisis rooted in distinctive national traditions or could it be the harbinger of a wider malaise? This chapter will look at the region's society in the early 1980s and at the Solidarity experience, before examining the issue of wider regional economic shortfall and in this light returning to the social scene to ask: how flawed were the developmental patterns of east European society and how serious a threat did they pose to the survival of communist regimes?

East European society *c.*1980

In 1951, the Trotskyist Glückstein estimated that it would take a five-fold increase of pre-war investment ratios just to absorb the region's *surplus* rural population into industry in the next two decades.[1] In this light the structural transformation which occurred under communism was dramatic. It expressed itself most basically in swift demographic convergence towards western norms. With improved health care, the death rate dropped dramatically to below 10 per thousand in all countries between 1953 and 1958; then a fall in the birth rate reduced population growth to a relatively modest 1 per cent a year by 1980, and considerably lower in Czechoslovakia and East Germany. Concomitantly, infant mortality fell. From being two and a half to four times higher than in Britain in 1950, all countries had reduced it to that of the British level by 1980 and by 1987 all but

Yugoslavia matched the British level of 1970, at just 18 per thousand. The convergence process was accelerating. Life expectancy, widely divergent not only with that in the west but also intra-regionally between the wars, had become more uniform at between 69 and 71 years by the late 1970s, just two to three years behind the most advanced countries. This excepts East Germany, on a par with West Germany, and Albania which demographically remained a land apart, with an annual population growth rate still of 2 per cent in the 1980s. Albania likewise was the only country where the massive interwar rural preponderance remained. Elsewhere the fall in the percentage dependent on agriculture by 1980 was roughly proportionate: thus from 34 per cent to 13 per cent in Czechoslovakia and from 78 per cent to 30 per cent in Romania. Urbanization had given Romania 14 and Poland 21 cities of more than 150 000 and quadrupled the size of once humble capitals like Belgrade, Sophia and Zagreb since 1940.[2]

Industrialization and urbanization brought a wholesale restructuring of east European society. Capitalists and large landowners were no more. Official accounts perceived three social groups: workers, peasants and intelligentsia. Of these the intelligentsia showed the steepest growth. First associated with the educated minority which had arisen outside the traditional lord–peasant nexus in the nineteenth century, the term's implication of enlightened hostility to a backward order made it congenial for communists, though their statistics simply used it in practice to denote those who had completed secondary schooling. While mass primary education had largely come about before 1939, mass secondary education was a communist achievement. Only 12 per cent continued schooling after an eight-year primary phase in east Germany in 1950, but 88 per cent by 1972; in 1980, 81 per cent of Poles from the ages of 15 to 18 were still receiving education. At the tertiary level, though it is difficult to standardize categories of university, politechnic institute and specialist colleges, numbers also rose, from some 150 000 in 1938 to 340 000 in 1950 and over a million by 1980. The ratio of highly trained personnel in the workforce thus swelled rapidly, enabling the servicing of a more complex society. By 1965–66 Polish doctors and dentists had already more than tripled in number over prewar levels, providing almost as dense a network per patient as in the United States. Along with the managerial and professional strata there was a proportionate increase in the ranks of clerical workers, primary school teachers, nurses, shop assistants and others of varying educational levels who came often to be categorized as non-manual employees beneath the intelligentsia proper.

The expansion of the working class was both quantitative, trebling overall by 1980, and qualitative, with a higher ratio of skilled to unskilled. While there was a tendency for members of the older working-class core to move into management positions, migrants from the countryside (half Poland's workers were country-born) teemed in the white monochrome high-rise flats which ringed the old city centres. With electricity and running water they experienced a step up from the rural poverty of the inter-war years, though not all workers shared these benefits: housing was the Achilles heel of communist social policy. A shortfall of flats compared to households was a permanent feature, the deficit in Poland in 1978 reaching 1.8 million. It helped account for the many east European workers who lived in hostels and the many others who lived in villages – about a quarter of Hungary's industrial and commercial workforce in 1980.[3]

In some ways, the closer contacts between town and country could be counted one of the positive features of the system. Collectivization of agriculture had put the great majority of rural workers in roughly the same league as their urban counterparts, as members of the socialized economy. Outside Poland and Yugoslavia, which had decollectivized in the 1950s, private farmers were rare, though they still owned about an eighth of the land in Hungary, Bulgaria and Romania.[4] Originally based on village units, the collective farms had been subject to further amalgamation in the 1970s, just as pressures had been stepped up in Poland in favour of the minority of state farms. Here socialist ideology was at work. But relative living standards had risen. Indeed, figures for 1970 gave Hungarian peasants exactly the same income as workers, ahead of Czechoslovak peasants at 98.1 per cent and Bulgarian at 91.5 per cent three years later. This seemed to promise the 'abolition of the difference between town and country' for which the *Communist Manifesto* had called. Even in non-collectivized Poland, where peasant income was estimated at 40–50 per cent of non-agrarian income in the late 1930s, it stood at 75 per cent by the 1960s.[5] In 1980, 97 per cent of Hungarian rural homes had electricity compared to 25 per cent in 1949. Rural prosperity owed much to the private plots collective farmers were permitted to retain, while using collective facilities, while Hungarian success also stemmed from the regime's permission for collective farms to engage in non-agricultural operations. It has been estimated that six to seven and a half million of the ten million Hungarians benefited in one way or another from the peasant plot. Another form of the intersectoral relationship, particularly in Poland and Yugoslavia, comprised the worker-peasants who commuted between factory and the plot they cultivated on their return. Such people made up a third of the Yugoslav industrial workforce.

The levelling of distinctions which characterized communist society operated most clearly in incomes policy. Pay differentials as between intellectual and manual labour narrowed sharply compared to prewar or contemporary western patterns, though traditionally plebeian Czechoslovaks paid intelligentsia posts (doctors, for example) only a fifth more than the national average in the 1970s, while for the Poles and Hungarians, whose nobility had once been national leaders, the differential was two-fifths. But the increased standard of living of all was clear, whatever adjustments should be made to official records of a three- to four-fold average increase in real wages in the region. According to emigré scholar Jaroslav Krejči, 56 per cent of Czechoslovak workers had occupied the two lowest income categories in 1937; only 1.1 per cent did in real comparative terms in 1968.[6] Thus the basis was laid for the fuller social integration which nationalist ideologues had talked of, but not achieved. Whereas children of worker or peasant origin were negligible in prewar Czechoslovak *gymnasiums,* the most elite form of secondary school, by 1979 they made up 32 per cent.[7]

Readjusting the educational system went together with the attempt to win youth and transform the situation of women. This had mixed fortunes. Monolithic bodies were formed to which most young people nominally adhered, as in interwar fascist systems. All east European countries had an umbrella sports organization with a huge membership, usually about a tenth of the entire population. Several of them instituted evocatively named 'Spartakiadas', whereby nationwide competitions eventually yielded vast numbers of finalists performing in the capital. In the 1975 Czechoslovak Spartakiada 180000 finalists competed in Prague, out of an original 1 529 000 contestants.[8] Communists loved figures and the gigantic; best of all they loved gigantic figures. In East Germany sport was declared a 'major subject' and was compulsory at university. In Czechoslovakia all pupils were categorized by their physical type, for which national attainment standards existed. Specialist boarding schools for talented athletes were another feature of the system. East Germany, with just 17 million inhabitants, came second in the medal table of the Olympic Games of 1976 and 1980. It is now clear that a dubious role in this was also played by the country's 600–700 sports doctors, a profession first developed in East Germany, which had founded the world's first sports university, with doctoral facilities, in Leipzig in 1952. At the grass-roots level it seems that sports participation was not necessarily wider in eastern Europe than in the west, partly because communist goals ran up against youth's predictable dislike of regimentation. Women, too, with fewer opportunities for leisure, made up only about a quarter of the members of the national sports associations.

The emancipation of women had been a key theme of the socialist movement from its inception. By the 1980s their position was undeniably transformed in several respects. Legal reforms had been quickly carried out, ensuring women's equal property rights, the abolition of the husband's leading role in the family and the removal of impediments on illegitimacy. Abortion rights were not granted until after Stalin's death. Women were free, and sometimes encouraged, to cross occupational boundaries, become train drivers, engineers, even crane operators. By the end of communism their share in the labour force had risen to 45–49 per cent in the four non-Balkan countries, including about three-quarters of all women, who dominated medical and welfare services and school teaching. In education, too, their participation increased by leaps and bounds, so that by 1989 they were to make up 55 per cent and 59 per cent respectively of Polish students at higher and secondary level. Yet advance in access to managerial positions lagged well behind, showing at best an upward creep, as in Polish figures for 1960–80: from one woman manager in twelve in state administration to one in five and from 7 per cent to 12 per cent in economic enterprises. Since female-dominated occupations were the most poorly paid, women's wages were outstripped by men's, despite constitutional prescription of equal pay. However, again ratios improved, with women's wages rising from about a half of men's before the war to some two-thirds by the 1960s and closer to four-fifths by the end of communism.[9]

By the 1980s socialist egalitarianism no longer wore only a frugal mask. Certain consumer durables like washing machines and, in towns, refrigerators had become all but standard. Leisure patterns had diversified. Burgeoning theatres and orchestras were, of course, part of the high-minded socialist vision from the start. One in two Poles and Hungarians visited the theatre at least once a year in 1960, far more than in Britain. Interestingly, these figures declined slightly thereafter, while visits to museums and less intellectual entertainments made great strides. The family television set had become generalized by 1980, with roughly one set to every three East Germans and Czechoslovaks, four Poles and Hungarians, and six Yugoslavs, Bulgars and Romanians. Half of all Poles and a quarter of Hungarians went abroad in 1975–78 respectively, compared to a few tens of thousands in 1960. Interaction was mainly with socialist countries, however. In terms of sheer scale, domestic tourists were the major indicator. In Poland in the early years of Gierek's policy of socialist consumerism (1970–75), these swelled from 23 to 125 million. The family car for weekend trips to the family country cottage had become a widespread reality for Czechoslovaks when one in seven persons had a car in 1980, instead of some 6 per cent ten years previously. The rate of increase was nearer four-fold in Hungary and Yugoslavia, to a car for roughly one in ten of the population. Yugoslavs' greater access to *western* travel was an important feature of its relative liberalization.

As these figures suggest, there were still differences in living standards, which east European analysts did not deny. For the Polish sociologist Jan Szczepański, however, the new system avoided the overlapping of wealth, power and prestige which he saw in capitalist society. Thus a worker-peasant might now have more prestige in a village than the biggest landholder, while the party had political power, and the church and the intelligentsia retained cultural leadership. Moreover, argued Szczepański, the restrictions on accumulation of family wealth and the fact it was no longer necessary (since the health care and education parents sought for their children were provided free) meant that what social differences remained would not become a basis for development of antagonistic classes. The Hungarian sociologist Zsuzsa

Ferge reasoned similarly. The socialist project was for the absolute improvement of living conditions and the relative decrease of differences between social groups, not about absolute equality.[10]

What was the nature of the differences still acknowledged to exist? With more affluence, basic matters like food no longer played much of a role. People across the board ate less bread and potatoes but more meat and sugar, and drank more beer, wine and spirits. Housing need not reflect income because state-subsidized flats had very low rents and the best supply of houses was actually in the poorer countryside, if often lacking amenities. However, household furnishings, including vacuum cleaners, could be a significant indicator of status and lifestyle. Divergences in lifestyle still made a boundary apparent between equally waged manual and non-manual workers. Thus non-manuals had more phones and cars, their patterns of socializing entailing wider networks, it seemed, than the family and locality-orientated manual workers.[11] In general, family size was the most significant indicator of living standards; non-manual households tended to be smaller than manual ones, which had the effect of countering their relatively low wages. While book reading and theatre visiting were activities more characteristic of intelligentsia members, certain features of intelligentsia lifestyle – which in countries like Poland had already incorporated elements of the old noble culture – tended to diffuse downwards, for example in the use of the polite form of address. Here eastern Europe's experience differed from the Soviet Union's, where the socialist greeting 'comrade' had made far more inroads into daily speech.

This did not mean a wider rejection of socialist ideas. In Poland before the onset of Solidarity opinion polls showed a majority favouring an absolute ceiling on incomes and defining democracy in terms of a just and equal society, rather than civil rights. Thus, in 1977, 78 per cent of young Poles declared in favour of a socialist world; in Czechoslovakia in the Prague Spring 89 per cent of respondents favoured continued socialist development and only 5 per cent a return to capitalism. Research in Slovenia (1971) showed strong egalitarian tendencies at all levels and particularly among skilled workers, at the heart of the communist project; only 3 per cent of Yugoslav university students thought a multi-party system was more democratic than their social self-management in 1969.[12] Yet the evidence suggests that support for socialist goals was by no means support for the communist party and could be turned against a party seen as failing to deliver on them. Only 38 per cent to 43 per cent would definitely have voted communist in multi-party elections in Czechoslovakia in 1968 despite the overwhelming support for continued socialist development mentioned above. Only 44 per cent said in 1977 that Yugoslav communist party interests coincided with those of the majority, though a mere 2 per cent denied that they did.[13] Plainly, in these two countries with the strongest natural base for communism large numbers regarded it with a certain

reservation. Again, the red thread running through the east European communist experience was not hostility to the regimes' developmental goals,
but distrust of communists and their means. The remarkable episode of the
Polish Solidarity episode once more showed up communist feet of clay.

Solidarity in Poland, 1980–81

In a communist experience divided into two phases by the suppression of
the Prague Spring, the Solidarity crisis falls halfway through the second
phase, sharing some traits with 1968 but in others anticipating 1989. Four
aspects in hindsight cast a searchlight into the future. These were the failure of the Polish economic opening to the west in the 1970s, the emergence
of an openly non-Marxist opposition movement, the dilemmas of a communist party lacking ideological conviction and the possibility of such a
party attempting a deal with the opposition on some kind of 'corporatist'
basis. All these themes were to come back in 1989. More, certain socialistic features of Solidarity in 1980–81, though the word was not used, help
explain the partial rehabilitation of former communists, as reborn social
democrats, in the east European politics of the 1990s.

Polish economic policy under general secretary Edward Gierek
(1970–80) was based on the need to appease the workers without calling in
question the command economy. The solution was found in an investment
drive heavily funded by western credits. Polish industrial production grew
by 70 per cent in 1971–75, ranking it tenth in the world, while real income
per capita grew twice as much as had been planned. Investment was also
way over target. This ill-considered tempo gave Poland a hard currency
debt which stood at $20 billion by 1980, by which time debt service charges
had risen to 82 per cent of exports. The world oil price hikes of the 1970s
and rise of world interest rates helped dash hopes for a Polish export industry which could pay back the debt to the west; Poland could not exploit its
western-derived technology as effectively as foreseen or even afford the necessary spare parts. As the economy nose-dived in the second half of the
1970s, agriculture also suffered, affecting food supply. Though private
peasants had gained from the abolition of compulsory deliveries (1972) and
inclusion in social insurance and old age pension schemes (1972/1978),
they felt threatened by the priority given to state farms at their expense.
Behind the contradictory policy towards private farmers lay continuing
assumptions about the inevitability of large-scale socialized agriculture,
which showed the difficulty of harmonizing pragmatism with inherited
socialist concepts of modernity. As the population became more frustrated
at the economic downturn, so resentment grew at disparities of wealth and
corruption, observable through the fifteen-fold increase of the turnover of
hard currency stores (1965–75), the foreign bank accounts now permitted
and the lifestyle of figures like the head of Polish Radio-Television, Maciej

Szczepański, with his mansions, yachts and call-girls. In 1980, 69 per cent of pensioners, a rapidly growing group, 55 per cent of private peasants and 46 per cent of employees in the state sector experienced a fall in real income. The first novelty of the crisis was that a Marxist regime should have got into such difficulties in part because of running up a huge debt with the west. Marxism-Leninism was supposed to be about saving people from the tentacles of capitalism.

The second was the nature of the opposition to the regime. The sociological predictions (see Chapter 1) of a new departure in the structure of east European politics were borne out. Solidarity was not a movement of reform communists but a trades union, whose right to exist independently of the party was the cornerstone of the Gdańsk agreement conceded by the Polish government to striking workers in the Lenin Shipyard on 31 August 1980. The occasion of strike action was the government's decision to raise food prices sharply, as it had been on the Baltic coast in 1970 and in central Poland in 1976. Solidarity was therefore the result of a tradition of worker militancy, combined with patriotic traditions roused by Pope John Paul II's election in 1978 and his triumphal reception by huge crowds during his visit to Poland in 1979. The movement's ten million members were led by a pious, humbly educated electrician, Lech Wałęsa, one of the worker recruits from a rural background of whom Connor had written. Such vast numbers also included massive professional and white-collar representation, however, including former reform communist intellectuals. Disavowing attempts to reinterpret Marxism which would cut no ice with a party indifferent to real ideological concerns, these intellectuals now turned directly to the masses and in the organization KOR (Workers' Defence Committee), set up by the ex-reform communist Jacek Kuroń, sought to give legal support to persecuted workers after the strikes of 1976. Kuroń's philosophy was that dissidents should avoid any direct challenge to the unreformable party-state's authority, which would simply invite the repression of 1956 and 1968; they should seek, rather, to create 'social space' by constructing their own networks in the interstices of the system. Aspects of this championing of individual creativity in the face of a repressive, philistine environment have been likened to the mood of the 1968 generation in western Europe.[14] There is room for debate, therefore, on the importance of intellectual influence in Solidarity's birth. The sociologist Roman Laba has vigorously traced Solidarity's roots to the calls for free trades unions by the 1970 Baltic coast strikers, denying what he sees as patronizing ideas that workers needed KOR's guidance.[15] Evidence can be adduced on both sides. KOR did see the relevance of its ideas of creating free networks to the union issue and was behind the journal *Robotnik* (The Worker), which championed the free trades union movement on the Baltic coast in the late 1970s, from which Solidarity sprang. In an opinion survey of October 1981, however, 48 per cent of its members defined Solidarity as in the first place a trades union, against 20 per cent seeing it primarily as a social movement (which had become KOR's perspective) and 19 per cent as an expression of Polish patriotism.[16]

Solidarity's problem was that the conventional trades union fight for the workers' share of the cake was unrewarding in a time of near economic collapse, brought on partly by its own wage demands and wranglings over the implementation of the Gdańsk agreement. National income fell 13 per cent in 1981. With working-class members embroiled in local disputes, intellectuals in the leadership increasingly inclined towards the social movement concept of Solidarity, with a contribution to make to the resolution of the national crisis through democratization. The Solidarity Congress of September 1981, 70 per cent of whose delegates were intellectuals, called for free elections to local councils and enterprise self-management, as steps towards the institutionalization of popular influence on the party-state. However, rank and file opinion continued to prioritize living standards, and latterly an end to the disruption and food shortages which threatened them, over moves towards a political party role. The impasse pushed the Solidarity leadership in the other direction, towards more direct political participation, in which voices were heard calling for free elections to the Polish parliament. These growing discords in the movement, which the moderate Wałęsa could hardly bridge, allowed the Polish communists to link the whole of Solidarity with the radicals and destabilization, so that increasing numbers came to blame opposition as well as government for the social malaise.

The party's weakness had, however, been exposed. Most members simply joined it to safeguard their social position or more particularly their family's. (This was true of the whole Soviet bloc; a startling Czechoslovak statistic from 1967 shows that 33 per cent of fathers were party members and only 4 per cent of the rest of the population.)[17] Hence in 1980–81 hundreds of thousands of party members resigned from the party, disproportionately workers, or remained but joined Solidarity, frustrating the party's early attempts to nip Solidarity in the bud. A movement for intra-party democracy developed that resulted in 90 per cent of the delegates at the Party's Ninth Congress of July 1981 attending for the first time. Only the inner bureaucracy, kept up to the mark by strong Soviet pressure, remained cohesive; the Polish Homeland Defence Committee recommended martial law on 13 September, well before general secretary General Jaruzelski preempted a Solidarity call for a day of action by introducing it three months later. Thus the 'Front of National Accord' which he offered on 30 October can hardly have been a serious offer to rein in the party's monopoly of power; for one thing, it proposed making Solidarity only one of seven interested parties. Jaruzelski's later argument that his declaration of martial law was the lesser evil, designed to avoid a Soviet intervention, has been called in question by evidence that he himself appealed for Soviet military support. The charge is not quite conclusive, though, as once Jaruzelski judged he could not avoid action Soviet aid was desirable to ensure a smooth operation. In hindsight his motives seem less significant than the fact that a general should have become party leader and proclaimed martial law in the name of a Military Council of National Salvation, replacing the party flag by the Polish flag on the party headquarters. Such an intervention of the military in its own communist state was an unprecedented humiliation for a Marxist-Leninist party and the party's subsequent restoration, without the felt need to revamp it as in Hungary in 1956, could only mean its leaders no longer took it seriously. This exposure of the communist party as a shell was the third way in which 1981 anticipated 1989.

The Hungarian crisis lasted a fortnight, the Prague Spring eight months, the Solidarity era sixteen months. Over so long a period the question of some sort of accommodation between licensed opposition and government naturally arose. As a trades union Solidarity held aloof from any such engagement, so as to avoid responsibility for government's problems. As the concept of Solidarity as a social movement gained ground among the leadership, however, so it edged nearer to playing a proactive role. In autumn 1981 it proposed a Social Council on the National Economy and even a second parliamentary chamber alongside the Sejm. This curiously foreshadowed the Round Table deal between the party and Solidarity of April 1989, which created a second chamber won by Solidarity so sweepingly that communist hegemony finally cracked. For the authorities' part, too, there were proposals that smacked of corporatism, whether sincere ones from minor figures or less sincere like Jaruzelski's Front of National Accord and subsequent meeting with Wałęsa and the head of the Polish Catholic Church on 4 November. Jaruzelski's deputy prime minister, Miecysław Rakowski, claimed after martial law that his sincere wish for an understanding with Solidarity had been unjustly traduced. It seems unlikely that he really meant to offer more than the 'consultative authoritarianism' of Kádár's Hungary, in Timothy Garton-Ash's phrase.[18] The fact that he was prime minister when the genuine Round Table deal of 1989 was struck, however, even more perhaps that in 1981 his divorced wife was a member of KOR and his son and daughter were living in Australia and Barcelona respectively, does add force to the view that communist politics were no longer taking place in Stalinist blinkers.[19] Some predisposition towards dialogue between autonomous social forces and the party state, even if shallow, was plainly already present in 1981.

That Solidarity's 16 months might carry wider messages for the communist bloc was not a general view at the time. Solidarity was widely seen as a uniquely Polish phenomenon, related to Poland's size and powerful national, Catholic traditions; it was noted that economic crisis had been avoided by Japan with an equally high investment rate and by Hungary with a greater per capita debt. Nor did 1980–81 seem to breed other communist regimes' fears of infection the way 1956 and 1968 had done. The advantage of hindsight shows that Solidarity did have a wider relevance. The Polish crisis lay in mishandling what was a general strategy of the socialist bloc, namely to fund consumerism through western loans rather than reforming command economies. This strategy had the backing of the Soviet Union, which hoped to reduce the burden of its economic support to its satellites. The Polish experience showed its potential dangers. Assuming, too, that the Rakowskis of this world were not just heedless monsters driven by an Orwellian logic of power (an assumption not much made when communists were understandably demonized), the ways by which they would have to redefine their relationship with the rest of society were anticipated by the late Polish 1981 talk of national accords and institutionalized partnership. It pointed, if yet dimly, to the Round Tables of 1989. Finally, the divergence between working-class and intellectual perceptions as the crisis worsened, together with workers' continued prioritization of egalitarian values, seen as social justice, helps explain the electoral successes of ex-communists in the post-1989 era.

Economic problems

Solidarity was about Polish patriotism, yes, but also the nexus between brittle living standards and notions of an autonomous civil society. This theme came to be generalized elsewhere through economic failure. By the 1980s the inability of the command economy to meet the needs of more advanced economies, compounded by an international environment of high energy prices and interest rates, had resulted in virtual stasis. Moreover, the hopes placed in socialist market solutions, like those of self-managing Yugoslavia or Hungary's New Economic Mechanism (NEM), had not been fulfilled. The remaining prop of communist legitimacy was crumbling.

Why did most east European countries continue with variants of the command model up until or almost until the collapse of communism? The Prague Spring reinforced hard-line suspicions that economic reform would have destabilizing political consequences, while communists' obsession with heavy industry as a vehicle of growth gave the managers concerned and the central planners linked to them a strong base from which to obstruct changes. But even given good will, there were both practical and theoretical difficulties in grafting reforms like profit-led remuneration and decentralized decision-making on to the existing structures. Thus the liberalization of Czechoslovak prices in the Prague Spring produced unexpectedly rapid inflation; the larger incentive bonuses for managers, which increased wage differentials at the start of the Hungarian NEM (1968–69), were not an easy pill for socialists to swallow. But full return to the Stalinist model did not occur. The common pattern by the 1970s was to retain or return to quantitative targets and 'plan hierarchy', whereby the central plan bound the regional plans and so on down, while reducing the number of indicators to be met and introducing an element of profit-based incentive. This largely followed the East German case. Indeed, after the wobbles of the early 1960s, the five-year plan targets of bloc countries for 1966–70 and 1971–75 were achieved, ranging from East Germany's 5.4 per cent to Romania's 11.3 per cent for the latter period.[20]

How are decades of such high growth figures to be reconciled with the lowly per capita living standards of the post-communist successor economies on record today? Communist gross figures included double-counting, of input materials as well as the finished product; Michael Marrese recalculated the 1970–75 growth figures down from an average growth rate of 8 per cent to 5 per cent.[21] Deliberate massaging of figures also took place, particularly in the GDR, to disguise the embarrassing gap with West Germany. Above all, much communist growth went to produce items like steel which were then used to make more of the same, at the expense of consumption and personal income. Even the more modest figures given for these Jaroslav Krejči thought greatly exaggerated, recalculating the share of personal consumption for 1956–70 from 60.6 per cent to 43.3 per cent of Czechoslovak national income.[22] Much of the 'surplus value' appropriated by capitalists from the workers, according to Marxist theory, he thought the state simply squandered – for example, 3–6 per cent of national income went through setting false exchange rate structures for exports. Waste continued: one-fifth of Czechoslovak capital funds in the early 1980s was tied up in 30 000 unfinished building sites.

The comeuppance was foreshadowed in the later 1970s and delivered in the 1980s. The plan results for 1976–80 varied from 1.6 per cent growth (Poland) to 7.3 per cent (Romania). Thereafter, Poland's net material product for 1988 has been put 1 per cent below the figure for ten years earlier, Hungary's barely advanced and real net personal income in the social sector fell in Yugoslavia by 26 per cent. The striking feature of decline was the collapse of the relationship with the west, foreshadowed by Poland. The balance of payments in western trade from the mid-1970s became sharply negative, leading to huge hard currency debts – $19 million for Yugoslavia (1981), $17 million for Hungary (1987) and swelling further to $38 million for Poland. Polish expenditure on research and development fell to half 1975 levels a decade later and the number of industrial licences bought from 316 in 1971–75 to just six in 1981–85, accounting for only 1.2 per cent of industrial production – a signal verdict on the strategy of modernizing into western markets. Meanwhile, compared to its prewar position, Czechoslovakia fell from tenth place to forty-second in world industrial production and East German living standards, from approximate parity with West Germany before the war, to an estimated three-quarters in 1967 and perhaps half by the late 1980s.[23]

There was irony in the Soviet bloc's dependence on the capitalist west for sources of innovation. The communist vision of the future had always pre-supposed the fecund creativity of a socialist society. In fact fetishization of the plan and heavy industry ruled. It is symptomatic of the latter that despite an official report saying it would be at least three times as expensive to mine an extra ton of brown coal as to save a ton by less wasteful use, the Polish plan for 1986–90 still envisaged increasing coal production by 14 million tons a year. Moscow's increasing reluctance to supply the region's energy needs below world market prices was part of a pattern whereby the terms of trade turned sharply against eastern Europe by 19 per cent in the region as a whole between 1970 and 1985. Despite Marxist international-ist rhetoric, the communist world's trading association, Comecon, proved a relatively weak instrument for mutual aid in a harsher international cli-mate. Only a super-plan could remedy this situation and this went against the grain of a system based on autarchic state planning and arbitrary pric-ing, besides raising sensitive issues of national sovereignty. Trade between Comecon countries therefore took place on a bilateral basis rather than multi-laterally, a situation not essentially changed by the creation of a con-vertible rouble as a unit of account and two international banks, for 'eco-nomic cooperation' (1964) and for 'international investment' (1971). By 1989 nothing had been done about the question of uniform exchange rates (a first step towards currency convertability) which had been postponed for ten years in Comecon's Comprehensive Programme of 1971. There was no meeting of minds between reformist Hungary, which wanted to push towards multilateral trade, and the Soviets and countries like Bulgaria, which were happy with existing, more or less barter arrangements. In 1975 only 5 per cent of Comecon's trade turnover was conducted multilaterally and only 0.04 per cent of its citzens were employed in another Comecon country. Declarations like Comecon's 1985 Comprehensive Programme to Promote the Scientific and Technological Progress of the Member Countries of the CMEA up to the Year 2000 remained largely statements of intent. In view of communism's modernist pretensions it is striking how backward the eastern bloc remained in computer technology and telecommunications, leading sectors in the advancing global revolution. While in West Germany the number of unskilled workers with a phone rose from 20 per cent to 58 in the 1970s, in East Germany only one home in seven had one in 1990. The average waiting time for a new phone in Poland was 13 years. Faxing played little part in eastern Europe because of the poor quality of transmis-sion.[24] East German attempts to go in for microchip specialization resulted only in a three billion marks annual subsidy.

A feature of the 1980s was the decline of hopes that all these oddities could be resolved. The Hungarian NEM, introduced in 1968, dispensed with plan hierarchy and fixed targets, using financial and tax regulations to keep managers in line. Investment funding remained largely in state hands.

Despite a conservative backlash reaching a peak in 1972–74, the above aspects of the reform survived and it was reinvigorated from 1978. Enterprises could issue bonds (1982); new enterprise forms were created whereby employees of state firms in their free time could set up cooperatives sub-contracting for the socialized sector or working for the free market (1982); a bankruptcy law was framed for failing state businesses, and the great bulk of state ownership rights were transferred to enterprises, now effectively autonomous (1985). These moves, however, had little effect on the slide of the Hungarian economy. The prevalence of exemptions, and price and investment controls meant that even before the partial degutting of the reform in the early 1970s managers found it more practical to pursue profit by cosying up to the planners than by market initiatives. Plan-bargaining over physical targets was replaced by bargaining over financial regulations. The heavy industrial sector continued to secure its subsidies and credits, subject to so-called 'soft constraints' rather than the 'hard constraints' which would have cut off the gravy train; the bankruptcy law was hardly used. Meanwhile, new cooperatives from the mid-1980s brought into the urban economy the kind of symbiotic state–private relationship which had already developed in the countryside, rather than amounting to a strong independent sector. Their sponsoring by the authorities was really a matter of bringing into legality a 'second economy' which already existed. It was through this kind of two-job economy – public and private – that Hungarians had managed to make both ends meet as growth stagnated.

In the 1960s and 1970s the Yugoslav model of self-managing socialism had aroused the most interest in reform-minded east Europeans. Yugoslavia was effectively a free market, where enterprises from 1965 were free to dispose of their profits through wages or reinvestment as they chose. The problem of 'soft constraints' turned out to dog the Yugoslav model also, however. Ethnic sentiment in the multi-national state meant that enterprises became identified with republican or local power structures, which for political reasons would not let them fail. At the international level Tito's prestige until his death in 1980 ensured a flow of funds unmatched by exports. Enterprise self-management, with workers' control of their own incomes, inhibited the intra-regional mobility of labour and technology: a rich region had no interest in welcoming workers from a poor one, who would lower the average income, while branch lines taking innovative technology into a new area would soon demand autonomous self-managing status, depriving the parent enterprise of benefit from its start-up venture. A self-managing economy also proved very vulnerable to externally driven inflation, making the oil price hikes the start of Yugoslavia's travails. The proof of the pudding is in the eating. Having grown at more than 5 per cent a year until 1979 Yugoslavia by 1987 experienced rising unemployment, a quintupling of inflation (to 150 per cent), and falls of 26 per cent and 20 per cent in real net personal income and labour productivity respectively.

It is legitimate, therefore, to talk of systemic crisis in communist economies in the 1980s. The ironies were unmistakable. A creed which saw heavy
industry as the acme of modernity had missed the modern technological
revolution. An internationalist movement dug in behind its inconvertible
currencies, multiple exchange rates and foreign trade monopolies against
the global market. Systems that had arisen on a promise to end the cyclical
crises of capitalist boom and bust had developed their own cycles, of start-
up and rush as investments piled up, followed by halt and slowdown, leaving the waste of unfinished projects and squandered resources. Of course,
academics are trained to spot inconsistencies, of which no society is free.
What was significant about communist economics is that the contradictions
were systemic; they arose from the attempt to dispense with real market
prices, modern mechanisms for raising investment capital (bonds, commercial banks, stocks and shares), wage bargaining, entrepreneurship and
enterprise-level international trade. The attempt to substitute for these factors or graft them back on proved insoluble at a competitive level.

A flawed modernization?

Eastern Europe's economic weakness in the 1980s confirmed the Marxist
premise that relates the fortune of a society to its economic base. As indices of growth slowed down or were reversed, governments were hard
pressed to maintain standards in fields like health and education which
were socialism's proudest achievements. Meanwhile, the Soviet bloc's claim
to be inaugurating a new kind of more advanced human society was
upstaged by rival models of modernization, in the Asian tigers and to a considerable extent in southern Europe too, in countries like Spain, Greece and
Portugal which now acceded to the flourishing European Community. If
the region was not heading to a glorious future, to what kind of society was
it heading? This question was increasingly put in what turned out to be
communism's last decade.

Statistics revealed that the great industrialization drive had limped
almost to a halt. The proportion of urban dwellers continued to grow in the
1980s, but more slowly than in western Europe. The state sector was no
longer inexorably expanding everywhere. Its share of national income fell
from 73.3 per cent to 65.2 per cent in Hungary between 1975 and 1984,
while numbers of those working in it in Poland fell by 485 000 (1980–88)
and rose by 547 000 in the non-state sector. As the vision of the great industrial future receded, its ecological legacy became more apparent.
Environmental effects had figured little in early communist priorities – a
1983 Albanian postcard proudly depicted a smokestack rising in a verdant
vale. Much Polish, Czech and East German production depended on brown
coal whose sulphurous fumes the regimes were too poor to filter. A Polish
ecologist commented that saving the environment would treble the cost of

the 1981–85 national plan. Fines for abuse of environmental regulations were too low to be disincentives. The principal impacts were dead forests (one-third in the Czech lands), river pollution, which in turn contaminated an estimated 21 per cent of public water mains in west Slovakia (1981) – and, of course, on health.

Thus vital statistics for the coal areas of western Bohemia ceased to be published and in general expectation of life worsened vis-à-vis the west, actually falling among middle-aged men. Medicines often became unavailable, like insulin in Yugoslavia where health spending at 3.5 per cent of national income (1987) was at its lowest ever point. In the search for funds Romania and Bulgaria introduced payment for certain services, for example cosmetic surgery. Mental health problems also drew increasing adverse comment, with 750 000 to a million people suffering from hypertension in Czechoslovakia (1984) and rising suicide rates, highest among unskilled workers. Those on low incomes were also at a disadvantage in societies where it was fairly common to bribe poorly paid health workers. A further disadvantage of the ostensible ruling class was that heavily subsidized state housing usually went to the better off. Szelényi's study of Hungarian housing policy in the 1960s argued that subsidized flats were an important means of attracting the desired managerial or technical personnel. Measures allowing holders of state housing to buy it up at low rates in the 1980s enabled this category, soon selling off their flats at near market price, to move from housing estates to the villas on the outskirts of Budapest, a status symbol similar to western norms.[25] Housing policy had long been an area in which the socialist state had withdrawn from ambitions of universal state provision, though much less so in Bulgaria and East Germany.

Education was another key sphere which suffered from economic decline. In Yugoslavia its share of national income fell by 44 per cent between the mid-1970s and mid-1980s. The head of the Hungarian Academy of Sciences complained in 1988 that his country was spending more on the military than on education, health and research put together.[26] There was also a longer-term problem involved. Communist educational policy, prioritizing vocational training for the masses rather than humanistic training for the elite, suffered from the phenomenon of rising expectations. Already by the 1970s vocational education was perceived as holding the vast new working classes back from the traditional career structure of *Gymnasium*, university and bureaucracy. When the authorities tried to strengthen the vocational element in education in Yugoslav Slovenia in the 1980s, they were met by mass parental protest. There was some justification for both sides. The urge to humanistic study was a part of the traditional class structure the communists had wanted to displace. But parents saw that hierarchy remained in communist society and they wanted their children to have access to it. In fact, eastern Europe did not make the transition to mass higher education that gathered pace in the west in the 1980s.

The percentage of the age group enrolled in higher education in the region averaged around 10 per cent, and with communist apparatchiks regularly gaining the academic qualifications they had not necessarily had before, the prospect of a conventional stratification emerging was real. In this as in other ways communist society resembled an old car which had been a revolutionary model in its day, but was now outdated.

The undermining of communist ideals by economic weakness and ideological shifts affected the 'woman question' too. In the absence of a subtler framing of the issue than that women's disabilities were all due to capitalism, when problems began to be encountered by the 1960s recourse was often made to old stereotypes. The ongoing labour shortage and awareness of social problems like juvenile delinquency combined to relegitimize some return to ideas of women's traditional role as child-bearer and mother. Women themselves often thought in these terms. Only a third of Czechoslovak women, mainly professionals, showed a wish to continue working unless they had to to make ends meet. The fact was that the drive to integrate women in the labour market had been as much to provide cheap labour for socialist reconstruction as to broaden their horizons; it meant men did not have to be paid 'the living wage' of old-style male trades unionism, namely a wage with which they could support their families. Fears began to be expressed because of the falling birth rate. Though only Ceaușescu's Romania significantly tightened up restrictions on abortion, increasing incentives were offered to women to ease child-bearing, in terms of child benefits and periods of up to three years' absence from the workplace. The problem with readmission of traditional notions of the woman's role is that they legitimized the 'double burden' of a day's paid work with several hours of unpaid housekeeping, child-minding and shopping. On average, women had half the leisure time of men. This problem had been predicted by socialist thinkers and was to be solved communally by crèches, canteens and laundries, and scientifically through labour-saving devices: hardly anyone in the 1940s dreamed of persuading men to wash dishes and nappies. But the mood of heroic collectivism soon passed; by the mid-1960s only 20 per cent of Czechoslovak workers had their main meal in the factory, as compared to 45 per cent of West Germans (1966), while laundries accounted for just 5 per cent of washing and economies geared to heavy industry were slow to produce domestic washing machines. Communist thinking on the role of women reflected its era and the severe, dark-blue-suited officials of indeterminate age who manned the minor desks of communist Europe's pervasive bureaucracy fitted neither traditional nor modern feminist views of a woman's role.

Until at least the 1970s an attraction of the communist world was to offer a recipe for rapid development. But by the mid-1980s Comecon's total exports to the west were exceeded three-fold by Taiwan and twice each by Singapore and South Korea. The moral could be pressed closer to home.

Czechoslovakia was on a par with Germany before the war and well ahead of latifundist Spain. Spain overtook her in private cars and phones per capita in her spurt of the 1960s, Portugal followed in the 1980s. Variations in geography alone cannot account for the remarkable differences in the point at which passenger kilometres travelled by air surpassed those by rail. In Ireland this was 1962, Greece 1969, the United Kingdom 1976, France 1992. In 1989 air transport thus defined was only an eighth of train transport in Czechoslovakia, a ninth in Poland, about a half in Yugoslavia. Here not just affluence but also the degree of integration into a wider world can be sensed. Eastern Europe had progressed but so had the others. Arguably, it remained as backward relative to western Europe as it had been before the war. A rurally employed population range from 34 per cent to 78 per cent in 1930 had fallen to from 12 per cent to 30 per cent, and more in Albania. But the western span, from *c*.18–30 per cent had shrunk to 4–7 per cent. The region seemed to have run out of steam with its ageing leaders. After the death of two leaders from the 1940s (Tito, 1980; the Albanian Enver Hoxha, 1985), there was still the Bulgarian chief Todor Zhivkov (1954), János Kádár (1956), Nicolae Ceauşescu (1965), Gustáv Husák (1969) and the new boy, Erich Honecker (1970).

As communist society aged, the body of work speculating on its nature grew. Regime Marxist positions maintained the gradualist thesis of movement to the ever more egalitarian, developed society, but in implicitly defensive and derivative terms; an able work like Zsuzsa Ferge's on Hungarian social policy of 1979 took its categories from western social science and refuted anti-communist criticisms in these terms. Meanwhile, western Trotskyists stuck to the facile line that communist societies were simply state capitalist ones in which socialism had not been tried. More interesting were east European dissident theses, voiced by Konrád and Szelényi, that a new society had indeed been formed, but a class-based one of a new type, founded on an intelligentsia using its monopoly of information to carry out 'rational allocation' of resources in place of the market allocation of capitalism. This intelligentsia was no longer just the party bureaucracy pinpointed as the new elite by the Yugoslav dissident Milovan Djilas in 1957, but incorporated alongside it technical-managerial and 'creative' strata. Much said above about educational advantage and elite privilege lends support to this view, but with important caveats. The erratic operation of east European planning acted to undermine ideas of 'rational allocation' by a Platonesque elite and, besides, in the 1980s economic decline diminished the size of the cake to be allocated. The Romanian dissident communist Silviu Brucan opposed the thesis of intellectual class rule as incompatible with communist regimes' actual 'workerist' policies, including the relative fall of intelligentsia salaries and cuts in cultural spending. He could agree with Konrád and Szelényi that workers were held back in allegedly workers' states but thought this applied most strongly to members of the pre-revolutionary working class who, he rightly pointed out, had been relatively rather well paid before the war. In Brucan's perspective, the actual basis of communist regimes and their workerist policies were the millions of ex-peasant workers. Whereas Konrád and Szelényi implied that intelligentsia rule was a betrayal of the socialist experiment, Brucan regretted its failure to emerge. The lesson of 70 years of communism for him had been of the need to modify Marx's thesis of the ascendant working class and recognize that workers could only rule if they produced an intelligentsia from their own ranks. But for ideological reasons communists had been unwilling to accept this logical consequence of their social development policy, and the result was stagnation. What did Marx's class theory mean in the society of the scientific-technological revolution where mechanics worked in agriculture?[27]

Such fundamental doubts among Marxists of the intellectual underpinnings of their creed grew as the 1980s wore on. Jan Szczepański wrote in a gloomy article of 1985 that he had expected industrialization to transform people's consciousness (as Marxism predicted). But under modern circumstances cultural ideas travelled so fast that the posited relationship of economic base determining intellectual superstructure did not hold; what really shaped consciousness were local communities and they were still trying, as much at a sub-conscious as a conscious level, to restore the values first upturned by the turmoil of the Second World War.[28] In this revealing reference to people's psychological need to renew contact with their past, Szczepański was implicitly opening up quite different sociological perspectives from those of the 1970s. In this new climate ideas began to sprout which not only saw eastern Europe as a class society but as one heading back to older, pre-communist forms. At their most basic, these ideas stressed that in a society lacking effective channels of representation and communication, individuals sought protection in familiar networks of kin, locality or ethnicity, which could be used to tap influence and connections. Social references could be more specifically historical. Ivan Szelényi, for one, raised the theme of 'embourgeoisement' among Hungary's farmers, tracing a line between prosperous peasants in pre-communist times and those who were setting up as small entrepreneurs in the freer economic climate of the 1980s.[29] His compatriot Elemér Hankiss speculated that as the communists would not voluntarily surrender power, eastern Europe would have to build a middle class in waiting from commercial and intellectual elements; embourgeoisement would have to precede democratization as had happened in western Europe in the eighteenth century. These pointers were not to a novel future but a known past. The irrevocability of the new order was not as axiomatic as it had been.

Communists, whether idealists or cynics, had always exuded the sense of irreversible change, of having set the past adrift from the flagship of history. Only odd references suggested an awareness of limitation, if not doubt, of the new order. Thus the prime minister of the Prague Spring,

Oldřich Černik, strolling a crowded one-time castle park, mused that the 'feudal lords' had left something that still mattered to the people, and added: 'Do you think we will leave anything of value behind us?'[30] The Yugoslav partisan and Tito biographer Vladimir Dedijer recalls his wife's envy, after taking their dying child to a hospital ringed by churches on hills around, of the pious local women who had the comfort of knowing they would meet their loved ones again – and adds that he never sought to persuade anyone out of their faith thereafter.[31] Religion was one of the strongest echoes from the past to resound. In fact, the Catholic Church had blossomed in People's Poland, doubling its number of priests and winning battles for the right to give religious instruction to willing schoolchildren and build churches in the new industrial centres. Contrary to initial communist assumption, Polish popular belief was nearly as massive a phenomenon in towns as the countryside, and showed a remarkable resurgence among the young: from 74 per cent to 96 per cent among students and schoolchildren together between 1981 and 1988. More than a third of young people by the latter date had participated in religious groups whose 'moral rigour' could fill the 'social vacuum' and perhaps enable a 'conservative modernization' in a society unprepared for the 'radical secularization' of the West and unresponsive to the 'patchy modernization' provided by the regime.[32] The Polish Catholic Church thus functioned as an alternative source of authority to the state. Elsewhere the 'Basic Communities' worshipping privately in Czechoslovakia and Hungary showed a will to a religious life untrammelled by church leaders' collaboration with the communist regimes. In Orthodox countries, where collaboration was the norm, their role was often played by burgeoning Protestant groups; there were 200 000 Baptists in Romania by the 1980s. In Yugoslavia too the relaxation in church – state relations which had followed the reforms of the Second Vatican Council was replaced in the 1980s by journalistic polemic and the arrest of clerics, including Orthodox and Muslim – after the Islamic Revolution in Iran.

A major issue here was regime fear of the fusion of religion and ethnicity to produce a combustible nationalism. That religion could be as much about identity as faith appears from the curious statistic whereby 93 per cent of Croats in one sample claimed membership of the Catholic Church but only 80 per cent believed in God.[33] The Hungarian Calvinist pastor László Tőkés, later to play an important role at the outset of the Romanian revolution of 1989, has written feelingly of the identification of Hungarian nationality with Protestant Christianity where he grew up in Transylvania.[34] The concreteness and beauty of folk artifacts became a powerful symbol of real identity in the decaying world of communist slogans; nationalism with its claim of ancient roots and its affective appeal salved spirits lost in the concrete jungle of the communists' underfunded utopia or wearied by 'the kind of declarative-repetitive discussions on nationalism which have exhausted themselves before our eyes,' in the words of a disillusioned Yugoslav.[35] Yugoslavia became the touchstone of communist hopes and disappointments on the national question. A nominal federalism on Soviet lines (1946) had become a genuine one, with confederal aspects by the 1974 constitution: Serbs' control of their historic land of Kosovo had been relinquished to the Albanian majority, Bosnians of Muslim tradition had been recognized as a separate 'Muslim' nation and the one remaining federal fund was to channel aid to the poorer regions. These formulae, compounded with economic shortage, led to tensions on all sides, of which the most symptomatic was the inflaming of a feud over how many Serbs the Croat fascist ustasha had actually massacred in the Second World War. The later founding President of Croatia, Franjo Tuđman, won his political spurs on this issue; the Serbian historian Đuretić electrified his countrymen by attacking communist equations of the genocidal, fascist ustasha with Serb chetniks who were merely fighting for self-preservation. Better than this corrosive moral relativism would be to be honest about past problems in the hope of initiating 'constructive social negations'.[36] This was a choice phrase for what turned out to be an invitation to civil war. The notorious Memorandum of the Serb Academy of Sciences of 1986 took up the cudgels of Serb nationalism when it effectively presented communist Yugoslavia's structures as a Titoist plot against Serbia's legitimate leadership role.

Đuretić's parody of the communists' attempt to defuse the bad blood between Serb and Croat after 1945 illustrates the fate of most of their nostrums. The list is long: 'people's states' in which ordinary people were treated cavalierly by irresponsible bureaucracies; the promise of universal health care which foundered on inadequate funds; the concentration on vocational training for the masses which appeared to block their rise; the mistaken assumption that religion would wither away far from the new industrial centres, that the end of capitalism would solve the 'woman problem', that youth would be won by sports clubs and lessons in Marxism-Leninism, that minority problems would be defused by autonomy and subsidy, which in the case of Kosovo irritated Croat and Slovene donors and Serb ex-hegemones without satisfying Albanians. Not all these failures were ignoble. Some of communism's failings which rankled most were less damning than they have often been depicted. The perks of the communist fat cats do not seem great compared to British golden handshakes and share options, and were in part unavoidable by-products of a system which outlawed normal accumulation of wealth. Dislike of communist inequality was a backhanded compliment to ostensible communist values. Most regimes, not just communist ones, become unpopular after a certain point. Two things particularly undermined communist eastern Europe. One was that the absence of an alternative was built into the system's utopian premise, and enforced by stultifying censorship. The other, and root of the utopianism, was the Marxist economic inheritance, which believed it possible to create plenty by planning away the most elementary instruments of economic life: markets and prices reflecting supply and demand.

Thus communist societies by the 1980s had gone as far as they could on their implausible premises. They had achieved changes that seemed remarkable by prewar standards but were no more remarkable than had been achieved elsewhere at less human cost and with greater freedom and wider prospects. A flawed vision had created a flawed society. Yet it would be wrong to say that it was already, for most of the people concerned, an intolerable society. They still struggled to achieve their dream of a better life; in Yugoslavia the number of cars actually went up by a third in the decade, through people's willingness to undergo privation for this status symbol. They were frustrated by flagging living standards, but we should remember that only in Poland were those standards better in 2001 than they were in 1989. Overall, there was a marked lurch towards pessimism and dissatisfaction in the second half of the 1980s, but as far as the majority were concerned it was more to apathy and gloom than to prerevolutionary militancy. Plainly the accelerating decline of the communist system, the erosion of sources of possible legitimacy, was a key factor in the collapse of 1989. It set the scene in which other factors might spark the final combustion. Among these were the reactions of communist apparatchiks themselves to what was happening. As in the France of the late 1780s the last years before the storm were marked by a sudden spurt of innovations which in hindsight contributed to the collapse of the system they were meant to save. At issue were not just the internal structures of communist power, but the international framework established in 1945 which had enabled Soviet hegemony over its western satellites.

3

The centre cannot hold

By the mid-1980s east European communist society was clearly struggling. Yet regimes without popular legitimacy have taken a long time to die in the past. Experience suggests that for the final collapse of an ailing system a movement on the part of the rulers is also crucial, often, as the Tocqueville thesis on 1789 argued (see p. 11), through the initiation of reforms which only inflame the problem they are intended to solve. This is what was about to take place in eastern Europe. Shifts in the international strategic and ideological climate, and the emergence of opposition groupings which could exploit a sudden crisis, were also important in taking the region to the brink of system change.

Gorbachev and the international order

Both sides of the cold war internalized the Soviet domination of eastern Europe as a geopolitical axiom. Even Churchill's famous speech of 1946 about great European capitals being cut off behind an 'Iron Curtain' had shown a curious fatalism in including Prague behind the curtain, at a time when Czechoslovakia was still a functioning democracy. When the new American ambassador arrived in Prague in 1945 he found an embassy staff vastly smaller than in Peru where he had also served.[1] Limited concern for the region and the realpolitik of a nuclear age led western policy to the Helsinki Final Act of 1975, a measure of détente which gave the Soviet Union the international guarantee of postwar borders it wanted – and saw as a legitimation of the Soviet bloc's position as a whole. In return the Soviets signed up to a basket of measures concerning human rights, which they doubtless accepted in the spirit of Stalin's agreement to the European Declaration of Rights at Yalta in 1945 – as empty rhetoric. The fact that the geopolitical division of Europe was internationally recognized and that the Soviets would suppress dissent in their sphere was the strongest single restraint on any attempts inside the region to change the status quo.

The west's historic perceptions were a matter of resentment for easterners, not least because they saw themselves as *central* Europeans. Attempts to revive the idea of central Europe in intellectual challenge to the division of Europe grew in the second half of the 1980s, particularly among Czechs, Poles and Hungarians.[2] But the impulse that really undermined the postwar geopolitical settlement came from the Soviet Union and the reform communism of Mikhail Gorbachev, albeit unwittingly. For there was a Russian Europhile tradition too, that of the westernizers who had battled through the nineteenth century with 'Slavophile' exponents of Russian distinctiveness; Marxists always claimed to share the secular, cosmopolitan traditions of the western Enlightenment. The history of communism has several times thrown up figures whose humanistic, rationalist inspiration is clear, men like Nagy and Dubček – and Mikhail Gorbachev.

Mikhail Gorbachev was born in 1931 of peasant stock and trained as a lawyer and agricultural manager before becoming a regional secretary at the early age of 39. His swift rise through the ranks must have reinforced his abundant self-confidence and given him at least a personal sense of the system's potential to deliver. Great energy and intellectual curiosity without, it seems, particular historical or philosophical reflectiveness, completed a personality which was shaped by the war and then the 'thaw' after Stalin's death, rare times in Soviet history which might encourage optimism about Soviet society's ability to overcome its authoritarian legacy. At the heart of Gorbachev's project was a faith that democratization and communism could go together in reforming a system whose weaknesses he knew from observation and from his intellectual contacts. He was the new generation, the educated leader sprung from the masses (he had two doctorates), who knew that a society whose secondary school graduates had quintupled since 1964 could no longer be governed in the same way. How radical a reformer he was at the outset in 1985 or indeed later has been disputed, but he exploited uncertainty about his intentions to balance skilfully between conservative forces and the party's liberal wing. By autumn 1988 he had transformed the old structures of power into a virtual presidential system, with himself head of a Supreme Soviet due for popular election the next spring. In the process traditional Marxist doctrine had been degutted by invoking its humanistic aura while jettisoning its economics and sociology. Proclaiming 'the priority of universal human values', foreign minister Shevardnadze could conclude in June 1988 that a policy of coexistence founded on 'such fundamental and universal principles as non-aggression, respect for sovereignty, non-interference in internal affairs etc., cannot be identified with class struggle'. Likewise the importance of 'the individual as well as of his self-realization and of his rights and liberties' was set at the centre of economic reform, and Gorbachev himself announced that 'a deeper understanding' of the relation of working-class interests to those of humanity gave the priority to common human values.[3] The intellectual turnaround was thinly disguised by appeals to Lenin's dictum always to seek the truth.

What did this mean for eastern Europe? Both main organs of the Soviet bloc, the military Warsaw Pact and Comecon, entailed disproportionate Soviet funding but arguably ensured Soviet priorities. The Soviets had 585000 troops in the region and 1400000 near their western border, as against some 900000 of their allies. Since nuclear weapons had diminished eastern Europe's significance as a buffer – the nearest American cruise missiles deployed in the early 1980s were a mere five minutes' flying time from Moscow – two chief motives remained for this massive force: to threaten a conventional strike against numerically weaker opponents, stressed by the west, and maintain internal cohesion of the eastern bloc, stressed by Pact commander Marshal Kulikov (1977–89). Some 80 per cent of requisite military expenditure came from the Soviets, running at twice or over the per capita contribution of her allies, which had not increased appreciably despite Moscow's chivvying. Bloc officers often received training in the Soviet Union and allied troops' loyalty was surveyed covertly by KGB agents and overtly by the Soviet military administration committee acting with its allied counterparts. According to a Polish source, the wishes of the Pact's Military Council were taken as orders by the Polish government but as advisory by the Soviet Commander in Chief.[4] The secretariat of Comecon's influential military-industrial commission was staffed entirely by Soviet citizens.

Economic relations in the bloc also made for heavy Soviet spending, though the extent of the subsidy involved is disputed. Marrese and Vanous's two estimates of 80 to 118 billion dollars for the 1970s have been scaled down by two-thirds by Marer and others. The main issue is whether the Soviet hidden subsidy extended not only to supplying east Europeans with energy which could have been more profitably sold to the west, but also to the Soviet Union's receipt of inferior bloc manufactures. In 1975 Comecon accepted the Soviet wish for annual adjustment of intra-bloc prices to reflect world prices over the previous five years; oil price levels in the 1980s meant that while the Soviet Union was still subsidizing its partners the level of subsidy fell, increasingly heavily after 1986. Both the Soviets and the east Europeans therefore felt the pinch. In Hungary's case a million tons of Soviet oil cost it 800 Ikarus buses in exports in 1974 and more than 4000 by the mid-1980s.[5] Meanwhile, as east Asian competition helped turn the global terms of trade against eastern Europe's engineering products in favour of Soviet energy, the Soviets' trade surpluses with their allies, allowed to accumulate, represented another form of credit. As always in economic relations there was room for both sides to feel aggrieved, with east Europeans resenting the Soviet priorities, which they felt throttled their development. At the most basic level, the Soviet Union paid to keep its allies quiet, as in writing off Polish debt after 1956 and 1981, and making economic concessions to Czechoslovakia after 1968. Had the time not come to put intra-bloc ties on a sounder basis?

It has been argued that the fate of the bloc was already under consideration before Gorbachev came to power. The mounting expense of the arms race, the American decision to site cruise missiles in western Europe in response to the Soviet SS20s, not least fears for the reliability of bloc partners appear to have produced some military tension in the Soviet leadership in the early 1980s; Staniszkis has claimed that this induced oscillation between military proposals for an offensive strategy against the west and nervous political reactions in favour of drawing in the horns of the troublesome Soviet east European empire.[6] Yet such moves can be read to show that eastern Europe figured for the Soviets only in the context of inter-bloc great power relations rather than as a problem in its own right, and this is how Gorbachev appears to have treated it. Despite the importance of the issues mentioned above, he gave them little initial priority, partly because of their sensitivity but mainly because of more pressing concerns: domestic matters and relations with the United States. By late 1987 he had negotiated an agreement on mutual withdrawal of intermediate nuclear weapons from Europe which reduced the need for a Soviet glaçis on its western border. It is possible that his rational, optimistic persona gave Gorbachev something of a blind spot where nationalism was concerned, leading him to underestimate eastern Europe's challenge for his project. His later attempts to reason Lithuanian protestors out of their nationalism remain one of the most tell-tale TV clips of his career. Be that as it may, in his first years as general secretary Gorbachev reaffirmed support for the use of force in 1981 and 1968 in the respective Polish and Czechoslovak party congresses, while phrases like 'concern for the common cause of socialism' (November 1987) might still be seen as euphemisms for the Brezhnev doctrine of socialist internationalism used against Czechoslovakia. Meanwhile the Soviet Union gave its Comecon partners notice it would no longer accept inferior goods and hundreds of special agreements regulated the product mix the Soviets desired, often entailing an upgrading partners could not easily provide. At this stage Gorbachevism for eastern Europe could still seem to mean primarily an end of the Brezhnev bargain which exchanged Soviet subsidies for east European acquiescence.

Early reservations, however, reflected Gorbachev's lack of complete control of the Soviet party rather than a lack of reform intentions. An unequivocal disavowal of foreign intervention 'under any pretext whatsoever' eventually came in March 1988.[7] Gorbachev had personal links to the Prague Spring through his university friendship with the leading Dubčekite Zdeněk Mlynář, whose funeral he was to attend in tears in 1997. His circle acknowledged a nexus between their own hopes and those of east

European reformists. Economic liberalization in Hungary and Poland was mentioned as relevant as a laboratory for experiments that if successful might benefit the Soviet reform project. Conversely, as the English-language *Moscow News* noted in 1988, difficulties of reform communism in Poland would be exploited by the opponents of perestroika in the Soviet Union. An analysis of the Soviet–east European relationship submitted by Soviet specialists to the first Soviet–American conference on the subject in July 1988 made no bones about the mistaken imposition on the region of a Stalinist model which had failed to stand the test of time, offering classic reform communist solutions: realistic prices and exchange rates in 'a qualitatively new model of a market type'. Eastern Europe was 'pregnant with crises' and in the interests of world peace the United States was warned not to try to exploit any recurrence of instability there for its own ideological purposes.[8] This fascinating document recognized the regional problem but showed the overriding priority for the Gorbachev camp of getting the relationship with the United States right, as a key to the successful resolution of other matters. Strategy to the west was not synchronized with policies in eastern Europe. Gorbachev's west-directed announcement of the withdrawal of 50000 Soviet troops from the region in December 1988 entailed a greater role for the native armies, but his regime had done nothing to strengthen their independence or supply them with the top-quality weapons they had traditionally lacked. Thus Gorbachev's radical rethinking of Soviet strategic goals had weighty implications for eastern Europe and his apparent failure to take these fully on board compounded the effect.

Perestroika and the fate of east European reform communism

The problem of Gorbachev's 'perestroika' as applied to eastern Europe was how to get its regimes to follow a line that explicitly said the Soviet Union would not dictate to them. The differentiated responses of the six states concerned, reflecting historic distinctiveness, showed the weakness of Gorbachevism as a force for overall bloc regeneration. In four of them the men in charge were with varying degrees of openness against Gorbachev's reforms. Of the two countries whose regimes were favourable, Poland was becoming increasingly unmanageable, while Hungary was slipping into the hands of communists who wanted to go beyond the Gorbachev vision.

Among regimes hostile to perestroika East Germany stood out. From being the ugly duckling in the communist camp, lacking clear identity and deserted by her people before the building of the Berlin Wall (1961), she had affirmed herself as the richest and best organized, reputedly the eighth industrial power in the world, no longer a client but a 'junior partner' in the words of a western observer.[9] Self-perception gave East German leaders a confidence to deny the relevance of the Gorbachev model. You did not have to wallpaper your room if your neighbour did, as one remarked;

Russia's merits lay in the struggle against fascism, another argued, not in its technology. By 1988 several Soviet journals aimed at youth were banned in the GDR. Because of the complex West German connection Honecker could plausibly argue that his country was a special case; he had yielded only reluctantly to Soviet pressure not to visit Bonn in the mid-1980s.

Romania's rejection of perestroika was also barely disguised. Her links to the rest of the Soviet bloc grew somewhat in the 1980s after the deple-tion of her oil reserves and loss of her special relationship with the west, including most-favoured-nation status with the United States in 1988. Ceaușescu's announced (but largely unimplemented) policy of knocking down villages to be replaced by agro-industrial complexes, together with the pollution and abortion scandals, were the spur here. However, in Gorbachev's 1987 visit, the Conducator's (leader's) speech was inter-rupted by applause some 50 times, while Gorbachev was heard in silence. The full paraphernalia of a Stalinist leadership cult and unreconstructed policies to match suited the taste of Ceaușescu and his wife, a shrewd but poorly educated pair of peasant background, in whom Marxist talk of man taming nature conjured up dreams of Promethean hubris which, sadly, they could indulge.

Czechoslovakia and Bulgaria's reservations were more discreet. While a leading Czechoslovak 'normalizer' scorned the 'so-called new policy',[10] the country's tradition was to keep its nose down and undermine at the grass roots what it dared not oppose openly. The press did not report Gorbachev's speeches in the stultifying fullness of communist journalism, and Czechs announced their own innocuous version of perestroika. When it was felt that Husák, so closely connected to the old Brezhnevite ways, had to go, he was made president (1987) and replaced by a man of similar ilk, Miloš Jakeš, who had been responsible for purging Prague after the Prague Spring. Todor Zhivkov's Bulgaria, most Russophile of the satellites, showed similar evasiveness. A stream of initiatives bade testimony to his devotion to the cause of reform. In fact, Zhivkov had no convictions either way, declaring after the fall of communism that he had not believed in it since the 1960s. Zhivkov's daughter's fate was a vignette of how personal life could develop behind a communist façade. Brought up in the elite and inducted into the Politbureau with a culture brief against Moscow's wishes, she responded to communist aridity by turning to cultural motifs of the nation's past and dab-bling in spiritualism before dying young. Her father in the 1980s sponsored a blatantly opportunistic campaign for the Bulgarianization of names and language of the country's sizeable Turkish minority, joining Ceaușescu and Milošević in the exploitation of nationalism. This wily operator had no point of contact with the high-principled Gorbachev.

In Poland and Hungary leaders were more receptive to the message of perestroika, but their control was in doubt. General Jaruzelski quickly became Gorbachev's favourite east European leader, with whom on his

1988 visit he signed an agreement for exploration of 'blank spots' in the history of Russo-Polish relations. On the whole, Gorbachev's confidence in Jaruzelski was justified. Since 1981 the Polish leader, realizing that only reform could save the Polish economy, had mixed repression with a search for ways of coopting the alienated Polish workforce. From 1986 these took centre stage, with an amnesty, the setting up of a Social Consultative Council and, in November 1987, an unsuccessful referendum asking Poles to sign up for belt-tightening economic reform in return for 'enrichment of the forms of socialist pluralism', a circumlocution worthy of the BBC's political satire *Yes, Prime Minister*. By 1987 Orwell, Kołakowski and the Czech dissident novelist Kundera were being freely published in Poland and the leading communist daily was discussing the concept of totalitarianism. These concessions, however, had not won the cooperation of disaffected workers, the economy continued to decline and the country, in April–May 1988 and again in August, was convulsed in strike waves. Moreover, experts were not convinced that the regime's latest economic proposals (1988) went further than earlier tinkerings or offered a reform comprehensive enough to prevent improvements in one sector being negated by linkages with unreformed ones.[11] Far from being a showcase for the workings of perestroika, Poland seemed to show a society that was terminally ill.

Of all east European countries it was Hungary to which Soviet reform communists turned most hopefully – 'the Hungarian reform has some global relevance', the Hungarian economist Kornai opined in 1986.[12] Ironically, Hungarian faith in reform communism withered away precisely at this juncture. The plethora of unavailing economic reforms of the mid-1980s (see Chapter 2) seem like the last gasps of a dying star, convincing the mainstream of Hungarian economists that as long as the nexus between administrators and the managers of large enterprises remained, so constraints on managers' ability to access public investment funds on 'soft', or non-commercial, criteria would remain. Indeed, decentralization was worsening the situation by making the new commercial banks more dependent on regional bosses, to whom they looked for repayment of the enterprise debts they had had to take over. Economic failure sapped social morale. The 'second economy' had created a 'second society' characterized by tired people making ends meet through working two jobs, state and private, and displaying little of the moral solidarity which was supposed to be socialism's strongest card. Figures ranging from 88 per cent to 98 per cent of the population thinking Hungary better than the west for bringing up a child, for health care and social morality in 1981 had shrunk to 50 per cent and less seven years later.[13] Economic opinion, as expressed in the document *Turnabout and Reform* (autumn 1986), became convinced that the only way to strengthen 'hard budget' constraints, which was seen as the key to the problem, was to restore the centrality of property and shareholders in it. Whether shareholders took the form of enterprises, self-managing workers or social institutions, a sense of responsibility would be increased and management would be subject to the concerns of 'external owners' (the shareholders) whose relationship to them was purely a matter of efficiency and profit, not a cosy administrative fiddle at the public's expense. This theme was ironic because one of socialist economics' original claims had been that eliminating 'externalities' would cut the waste of industrial espionage and distortions of predatory competition. The debate on *Turnabout and Reform* – which initially the Party refused to consider – was partly generational and led to the decision to call an extraordinary party congress in May 1988 at which Kádár, who had repeatedly denied that there was any crisis, was eased from power. A party commission set up to consider economic reform reported in December, effectively endorsing the principles outlined above. This was reformism but hardly of a socialist kind.

Thus there was a disjuncture between Gorbachev's reform communism and what was going on in the region. That he should still appear to look to the Hungarian NEM foundering in its homeland is testimony to the speed of events, to his own optimism about a viable socialism and no doubt to the superficiality with which a superpower observed a diminutive ally. Gorbachev wanted to encourage reform tendencies in eastern Europe and was as well received there as elsewhere, but it seems unlikely that he understood the region well and his impact helped stimulate strands of critical and dissident opinion far more wide-ranging than anything that existed in the Soviet Union.

The dissenting intelligentsia – the basic ideas

It was the 'dissidents', not intra-party debates, that attracted most western journalistic interest. After all, as one *bon mot* put it, westerners lived in a civilization; east Europeans lived in a drama.[14] Yet judging the relationship between the intellectuals who constituted the bulk of dissidents and the largely voiceless mass of the population is not easy. Polls permitted in the more liberal communist countries, Poland, Hungary and Yugoslavia, show a steep slide in support for regime institutions from the middle of the 1980s, but from a notably high base in previous years, a factor which will be discussed below. East European dissidents themselves did not claim to know the masses were on their side. Any attempt at revolt, the Czech playwright Václav Havel wrote in the late 1970s, would not only not be supported by them but would probably strengthen their bias towards the regime.[15] The people's concern was with material improvements, the Polish novelist Kazimierz Brandys noted in his diary in 1979.[16] Doubts about attitudes of the man in the street were common among intellectuals until the very end of communism. Yet they were interspersed with other comments to the effect that there was some sense of the 'ideal' in the masses, in Havel's words 'a potential, which is hidden throughout the whole of society' to cleave to the truth rather than official lies.[17] For the Polish dissident Adam Michnik their capacity to become involved was demonstrated throughout Polish history, as well as by Solidarity – were not the Warsaw street demonstrations of 1891, first since the crushed rising of 1863, an 'emergence from nothingness'?[18] Similar surmises were general among intelligentsia activists, psychologically necessary to them and with the hindsight of 1989 justified. Yet until then opposition activity was largely a matter of small groups of traditional 'intelligentsia' character, keeping their little crafts afloat, in another Havel observation, in the vast ocean of communist-manipulated life.[19]

The key role of an intelligentsia reflects the part played by writers, journalists, academics, students, artists and the like in the national revivals of the nineteenth century, from which they had drawn a deep sense of social and national mission. Seeking historical legitimacy, communists had only encouraged this tendency by trying, increasingly unsuccessfully, to coopt intellectuals, thereby preserving them a distinct, prestigious status lost in the more fluid, commercially orientated west. The Hungarian dissident György Konrád could simply assume the 'cultural and moral stature' of intellectuals as their means of exerting pressure on the regime;[20] university professors were very close to the top of most people's lists of admired occupations. The pro-democratic dissidence which fed into 1989 was associated particularly with the north-central tier of Hungary, Czechoslovakia and Poland. Yugoslav intellectuals' critique of communism became increasingly bound up with the nationality questions which divided them. In Romania the harshness of the Ceauşescu regime and absence of a strong tradition of dissent meant that no currents along central European lines developed. The leading critic, Paul Goma, agreed to go into exile, and Romanian intellectuals' contempt for communist crudities was expressed at a rarified, philosophical level. The East German case was somewhat different. Here dissidence remained longer in the reform Marxist mould and showed its weaknesses, mixing, in the case of Bahro, unreconstructed Marxist sociology and new-fangled cultural utopianism to posit a single but reformed communist party as a 'collective intellectual' composed of all 'genuinely developed individuals'.[21] By the time he emigrated to West Germany a more promising development was occurring, linked to the Lutheran Church, the only relatively independent institution in the state, which gained from the fact that theology was the only form of higher education open to persons not trusted by the regime.

The core of the dissident movement which anticipated 1989 centred rather around western-style ideas of citizenship and 'civil society'. Its leading figures displayed concerns and nuances relating to their own national society, but more important were their common preoccupations. They shared an analysis of communism as much moral as political and a view that direct confrontation with the system was out of the question. They grappled with the problem of institutionalizing a middle course between revolt and collaboration, so that individuals were not left to face the system alone. Almost all saw themselves as men of the left or at least progressives. Most, indeed, were ex-Marxists and the main exception in this respect, the Czech Havel, son of a well-to-do businessman, shared his country's majority left-leaning, secular-minded orientation. Havel, Michnik and the Hungarian György Konrád were representative figures who will be given the major attention here.

The common analysis, contrary to some western views of the 1970s, was that communist societies were abnormal dictatorships, which span deceitful webs of regulation and legality to mimic the humanism they professed. In suppressing individual and national freedom through blotting out or distorting the past, communism revealed itself as essentially an alien spiritual force, aiming to erode human personality so as to shape subjects to its will; at the national level it produced a deep moral crisis of society. The denial of means for people to live an 'authentic' life of their own choosing meant that they existed as in a state of waiting, looking longingly to western societies as pointers to what normal life might be, a perception paralleling what has been said above about communist eastern Europe's inability to generate its own intellectual categories. Alongside lack of freedom, communism's most destructive feature was lack of reliable information, which compounded the moral morass by depriving people of a compass to measure genuine achievement. One could tell what was a lie, said Brandys, but not what was the truth.[22] The fiery Michnik spoke of totalitarian society; Havel of post-totalitarian, but one mounting a total assault on human beings against which they stood alone and isolated. The chief weapon in this assault was to break people's self-respect by making them live a lie, complying outwardly with an ideology no one any longer believed but which was so much part of the landscape no one could imagine challenging it; here Havel used his famous illustration of the greengrocer who posts in his shop the notice 'Workers of the World, Unite!'[23]

Dissidents believed that ultimately the communist system would not last but they opposed a frontal attack upon it; the revolutionary romanticism of intellectuals who worshipped 'the deed' led equally to authoritarianism. The immediate goal was to find a means of living with dignity within the system. This was Kuroń's doctrine of social space, Havel's of 'living in truth', as the greengrocer would be who took down his empty slogan. The difficult thing was to encourage individual acts of courage without alienating those who did not yet feel able to take them. In Poland, which had inherited very active traditions of resistance to alien rule from the time of the partitions, this could be approached through the past, as in Michnik's penetrating historical essays. In speaking out for a historic compromise between the Catholic Church and the free-thinking Polish left, Michnik skilfully set the ground rules for an anti-communist national coalition that could span traditional left–right categories. Czechs had been historically less assertive, which helps explain Havel's mordant exposure of the collaborationist tendency in his plays, where timorous intellectuals end up discrediting themselves as they allege that the moral sufferings they endure in pragmatic comfort are infinitely greater than those of the holier-than-thou protagonist in his prison cell. Czechs had, however, inherited with Poles a late nineteenth-century tradition of 'small deeds' as opposed to revolutionary romanticism. Since communists sought to control the whole of society, regaining moral autonomy in any part of it, however ostensibly non-political, had a political consequence. This was the theme behind Konrád's provocatively entitled work *Antipolitics* (1984) which made plain that an 'antipolitician' was far from being someone uninterested in politics. Dissidents' emphasis on small deeds has often been contrasted with the revolutionary utopianism of the communist generation. Yet Havel at least had a utopianism of his own. He did not oppose revolution because it went too far, he said, but because it did not go far enough. At bottom, communism was just a cruder case of the alienation which modern technology and consumerism produced in human beings. The changes Havel ideally sought pointed away from the consumer society altogether.

By building up independent social life and standing on the basis of the regime's legalism and the rights it purportedly enshrined (reiterated by the Helsinki accords of 1975), dissidents hoped to pressurize communist authorities to be less cavalier in their procedures. In the longer term, communist institutions might be so hollowed out that a peaceful transition occurred to a more democratic order. There was some tension between the refrain about the futility of aiming at a change of system and such eschatological optimism; in practice dissidents were mainly absorbed in far humbler tasks of setting up and sustaining the basic building blocks for autonomy in a hostile climate. Only Konrád directly laid out a political scenario for the region's liberation, positing an American offer to withdraw its nuclear weapons from Europe in return for European self-determination.[24] Influenced perhaps by the still 'feel-good factor' of Kádár's relatively prosperous, liberal Hungary in the early 1980s, Konrád was less concerned than the intensely politically involved Havel or Michnik with the problem of reconciling intelligentsia attitudes with the needs of potential social movements: it was time for people to grow up and act like rational adults or at least listen to the intellectuals whose task it was to think. The difficulty with this somewhat patronizing position was that Konrád said nothing to suggest his intellectual circles had thought out a solution to the economy, which was the key problem of the day. In this he was typical of dissident attitudes in the 1980s. When the economy came up, in keeping with their tendency to the left, the thinkers reviewed here mainly named workers' self-management as the panacea.

As for the international situation, all dissidents agonized, Poles especially, over the Russian character and whether these Eurasians were just alien or could accept a compromise which recognized their smaller western neighbours' right to an autonomous life. Yet dissidents also doubted the west which had abandoned them to the Soviet sphere at Yalta and they were uneasy at signs that Reaganite Americans thought they could bully or bankrupt the Soviets into submission. For Konrád the difference was that the Russians were an actual problem and the Americans only a potential one. Havel spoke of the 'banalities' of western journalists; Brandys of American naïvety. Thus western concerns like homosexual rights seemed trivial to Brandys, though he was repelled by Russian intellectuals' similar indifference to Polish plaints, along the lines: if you Polish writers are not in danger of arrest, what are you worrying about? All in all, hope for an international dimension to east European liberation seemed rather optimistic when emotional and intellectual sympathies were so far from matching. A conundrum was that most east European dissidents were leftist in assumption but could not stomach what they saw as western progressives' naïvety about Soviet socialism; western conservatives shared this scepticism but were quite happy with the entrenched cold war attitudes that kept Europe divided. As a result the western movement for European Nuclear Disarmament (END), under the leadership of the British Marxist historian E.P. Thompson, encountered some distrust in its attempts to cultivate contacts behind the Iron Curtain, as Havel's essay 'Anatomy of a Reticence' (1985) showed. The reticence was towards the western peace movement. International deadlock added another conundrum to the dissidents' task as they groped towards an unknown future in a multi-faceted situation, unable to know where the key to deliverance might lie: in the often inscrutable mood of the masses, their countries' histories and traditions, international alignments, or the resourcefulness of their own strategies.

Dissent in action – movements of the 1980s

What, set in this context, did dissent achieve? Intellectually and morally, the analyses of Havel and Michnik among others were striking testimonies to the human spirit under stress. The shape taken by Solidarity owed much to the thinking of Michnik, Kuroń and KOR. Havel's ideas provided an underpinning for Charter 77, launched in Czechoslovakia in 1977, which while never becoming a mass movement succeeded in keeping together over 1200 signatories of widely varying views as the public face of civil society in an autocratic state. It provided a continuous service of free comment through its hundreds of numbered communiqués (and those of its sister organization VONS, for the defence of the unjustly persecuted) and was the focal point for a network of independent intellectual activity that produced more than 600 books by 1985 and several academic periodicals;

a bibliography published in 1980 listed 180 underground historical articles. If Hungary saw no comparable umbrella movement, it was because
Kádár's somewhat more liberal regime left freer rein to individuals to do
their own thing. Such, besides Konrád, were the documenter of life as a
factory worker, Miklós Haraszti, and the son of the 1949 show trial
victim, László Rajk Jr, who challenged the official choice in 1985 parliamentary elections, which allowed for multiple candidatures.

Yet Haraszti, writing later, spoke of the atmosphere of fear surrounding
unofficial activity well into the 1980s. Overt opponents of communism still
remained a tiny proportion of the population, limiting their activities
mainly to documenting regime repression. Even Poland was not so far from
this pattern as the recent existence of the mass movement Solidarity might
suggest. An underground organization, 'Fighting Solidarity', survived martial law, to be sure, while above ground Lech Wałęsa provided a figurehead,
too internationally prominent as winner of the Nobel Peace Prize (1983) to
be subject to normal harassment. However, keeping the underground going
was coming to seem to some of its activists little more than a gesture of defiance for its own sake. Membership of the official union rose steadily;
Solidarity's occasional calls for symbolic action were only patchily heeded.
Regime tactics of persecution and amnesty, tested after 1956, were being
applied with some ruthlessness; the murder of a prominent pro-Solidarity
priest, Father Jerzy Popiełuszko, in the autumn of 1984 showed that the
authorities meant business. In reputedly liberal Yugoslavia the later
Bosnian president Alija Izetbegović was sentenced to 14 years for
'Panislamic activities' in 1983, one of many religious figures jailed. Nor did
the fame of Milovan Djilas stop police breaking up a seminar with foreign
guests in his apartment in 1984. In Romania and Bulgaria there was no
organized dissidence. Even in London exile the leading critic of the
Bulgarian regime, Georgi Markov, had been killed using a poisoned
umbrella.

In all this a marked change occurred in the second half of the 1980s,
more particularly from 1987. Padraic Kenney has brilliantly documented
the interlocking features of a rejuvenated opposition which came to give
public protest a certain profile in major centres (and on ecological matters
in some minor ones) in advance of the dramas of the autumn of 1989.
Probably first in importance was the emergence of single issues like environmental pollution, nuclear weapons and human rights which could give
dissent a focus for action, not just the chronicling of repression. With variety of issue came ideological pluralism; religious mixed with non-religious,
liberals with nationalists, anti-communists with single-issue activists, even
anarchists with conservatives. There was rejuvenation in a literal sense in
the infusion of the energies of teenagers as well as students, for whom even
Solidarity was history. Often they brought an irreverence which contrasted
with the heroic pathos of earlier opposition, parodying the system rather

than denouncing it. A marked exchange of ideas and contacts between the northern tier countries in particular was observable. The heavy-handed response of the authorities reminded youthful spirits that they did not live in a normal free society, while gradually becoming less punitive so that small, even not so small, victories were steadily won. Thus regimes reaped the worst of both worlds.

The peace issue had a universal appeal. The rival deployment of Soviet SS20s and American cruise and Pershing missiles in Europe became a leading theme of international politics in the 1980s. Not all peace groups were ostensibly oppositionist from the start. The Hungarian group Dialogue (founded in 1982) at first tried to keep its independence from both official and opposition camps, in the spirit of END, whose leader Edward Thompson it invited to Budapest. The East German peace movement had its roots in the church–state agreement of 1978, intended to bring the Lutheran establishment under closer control, while devolving some responsibility to it in this area. In fact the church proved difficult to manipulate. It provided a framework for groups meeting on its premises to organize regional 'peace weeks', state-wide 'peace-workshops', 'women for peace' and the like where freer spirits gained confidence in independent self-expression and network-building, so that from 1986–87 diversified groups targeting human rights and ecology matters could emerge from under the church's umbrella. The Peace Movement Working Group in Slovenia (1983) with its Peace Street Shops and campaigns against military toys was more overtly oppositional from its inception, all the more so the Freedom and Peace group (WiP) in Poland (1985). Both agitated on behalf of young people imprisoned for conscientious objection to military service. Test cases in Hungary and Czechoslovakia in 1987 also highlighted the importance of the military service issue and led to a dropping of the charges in the case of a prominent advocate of Czecho-Polish dissident cooperation, Petr Pospíchal, which had aroused some international attention. This internationalization took east European dissent beyond the distrust which had dogged its earlier relations with western disarmers. Easterners ceased to play second fiddle to END and their own official peace movements, organizing successful international conferences in Warsaw and Budapest (1987); 200 east Europeans signed the Helsinki Memorandum in 1986.

Sharing the wide appeal of peace as an issue was the environment. Resistance to a joint Czechoslovak–Hungarian project for a dam on the Danube began with biologist János Vargha's Danube Circle in 1984 and had already won 10 000 signatures by the next year, to no avail. Then the 1986 Chernobyl nuclear power plant disaster in Ukraine gave environmental causes a fillip, stirring Slovene and Polish demonstrations and bringing calls for freedom and peace into movements against a Polish nuclear power project, a polluting metallurgical plant and waste dumping plans; a fifth of a small town's population marched on the last case. Some 300 Chomutov residents wrote inviting the Czech prime minister to visit their polluted town (1987); two years before, activists had been threatened with long jail terms on this score. Charter 77 made the environmental issue the touchstone of a switch to a more activist stance, organizing its first semi-public forum on it in June 1987. The Danube dam at Gabčikovo–Nagymaros remained the biggest cause, however; 40 000 demonstrated against it in Budapest in September 1988 and 140 000 signed a petition delivered to the Hungarian parliament the following February.

The tone of much of the activity of the late 1980s could be as important as its content. A group like the Polish Orange Alternative echoed the alienation of young people no longer accessible to grand rhetoric, whether of government or opposition. In its 'happenings', where participants dressed up as red-capped elves ('little red people' in Polish) and made ranting speeches in pseudo-communistic language, the authorities were held up to ridicule in a way which recalls the dual undermining of the *ancien régime* in pre-revolutionary France. Robert Darnton has shown that the sardonic pasquilles on the less than noble lifestyles of the nobility probably had wider influence than the philosophes. The occasion of Charter 77's formation had been the trial of the Czechoslovak rock group Plastic People for indecent lyrics; in 1985 a commemoration of John Lennon's death by the mockingly named Lennonists in Prague turned into a peace demonstration. *Szkoła*, a spirited periodical for schoolchildren which took as many pains with its colourful graphics as with its articles, printed 5000 copies by 1988; the green youth movement *Wolę Być*, has been called the equivalent of 'freedom and peace' for 16 year olds.[25] The Czech Children issued a manifesto calling for a Czech monarchy, black humour which the communist party daily reprinted for real. The powerful Slovene dissident movement of the 1980s grew out of the journal of the Union of Socialist Youth, *Mladina*, whose editors successively moved into the opposition camp. Already the 'postmodernist' mood of youth rebelling against previous conventions had been caught by the weird Slovene heavy metal band Laibach (after the German name for Ljubljana) whose provocative performances were laced with Nazi imagery. But modern and traditional/national sensibilities were aroused when *Mladina* journalists were tried in a Ljubljana military court, in Serbo-Croat, for insulting the Yugoslav National Army, a *cause célebre* of 1988.

Thus through much of eastern Europe, rock music and jazz, youth groups, ecological issues and peace became focal points of free activity, illustrating the point that under an authoritarian regime anything can become political. The habit of independence came step by step. In 1981 it did not occur to Hungarian students refused permission to found an independent representative body that they might organize it themselves, but in

1988 the youth movement Fidesz simply set itself up as an alternative to the official youth movement in defiance of the Hungarian authorities. (By 1998 Fidesz had transmogrified into Hungary's governing party.) From about 1987 the 'fences of fear' in one phrase had collapsed.[26] From that time the formation of independent groups in more 'liberal' communist countries began to escalate and the press became bolder. A meeting of 150 intellectuals at Lakitelek that autumn laid the basis from which the Hungarian Democratic Forum was to emerge, the winner of Hungary's first post-communist election. But even in more regimented regimes the shift can be seen. Realizing their attempt to use the church to contain dissidence was not working, East German communists went on the offensive, leading a Lutheran Bishop to accuse them of obstructing the process of reform (February 1988).[27] Slovak Catholicism was the strongest force behind the largest single manifestation of discontent in hard-line Czechoslovakia, the 500 000 signatures (eventually) for a Czechoslovak petition for religious freedom. Religion stiffened resistance generally, not just in Poland. Likewise ecology was a pervasive issue – a 'productive symbol' for party formation in late communist eastern Europe, as it has been called.[28] A Czechoslovak government report spoke of some 20 opposition groups on this issue with 500 activists and some 5000 sympathizers. In Bulgaria the issue provided the spur to the formation of some of the first autonomous associations in 1988–89.

Yet these movements remained small-scale. Many of the demonstrations listed by Kenney numbered no more than a few dozen individuals. The anarchic, at time hippy and almost unpolitical influences upon them spoke to divergences, even estrangement from the longer-standing opposition, which in turn looked at these unpredictable youthful energies with misgiving. When virtually anything could be taken up as a symbolic reference point by Orange Alternative – say red stockings or sanitary paper – this uncomfortably relativized the force of traditional symbols revered by earlier generations of Polish opposition patriots.[29] The fact is that for all the issues raised in this chapter right into 1989 hardly anyone inside or outside the region anticipated that communism was about to fall.

The outlook

In hindsight it is clear that the late 1980s were repeating a pattern. In politics as in geology major earthquakes are regularly preceded by a flare-up of activity: the years before 1789, 1848 and 1914 all show the portents. From 1987 in eastern Europe, the number of non-official groups, frequency and size of demonstrations, variety of issues raised and boldness of language used rose sharply. Economies nosedived, looming into hyper-inflation in Poland, falling sometimes too rapidly even for experts to follow, as in the galloping ten-billion-dollar debt which Bulgaria's rulers disclosed to the world in 1990. Countries previously hardly touched by organized group dissent, like the GDR, were drawn in, while in those that already had a more liberal climate the press was filled with expressions of disenchantment and gloom. The communist world was on the defensive. The post-1989 rhetoric of excising the malignant cancer of communism overlooked the extent to which communism had faded as a real social force.

This was true at every level. There was a steady shift away from the exclusive privileging of state ownership to concepts of multiple forms of enterprise and commercialization. Communist industrial associations no longer represented the old Marxist faith in the rationality of large-scale planning but were lame attempts to replicate the research and development resource base available to western multi-national conglomerates. In the desperate need to cut back shortages for large urban populations, the classic communist strategy of squeezing collectivized peasants in the interests of forced industrialization was yielding to ever more incentives for peasant production, increasing opportunities for corruption. Socially, membership of the mass socialist organizations was tailing off as western-style voluntary associations grew in number; a Hungarian minister could praise the role the churches might play in combating social problems; another pooh-poohed the idea that communists wanted to export their ideology when it had patently not solved their own difficulties. The media of the prestigious western world impinged ever more on the region. The GDR, sharing a language with West Germany, had given up the attempt to shut it out since the early 1970s, partly because it was also patronized by the elite. The daily official news at 7.30pm was thus sandwiched between the news programmes of two West German channels, which set their schedules partly with an eye to the East German viewer. Czechoslovakia rarely jammed the BBC or Voice of America, for all its hard line. The forest of TV antennae for foreign reception on Romanian rooftops has been described as the first overt collective defiance of Ceauşescu's regime, curiously unpunished by the Securitate. So dire was Romanian television after Ceauşescu curtailed it to save energy, keeping mainly the propaganda function, that the most popular Bucharest university adult learning language course actually became Bulgarian, TV Sofia being the only foreign channel accessible in the capital.[30]

The intellectual repudiation of Marxism is perhaps the most striking feature of communism's retreat. The extent of this dismissal cannot be underestimated, not only for an understanding of 1989 but also of the revolutionary aftermath: its main thrust was directed against any idea of a third way between a failed communism and western capitalist democracy. It was not the lack of institutional and accountable representation of society's interests in communism which was at fault, wrote the Polish academic Staniszkis in a work conceived in these years, but the absence of interests themselves. The communist legal theory of collective ownership could not be made operable as an economic reality; the state's attempt to substitute itself through planning for the play of interests meant incessant bureaucratic intervention to maintain a lifeless corpse, resulting in a de facto anarchy whose opacity and manipulability preserved the power of the elite. The obverse was the need to recognize the exclusive nature of property rights.[31] For the doyen of Hungarian economists, János Kornai, the key to what already in 1986 he was calling naïve advocacy of socialist market reform (he had been its leading champion), was the mistaken belief that if planners could fix correct prices the market could then take over. This concept, going back to the father of Marxist reform economics, Eugen Varga in the 1930s, Kornai dismissed as the illusion of armchair Platonic philosopher kings.[32] While regime ideologists continued with ever less plausible attempts to couch Marxism in the universally pervasive western categories (the Yugoslav Dragičević's 'postmodern' goal of 'communist individualism', beyond the classes of mass society, for example),[33] more independent thinkers were moving towards quite a fundamentalist acceptance of western concepts of economic management and social motivation, mediated through the centrality of property rights. As yet, many still disguised their radicalism with the figleaf of reform socialist phraseology.

Three main approaches to the region's future among a kaleidoscope of views may be perceived among observers of the late 1980s. One, taking a historical perspective, held that the communist world might share the fate of the late Ottoman empire, the sick man of Europe that was nonetheless a long time dying. Eastern Europe might experience a kind of 'emancipation in decay' like the nineteenth-century Balkans.[34] Another, relatively optimistic view clung to the hope that elements of civil society could gradually be grafted on to the communist polity, along the lines of Havel and Michnik and Jacek Kuroń's KOR. The boldest version of this thinking came from the Hungarian János Kis, whose 1987 samizdat proposal aimed to reconcile the party-state and civil society in what has been called an 'authoritarian *Rechtsstaat*': the party would control a new, second chamber of the Hungarian parliament and have a veto over new groupings hostile to it, but the lower chamber MPs could be chosen freely, though not as representatives of parties.[35] The third approach was more pessimistic, believing there was no way of escaping the fact that communism could not reform and that communists would use force to stay in power. Even Gorbachevism was a façade in some of these views. If the forces of civil society *were* strengthening this only made a dangerous confrontation more likely. Ostensibly, the Polish and Hungarian regimes might have come to advocate 'national solidarity' by 1987, seeing that they needed to recoup popular support if they were to overcome mounting difficulties, but since the gulf between them and society was unbridgeable this attempt to play the national card would fail and the situation would end up more polarized than before. By mid-1988 it seemed to many observers that this latter prophecy had been borne out in the Polish wild-cat strikes of early spring and summer and that a vicious circle existed of spiralling economic decline, breeding resentment that made any cooperation for a way out highly problematic.[36] With Staniszkis pointing to the militarization of communist rule and the economic reformer Kornai to the still substantial body of those who would prefer the status quo, advocates of change gave themselves no illusions. The Hungarian leader Grósz, turned by the pace of events from would-be reformer to hard-liner in the space of a year, by late November was threatening a crackdown on the 'White Terror'. In Yugoslavia, once relaxed, even supercilious, in its communist reformism, there was apocalyptic prophecy of strife which did indeed come to pass.

It can be now seen that outside Yugoslavia this third view was overly pessimistic and that the developments surveyed in this chapter had the potential for a more benign outcome. Four themes have been covered here: Gorbachev's perestroika, the response of east European communists, the rise of a democratic opposition rooted in notions of civil society, and the ferment of new movements and attitudes in the later 1980s. With the benefit of hindsight the two communist-orientated themes worked against each other; the opposition-orientated themes complemented each other. Gorbachev embraced an ideology of reform communism which seemed fresh in the Soviet Union but was repudiated by conservative communists in eastern Europe and intellectually dismissed by almost the entire intellectual establishment in the countries that had gone furthest down the road to reform: Hungary, Poland and in its own way Yugoslavia. His faith in socialism's creative potential found no echo there, let alone in hard-line states appalled by perestroika.

On the other hand, the weaknesses of the opposition could also make for strengths. Older dissidents' fear of losing out to the brasher energies of alienated youth made them readier to parley with their communist enemies, a tactic which was to prove fruitful. Actually, the activity of newer groups helped more traditional dissent in making swathes of the population more attuned to ideas of protest. The new opposition's ability to turn almost any issue into a 'happening' bore out established dissident ideas about the potential for a non-political politics. If research has shown that the masses were overwhelmingly motivated by material issues rather than loyalty to dissident intellectuals, for whom many of them had little time, this did not undermine reformers as much as contemporaries often supposed. What oppositionists tended to overlook at the time was that regime figures too were depressed by economic failure and impatient of their own prevarications about bright skies ahead. They were not impervious to the intellectual climate referred to above. Clinging to power regardless was no longer so automatic a response. Of course, there had to be an escape route. Regime figures feared vengeance as much as oppositionists feared repression. In 1988 both sides still felt the deepest distrust of the other. Contemporaries and later commentators are agreed that several paths of development were still open. The moves that opened the first breach in the communist monolith came in the countries Gorbachev had seen as allies, Hungary and Poland. Together they set a precedent for peaceful transition which contributed powerfully to the more dramatic events of autumn 1989.

4

The demise of communism
Breach and balance sheet

Poland and Hungary, where opinion was freest, were the societies where the transition to a post-communist future began. It is a process hard to pin down. Seen from a distance a mountain range appears to rise so sharply from the plain that travellers, drawing nearer and finding themselves among foothills, are often surprised to realize they cannot tell whether they have reached the mountains or not. What is not surprising, to pursue the analogy, is that Poland and Hungary should have been the foothills of post-communism in the Soviet bloc. They had been the east European countries which historically had most fought their Russian neighbours, Poland the most often, Hungary the most recently; by the late 1980s, the former had the largest debt in the bloc, the latter the largest debt per capita; their sociologists and economists provided the system's most explicit critics. Most notably, they were the societies where the move from orthodox communist economic management towards commercialization and pluralism of forms of ownership had gone furthest. Both of them found their way to forms of action which against expectation provided for a peaceful and negotiated course out from the unhappy deadlock.

Poland: to the Round Table and 4 June 1989

The bitter strikes of April–May and August 1988 seem to have been crucial both for the Polish authorities and for Solidarity. The former saw they had no hope of social cooperation on the economic crisis along present lines, while the latter, who had not initiated the strikes, feared for their hold on the febrile opinion among younger workers. By a typical virtuoso performance, Lech Wałęsa got the Gdańsk shipyard back to work in May but gave himself no illusions; 60 per cent of society and maybe more, he commented in this period, did not give a hoot for him, pluralism or Solidarity.

Kuroń estimated that 12 to 20 per cent of Poles were unequivocal supporters of the authorities, 20 per cent supported the opposition, while the rest
wanted peace and quiet.[1] Thus there was little room for triumphalism on
either side. On 31 August 1988 the minister of the interior general Kiszczak
met Wałęsa, offering talks between government and opposition if the current strikes could be ended. Wałęsa managed to get the strikers back to
work and gradually official media came to present him as a possible factor
in the solution to Poland's malaise rather than its cause. As talks about
talks proceeded, 85 per cent of regional party secretaries in an autumn
sounding voiced their opposition to any concessions touching on the
essence of the system. Yet a party central committee plenum in January
1989 authorized plans for Round Table discussions between government
and opposition, which began on 6 February and concluded in April. By
their terms Solidarity was re-legalized (17 April) and partially free elections
fixed for 4 June. Only 35 per cent of the seats in the Sejm were to be contested, meaning the communists and their satellite parties retained a majority, but all 100 seats in a new second-chamber Senate had to be filled and
Solidarity was permitted to launch its own newspaper.

How did this unprecedented breakthrough come about? The recollec-
tions even of reform-minded communists stress, alongside their realization
that major change had to come, their continued deep distrust of Solidarity's
unformed ideas (as they saw them) and of the genie of unreconstructed
nationalism these might release, endangering the relative freedoms Poland
enjoyed in the Soviet bloc. But Solidarity in 1988 had barely a tenth of its
members of 1981, Wałęsa's poll rating had been falling relative to
Jaruzelski's in the autumn, the election date gave the union little time for
preparation and the communists expected them to take at most 40 per cent
of seats in the Senate, which would be a mere talking shop, particularly as
nearly all other leading figures of the 1980–81 period denounced Wałęsa's
tactics as a betrayal of the workers and advocated abstention. For
Jaruzelski this was a price worth paying for inveigling Solidarity into
responsibility for the economic mess, perhaps with a number of economic
portfolios. His bold threat to resign and Gorbachev's very clear December
1988 reiteration of the theme of Soviet non-intervention (the Soviet party
propaganda chief had already said in September that Moscow had no
objection to Solidarity's re-legalization) helped sway the January central
committee plenum. The communist Round Table participant Ciosek's comments that, besides, communists were tired and wanted to know the real
truth, may reflect a psychological factor for the party's more flexible wing.[2]
The fact that the Round Table provided for fully free elections next time
round in 1994 should be noted.

Solidarity leaders had even greater difficulty in retaining the loyalty
of their base; Michnik describes the anguish of the inaugural handshake
with general Kiszczak before the cameras. Their spokespeople were more

passionate, less cynical and unconvinced that legalization would follow the surrender of their ideological virginity through parleying with their oppressors; often they thought of the talks as a somewhat more liberal episode which might well be reversed as in previous cases when communist regimes had felt obliged to make tactical retreats. Yet the American ambassador urged them to see the government's weakness and the chance this offered; the Wałęsa leadership was firmly for negotiation; even the underground under martial law had viewed its actions as part of a campaign for an agreed settlement; and in the last analysis such a settlement rather than revolution had been the tenor of Polish opposition since the 1970s. Moreover, a sense of common Polishness and desire to avoid bloodshed played an important role. Poland's violent history held out warnings against revolutionary romanticism and beckoned towards the less well-known streak of realism in Polish national traditions after 1863. The Catholic Church was a crucial mediator, its hierarchical organization making it more congenial to the communists than unpredictable Solidarity. Finally, the negotiations were not without flashes of humour which eased the undoubted strain. To Ciosek's comment that Poland was a sick dog but the democratic cure might kill it if administered too quickly, Bishop Orszulik replied that this dog had spasms just seeing the syringe; Goethe, recalled a communist participant, had once met a fierce enemy on a narrow forest path who said he never yielded the way to fools; 'I always do,' replied Goethe and turned on his heel.[3] The Round Table was indeed a remarkable balancing act in which only both sides' sense of weakness, desire for a deal and willingness to avoid totems of past grievance kept the show on the road and averted an explosion from the rank and file. For the deal to work, reformers in the party had to trust that dissident moderates would not combine with radical opposition in the workplace, and that they themselves would not be undermined by their own hard-liners. The constellation of forces in Poland favoured this, enabling agreement.

However, the very fact of a deal has led some commentators to see the Round Table as a device which cheated the Polish people out of a full victory over the communist beast. Particularly in the eyes of the national-catholic right, it has come to represent a deal between Solidarity liberals and younger communist opportunists, who had little interest in Marxism other than as a source of power and of the secular world-view they shared with men like Michnik. An example would be Alexander Kwaśniewski, since 1995 Poland's president but then a communist minister and participant in the talks. There is indeed a *prima facie* case that wherever two previously strongly opposed camps reach an accord, the process is smoothed by some coming together of social interests too. One view of the origins of the revolution of 1789, in a fusion of liberal nobles and rising bourgeois into a new monied elite, provides an intriguing parallel to the charges about the roots of nomenklatura survival in post-communist eastern Europe.[4]

These charges draw some plausibility from the way communists reacted to the collapse of socialist economics in the final stages of their rule. Poland's economic crisis of 1979–82 had already produced by the mid-1980s a willingness to reduce red tape in the way of private enterprise and to extend the leasing out of state enterprises in clearly defined consumer sectors like retail stores, hotels and car repair. The purpose of this 'twin-track' approach was to provide the state sector with a modest dose of competition and a cheap source of supply, while creating some low-paid labour to soak up excess labour which large enterprise needed to shed. Under the last communist prime minister, Miecysław Rakowski, laws of December 1988 and January 1989 took the recognition of plurality of forms of enterprise much further, greatly increasing 'capitalist' elements. State enterprises were transformed into joint stock companies under autonomous boards of directors (commercialization); the hiving off of sections of firms into private managerial concerns grew apace; institutions like banks and insurance companies were encouraged to develop cross-ownership in them; the Soviet-style banking system was replaced by a network of commercial banks: in general, free rein was given to members of the economic 'nomenklatura' to appropriate state assets in ways which gave them material interests in a radically reconstructed order.[5] Indeed, contemporary surveys showed that communist party members were the group in Polish society most in favour of free-market values![6]

Was the Round Table, then, a stitch-up between old party nomenklatura and prospective Solidarity technocrats? In a longer perspective, the re-shaping of the economic map in late-communist Poland must have smoothed communism's passing. But in the shorter term, to see new coalitions of interest emerging in the Round Table talks such as may arguably have emerged several years later is to foreshorten historical events. In fact, in the economic sphere the Round Table looked backwards rather than forwards. It did not advocate the laissez-faire and privatization policies which were to follow shortly, maintained farm subsidies, relaxed union regulations and provided for wage indexation, if at 80 per cent of price rises rather than the 100 per cent demanded by the official unions. Thus its economic terms still reflected the socialistic assumptions a trades union movement might share with a Marxist party. The Round Table negotiations were preeminently a political process, aiming to find political mechanisms to get round what had stymied all previous attempts at reform in communist eastern Europe: the absolute power monopoly of the communist party. They depended for success on the political factors outlined above. That they took place at all reflected communist recognition of their system's long-term failings; the most important thing about them, though, was that they produced an agreement.

In the event, on 4 June 1989, Solidarity candidates won all 100 seats in the Polish senate and 160 of the 161 seats open for their candidature in the lower house of parliament, the Sejm. The first breach in the communist monolithic power in the region had been made.

Hungary: from reform communism to post-communism

In hindsight Hungary was even more a candidate for breakthrough than Poland. Many of the processes associated with post-communism had already begun there in the long-drawn-out crisis of the 1980s. Between 1980 and 1986 the Csepel steel workforce in the heart of Budapest heavy industry decreased from 26 000 to 10 000. Already in 1985 a third of Hungarians' working time was spent in the private sector; from 1987 membership of socialist-style mass organizations (trades unions, youth associations) was falling while voluntary associations were growing. Increasingly social policy was being reshaped to western models: unemployment was first acknowledged in 1987, destigmatized in 1988–89 and unemployment benefit offices set up in January 1989.

This was the climate in which the ageing Kádár had been pushed out to make way for Károly Grósz in May 1988. The politics of what followed, however, were determined by the fact that Grósz was no longer the driving force in Hungarian communism. Several leading figures, most influential among them the arch-liberalizer Imre Pozsgay, were more concerned with strengthening their own positions in advance of the planned 1990 elections rather than coordinating a common strategy. Pozsgay had participated in the Lakitelek meeting of autumn 1987 (see p. 61) where populist, provincial Hungarian traditions were expounded rather than the Marxist internationalism of the previous 40 years. This struck a chord with Pozsgay: in an article of winter 1988 he described his 'long years of painful drudgery to become aware that the nation was the community which could keep a people on a high level of emotional and moral commitment'; the socialist countries were mistaken to take their 'raw communism' in Marx's phrase for advanced social development; a 'dialogue with the public' and end of the unchanged 'monolithic institutions' was necessary.[7] In June 1988 independent MPs submitted to parliament a 'democratic package plan' drafted by Pozsgay associates covering electoral law, the status of the communist party, association and assembly, trades unions, human rights, a constitutional court, draft constitution and a new office of President – comprehensive indeed! As Pozsgay's section of the party secured a majority in parliament this institution came alive in the winter of 1988–89, passing a press law and a law for freedom of association, including political parties. A new company law facilitated the same 'commercialization' process of joint-stock formation and hiving-off of enterprise assets by managers as was taking place in Poland.

The democracy package plan now became official policy, while pluralism proceded apace, with the formation of the liberal Alliance of Free Democrats in November, recreation of the Independent Smallholders in January, first national convention of the Hungarian Democratic Forum in March and many other revived or new parties. Grósz began to hold speeches on the dangers of a 'white terror' and would have developed mechanisms of repression (the Workers' Guard, the riot police, the Ferenc Münnich socialist brigade named after a 1956 hard-liner) if the minister of the interior and probably the army had not opposed this. In January 1989 Pozsgay upped the stakes by calling the 1956 'events' a popular rising. The Central Committee plenum in early February rebuked him only mildly, choosing to interpret previous party statements about 'socialist pluralism' as an endorsement of multi-partyism. Grósz still thought in terms of a transfer of power to new political forces which would be 'amenable to [our] influence'.[8] However, the tide was flowing the other way. The 'freedom of political platforms' conceded by the February plenum led to 'reform circles' being set up inside municipal organizations which formed the base of Pozsgay's Movement for a Democratic Hungary, established on 7 June. This was after Grósz had been forced to share power in a four-man leadership and just before Hungary's own tripartite Round Table got under way – with delegations of the party, the political opposition and social organizations. The results of the Round Table talks from June to September 1989 amounted to a blueprint for a new, post-communist order. Pozsgay had already put down a powerful symbolic marker by ceremonially cutting away a portion of the wire fence on Hungary's western border with Austria in May.

Social organizations were separately recognized in the Round Table because the Hungarian democrats realized that unlike their Solidarity counterparts they could not plausibly claim to represent the rest of the nation. Organized opposition was too recent and numerically weak. In the Hungarian case, however, the drive towards post-communism could be found in important sections of the party itself. There is no other way to describe Pozsgay's strategy, under whose pressure reform communists of Grósz's ilk were forced into giving real content to their mealy-mouthed talk about 'socialist pluralism'. Steps to institutionalize norms of parliamentary democracy and a market economy went considerably further in Hungary than in Poland, and before the breakthrough of summer 1989 observers contrasted the 'realistic' Hungarian approach to civil society from above to the 'unrealistic' Polish approach from below, through Solidarity's challenge to the party regime.[9] In fact, both approaches matured at about the same time, suggesting the inherent strength of forces involved which would find a way to effective expression somehow or other. Political scientists have compared the Polish and Hungarian Round Table processes to the negotiations ushering in democratization in Spain and parts of Latin America in the 1970s, where also moderates both in regime and opposition had to prefer compromise with their counterparts in the other camp rather than doubling up with hard-liners/radicals on their own side.[10] As more work is done on them and particularly on their many sub-groups that dealt with different aspects of the settlement, so they are likely to be seen as a first-rate source for the inner decomposition of the communist project before the better-known dramas that were to follow.

The collapse of communism: towards a balance sheet

The events of autumn 1989 introduced many distinctive factors into the communist end-game to be discussed below: crowd mentality, the domino effect, the telescoping of the decision-making process, the role of conspiracy. Yet these can be readily separated off from the longer- and shorter-term issues which have been the subject of this opening section. Enough evidence should be available for generalization on the processes leading to communist collapse.

System collapse typically involves two interacting processes: an increase in the will and/or the power of the ruled to challenge the legitimacy of the status quo, and a decrease in the power and/or the will of the rulers to maintain it. Both processes can be seen in eastern Europe, but the balance between them was influenced by the revolutionary nature of the communist regimes. For the ruled the key issue to explain is not why they ceased to accept communism's legitimacy, which most of them had never believed in, but why they acquired the confidence to give up acquiescence and defy its power. For the rulers, contrariwise, the issue to be explored is not power but legitimacy. Communists created probably the most remarkable power structures ever known, which remained fully functioning in the late 1980s. Yet as recent revolutionary regimes they could not look for legitimacy from the weight of tradition but only from the achievement of their revolutionary goals. Popular opposition to the nature of communist rule had burst forth many times, most notably in 1956, 1968 and 1980. It took new forms in the 1980s. What was most strikingly new, and will be addressed first, was why the communist elite no longer had the self-confidence to crush it as they had before.

No doubt the chief reason some communists sought new paths in the late 1980s was that the communist utopia had failed. A one-party state could not live up to Rosa Luxemburg's ideal that 'freedom is the freedom to think differently', proclaimed on a dissident banner in East Germany in 1988.[11] Prosperity could not be planned in the absence of normally functioning markets and prices. Of course, this failure was not a sufficient condition for collapse, only a necessary one. North Korea still survives as a Marxist-Leninist state despite its atrocious record. Some might challenge, too, the suggestion that the communist system was a flawed utopia, arguing that it delivered eastern Europe higher living standards than freer markets gave the region before or for some years after, let alone much of the so-called third world. Particularly in the 1960s and 1970s, when it was North, not South Korean footballers who excelled in the World Cup and Soviet influence was expanding in the ex-colonial world, many western scholars preferred to see communism as a strand in worldwide attempts at modernization and development rather than an ideological delusion.

However, for all the 'separate paths', 'thaws', 'springs', 'liberalization', 'polycentrism', 'socialist pluralism', 'new economic models', 'socialist self-management' and finally 'perestroika' which attempted to detach the attractive goals from the early excesses, the conclusion of thoughtful east European reformers themselves by the late 1980s seems correct: namely that the basic features of the utopian project did not change. It remained a one-party system unable to drag its economy from a nexus of managers and planners or (in Yugoslavia) regional bosses, whose interests counted for more than market rationale. The idea, quite common from the 1960s onwards, that the utopian ideology was no longer taken all that seriously rested on the misapprehension that a one-party state could ever take lightly the only justification for such a bizarre monopoly – the ideological justification that only the party had the truth. The very number of attempts made at regeneration shows how desirable the goal of a rational, planned society seemed, but also suggests the inevitable disenchantment that had to follow when it remained elusive. That is why this study has taken a historical approach, aiming to show the successive stages by which illusion after illusion was stripped away until the original energy sustaining the experiment had burned itself out. If ever there was a chance that people's attraction towards communism's developmental goals might have overcome rival allegiances, it was squandered by the brutality of the Stalinist years. Stalinists like Józef Berman had shrugged off unpopularity with reference to past violence by progressive minorities like the Jacobins whose cause had been accepted in the end, but history had speeded up and communists were not to have the time for new generations to shed their forefathers' revulsion.[12]

Ironically, the very extremity of Stalinist fundamentalism helped prolong the utopian system by making ordinary one-party power monopoly appear moderate in comparison. The existence of past 'errors' to which difficulties could be attributed made it possible for would-be reformers to go back beyond Stalin to Lenin, from Lenin to Marx and from the old Marx to the young one, and much water had to run under the bridge for any one-time believer to become convinced of the problematic nature of the source itself. Faith in communism usually took time to drain away. A step on the road was the crushing of the Prague Spring, which destroyed the chance of a reform communist meritocracy and trapped communism in 'workerist' traditionalism. For all the flexibility noted by Havel, the remarkable ability of communist bureaucracy to function through people who did not actually believe in it, it was not a system manipulated by an inner core of fiendishly clever and amoral Orwellians. A key feature of Brezhnev's 'really existing socialism' was observed by both Brucan and Connor, namely the role of ex-peasant workers as a natural base of communism. Communist movements were closer to conventional political parties than one might think, with their fair share of the sentimentalized ideology, traditions and shibboleths which make political parties often appear unmanoeuvrable, indeed, stupid bodies. Why, for example, did communists respond to all crises by trying to increase their working-class membership, a fruitless tactic which ran up against the fundamental problem of Marx's original concept: the quixotic bestowal of social leadership on a class nearly all of whose educated members wanted to leave it? The point here is not that communist parties really were parties of the working class. It is that ideology prevented them from becoming parties of the intelligentsia either. Thus 1968 blocked a theoretical line of development when the Soviet leadership prevented the Czechoslovak Party from yielding the reins to a socialist-minded intelligentsia which it had itself largely produced. It ensured that communist polities would flounder as amorphous societies where in the absence of guaranteed individual rights people came to seek their security in groups, using connections to access power and benefits. One reason communism survived as long as it did was that it took time to work out what kind of society one was living in and energy-sapping effort to find ways of surviving within it.

A limited parallel may be made. Austrian enlightened despotism likewise opened up new social perspectives but by the time of Metternich rulers shrank from their consequences, producing their own 'era of stagnation' in Gorbachev's famous phrase. Of course, communism was operating at another stage of the 'modernization' process and had more ambitious economic goals. But it could not achieve them, not altogether because of lethargy. Communist bureaucracies never ceased to meddle, with changes of targets, adjustment of indicators and localized experimentation. Much of their practice was in fact by trial and error, since Marx had left no blueprints of a socialist economy. Szczepański included too many plans going wrong among the factors which had led to disenchantment.[13] The picture is now clear of an economic order that, far from being planned, operated through a series of make-shifts necessary to bring utopian designs into some contact with reality. There is widespread scholarly agreement that though late communist states were authoritarian, sometimes tyrannical, they were actually rather weak in terms of their ability to attain their social goals. Time-scales of disenchantment varied. Stalinism already showed that communism did not mean superior morality; 1968 eroded faith in a Platonic politics of enlightened consensus; economic disillusionment, including disbelief that the system could get better, did not become pervasive until the 1980s. But it was the most deadly.

Explanations of the demise of communism must be multi-causal. The economic stagnation of the 1980s is a convenient entry point into the chain of interacting factors which cumulatively produced a new situation. It undermined communism's ability to deliver on its social policies, a short-fall the more resented after the expectations aroused by socialist consumerism and détente in the 1970s. Together with the advance of the East Asian tigers and the lag in computers and telecommunications, it damaged communism's claim to be the cutting edge of modernity, the belief Kołakowski has said communists clung on to longest: that the future was communist. It spurred greater openness to the western world, partly from the need to supplement inadequate native resources, partly because of the decline of ideological hubris – hence Gorbachev's 'new thinking'. The resultant regime relaxation allowed greater play for dissidents, which encouraged wider swathes of the population to risk the challenge before Havel's putative greengrocer of 'living in truth'. This in turn put more pressure on regimes, whose greater dependence on the outside world made them progressively less able and/or willing to respond through repression. Oppositional organizational networks grew accordingly. The general picture is plain enough, if debate remains on the relative importance of particular links in the chain.

Thus American conservatives have argued that it was President Reagan's exploitation of Soviet economic weakness, by challenging the Soviet Union to match greatly increased US defence spending (and the 'Star Wars' initiative), that broke the camel's back. It is true that Soviet leaders were aware of the strain of great power competition on their stuttering economy and that the American right's free market doctrines also now launched their bid for global dominance. If western Europe began to retreat from Keynesian economic pump-priming and to consider the postwar welfare state too expensive to maintain, how much more problematic was the funding of east European social policies? But there are several problems with seeing American right-wing pressure as the mainspring behind the introduction of perestroika. The American military squeeze came in the first half of the 1980s, before Gorbachev came to power; Soviet military spending in fact held up until 1989. The Soviet economy was damaged more by falling oil prices than (inconsistent) American economic pressure. Besides, most rulers of great powers have been more prepared to risk their economy than their international prestige. Gorbachev's introduction of perestroika can be explained in terms of the reform communist tradition to which he belonged. (His press secretary, asked in 1987 what was the difference between perestroika and the Prague Spring, answered simply: 19 years!) Timothy Garton Ash has plausibly argued that, while awareness of American technological strength might have inclined him to seek accommodation, it was much easier to make concessions when there were also western social democrats around like Willie Brandt and Olof Palme, whose values mirrored perestroika's rhetoric of the common European home.[14] Reaganite argument thus appears to be only a gloss on the broader theme of Soviet economic decline. Gorbachev broke the mould, not American hawks.

Gorbachev's was therefore a crucial role. His critical attitude to traditional regime stances unsettled the rigid power relations which had conditioned people's acquiescence, while his personal make-up inclined him to underestimate the difficulties along the path he had set. The condescension of an imperial power and his own limited sense for ethnic issues compounded this underestimation as far as eastern Europe was concerned. Was Gorbachev simply foolish to believe he could reform a system rooted in utopia? He and other reform communists could point to apparent strong public-opinion support for socialist values and the massive popularity Gorbachev personally experienced during his visits to eastern Europe. It is at this point that reform communists misread the signs, failing to distinguish between two issues that, by a key thesis of this book, ought to be kept apart. Poll surveys recorded opinions about social ideals – support for egalitarianism and state welfare systems – not about a party. The ambiguity that had aided communism in its rise to power misled its leaders in its decay: the confusion between socialism as a general progressive, developmental principle and backing for the communist party. The leftish orientation revealed by the polls was not faked; it helps explain the electoral successes of the Polish left (and its counterparts elsewhere) in the 1990s. But it said little about attitudes to the unreconstructed communist party. Party loyalties everywhere, until very recently, have been a matter of families and generations. If the communists hoped to break through the barriers of habit, religion and patriotism that had stopped people identifying with them before (what German historians have called *Resistenz* or immunity from indoctrination), they blew their chance in the Stalinist years. Yet they were not alone in overestimating their strength. Neither western observers nor Solidarity spokespeople anticipated the completeness of the communist electoral rout in Poland on 4 June 1989.

However much Gorbachev's naïvety about the prospects of reform communism in eastern Europe can be explained, naïvety it remains. Could he afford to address the United Nations on 'the compelling necessity of the principle of freedom of choice' (December 1988);[15] promise to clear up 'blank spots' in Soviet–Polish history (Katyn and the secret protocol of the 1939 Nazi-Soviet pact); or allow, as a sign of virtue, statements that the Soviets no longer had a blueprint for socialism to impose but invited people to come together to think up a new one – as if a liberal capitalist global alternative did not already exist, for which leading east European intellectuals were signing up? Shrewd observers have noted how in these last years technocrats used to expressing their reservations in code began to encounter and be enthused by the robuster language of the dissidents.[16] In 1986 Kornai had reserved 'the right to doubt' whether socialist economic reform could go beyond the Hungarian present, on whose shortages (15 years' average wait for a phone, two or three for a new car) he expatiated. In 1988 he began an article by asserting his belief in individual liberty as a primary good, a notion he said had been taboo in socialist countries for decades.[17] He was clearly on the way to his scornful dismissal of the 'fiasco' of market socialism in an economic programme for the forthcoming Hungarian parliament in the second half of 1989.[18] The distinguished Polish economist Brus followed a similar trajectory. Still arguing the superior potential of a socialist economy in exile in the early 1970s, but noting in 1986 that there were inherent difficulties in achieving a turnaround, in 1989 he retracted every argument he had advanced in socialist economics' defence.[19]

Plainly, Gorbachev was not the inspirer of all this. Powerful movements critical of official structures had preceded the great outbursts of 1968 and 1980 without needing a reformist course in the Kremlin. But the less repressive climate his policies helped shape catalysed aspirations towards organized dissent already there – though Kenney notes that to contemporaries the authorities often did not seem to be becoming more conciliatory at the grass roots.[20] Emancipated from unrealistic reform communist or eurocommunist dreams of regenerated Marxism, dissidence now distilled attractive syntheses of regenerate liberal democracy, where responsible, property-owning citizens had direct incentives to negotiate basic legal and institutional guarantees for their common good. Single-issue groups on iconic modern issues like nuclear weapons and the environment, together with youthful irreverence and reviving religious and national sentiment, provided further channels to irrigate a parched landscape of traditional socialism. Alongside the handful of older networks, like Charter 77 and Solidarity, a host of new ones was in place by 1989, in all but Romania and Albania, experienced in organization and debate, and potentially capable of mobilizing more widely. A further advantage of the underlying 'civil society' rather than reform Marxist ideology of these networks was to link eastern Europe more directly with the western world whose image and values exerted so much more powerful an appeal on the region than the Soviet Union. The failure to create a self-sufficient and attractive socialist world is perhaps what would most have surprised and disappointed communist pioneers. The glamour of the west operated both at the popular level and the intellectual one. The oft-mentioned Hungarian economist János Kornai, for example, taught at Budapest and Harvard.

Perestroika and east European social movements were therefore independent forces. The switch in the tenor of the latter from hatred of a cruel ideology to mockery of a failed one, the upsurge of confidence that the vital, pluralistic west and not the grey communist world was the way of the future were the products of a wider process than Gorbachevism and would no doubt have occurred without him. Far from reformists being led on by Gorbachev, Pozsgay after the 1989 turn-around commented that if he had known how fully Gorbachev was committed to non-intervention, he would have gone faster. Yet Gorbachev's role ceases to be crucial only if it could be argued that the fateful events in Poland and Hungary in 1988–89 would still have occurred without him. Would a more conservative figure in the Kremlin have licensed the Polish Round Table, the Solidarity government or the opening of the Hungarian–Austrian border? It is hard to think so. A hard-line stance would doubtless have made the whole socialist bloc still more brittle, but the dénouement would have been delayed. Though the increase in tempo of social activism since 1987 is notable everywhere in hindsight, it had not reached the mass or achieved sufficient cohesion to bring down unresponsive regimes. The crucial importance of Gorbachev and economic decline must complement any presentation of dissidence as a trigger to the events of 1989.

In hindsight we can see discords in the movement leading up to the revolution. Not all dissidents lauded as victims of illiberal regimes turned out to be much interested in liberalism: this applies particularly to the Yugoslav situation and extreme nationalists of the 1990s like the Bosnian Serb Vojislav Šešelj or the Croat neo-ustasha Dobroslav Paraga. Another comment has a wider bearing. The 'civic society' discourse of the critique of communism, pointing to a society based on human and citizenship rights and the rule of law, was classic liberal doctrine, reminiscent of reformers' themes before the revolutions of 1789 and 1848. Yet, as happened with those revolutions, it did not provide as full a blueprint for a new order as its advocates thought. It had little to say about economics, which became a central issue in the reconstruction of post-communist societies after 1989. Many dissidents desiring a society based on participation and citizenship tended to link such participatory ideas with elements of worker self-management, thus reflecting their left-wing background and the workerist, egalitarian traditions which had developed in communist eastern Europe. Yet self-management had proved economically inefficient in Yugoslavia and been rejected as impractical by Hungarian economists in socialism's last gasp in the mid-1980s. There was a disjuncture in the oppositionist programme between its clear liberal politics and its still unclear economics.

Even the politics was arguably not as liberal as its stress of individual civil rights sounded. Collectivist notions were strong in eastern Europe: from its powerful national traditions; from a sense that communism had atomized society, which needed to be put back together; and last but not least because communism had created a fairly undifferentiated society lacking much basis for individualism. In other words, the language of the anti-communist opposition seemed to echo west European, largely individualistic, liberal-democratic beliefs but the situation on the ground was more complicated, with nationalist, religious and socialist strands stronger than in the west. This was particularly true of Solidarity, the most powerful opposition force in the region and itself more a collectivist than a liberal movement. However, largely unnoticed at the time, a minority tendency was growing in the late 1980s to resolve the contradictions just noted by adopting the classical liberal programme in economics as well as politics. The Polish writer Dzielski in his 'Who are the liberals?' had said in the early 1980s that the key problem of communism was not its totalitarianism but its attempt to control the economy.[21] Staniszkis's conversion to the free market should be seen in this context. In reaction to Solidarity's failure in 1980–81 some criticism of its collectivist stances began to be made; Poles were a very leftist nation, wrote the conservative Werbicki in 1985, and did not really want to get rid of the socialist system.[22] Indeed, Solidarity, influenced by the shift of mood, itself called in a 1987 document for economic privatization, losing some working-class support thereby. These incipient rifts in the opposition ranks were to become yawning fissures after the revolutions. Suffice it to say here that the attractive slogan of mainstream dissidence – 'civil society' – did not stand duty for an agreed or comprehensive blueprint of what would replace the flawed communist order.

In retrospect, communists and the people they ruled were probably less far apart in 1989 than either side supposed. The communist experience had reinforced the region's strong collectivist traditions, expunging the anyway weakly rooted spirit of individualistic capitalism. The stereotyping of communists as both fanatical ideologues and cynical careerists, united by lust for power, wrongly ascribed the driving will of the early Stalinist true believer to the grey apparatchiks more characteristic of the 1980s. Communism's signal success had to been to inculcate in supporters and opponents alike the idea that it really was historically unique, a creed so strong that it could override the normal workings of human nature to which all human belief systems are subject. Many communists, however, were not immune from the disillusionment, wounded nationalism and sense of tedium of the general population. Special circumstances meant that this process had gone further in Poland, Hungary and Yugoslavia than elsewhere. It was very important that many communists in these countries could see a way out and thus did not feel their only option was further repression. With their better overall education and access to the actual workings of the system, it is not surprising that they were as quick as anyone to envisage a kind of post-Marxist third way to which they could adapt as well as their opponents – in Yugoslavia, of course, the escape route of Milošević was to be nationalism. The evolution of Chinese communism or indeed eastern Europe since 1989 shows such hopes of longer-term survival not to have been fanciful. What was unrealistic was for reform communists to think that they could control the transition itself and deny their people the cathartic moment of outrage at the repressions, hypocrisies and failures of 40 years.

II

COURSE

Revolution and system change

5

Autumn 1989

The fall of communism in eastern Europe will always be linked with the astonishing events of autumn 1989. What autumn 1989 signified was one of those rare moments in which deeds are done that in all normal times are unimaginable; the largely bloodless uprisings against oppressive regimes made talk of the unfathomable potential of the human spirit part of the discourse of a sceptical postmodern age. The following chapters of this section of the book will take the story back to earth, detailing the dispiriting Balkan follow-up and the difficulties of reconstructing eastern Europe after unprecedented system failure. This chapter deals with the initial exceptional explosion: the dramatic mechanisms which transformed the long-term malaise already described into exultant protest, and the problems of defining the exceptional and explaining why it caught the world by surprise.

The Polish and Hungarian example

The autumn upheavals were linked to, but transcended, the earlier breaches in communist hegemony in Poland and Hungary. Dramatic as these breaches were, it is not quite clear what they would have led to if the autumn revolutions had not supervened. The Round Table deal struck between the Polish communists and Solidarity proved strong enough to survive Solidarity's comprehensive electoral victory on 4 June, made the more stunning when the communists got a mere one seat for their 28 per cent of the vote because of the first-past-the-post system they themselves had chosen. However, the communists resisted the temptation to override the elections and Solidarity did not exploit them to block parliament's pre-arranged choice of Jaruzelski as president; he scraped through by a single vote only with the help of some adroitly cast Solidarity ballots. Because only 35 per cent of seats in the Sejm had been contested the communists and their allies had the numbers to form the new government, but not the moral authority. Eventually, Wałęsa bade for the defection of the United Polish Peasant Party which ended 40 years' subservience to communist rule by agreeing to join a Solidarity government. In a phone conversation of 22 August Gorbachev urged the communist party prime minister Rakowski to accept a minority role within it,[1] making the Catholic dissident Tadeusz Mazowiecki the first non-communist premier in eastern Europe since 1947.

Yet was this already the thin end of the wedge of communism's demise? In view of Poland's incipient hyperinflation crisis it had taken Wałęsa over two months to accept the possibly poisoned chalice, while Solidarity's acquiescence in communists remaining head of state (Jaruzelski) and ministers of the interior and defence showed their continued deference to the Soviet Union. The scenario was not inviting. Isolated in the region, they would either have felt unable to enact a western-style programme and disillusioned their voters or, less likely, they would have risked what they in fact did and produced the catastrophic economic downturn of 1990–92 without the buffer of neighbouring regimes also committed to free market policies.

Of course, they would not have been quite isolated because of scarcely less spectacular trends in Hungary. As a result of the Hungarian Round Table talks concluded in September 1989 a preamble to an amended constitution passed by parliament on 23 October spoke of promoting 'the peaceful transition to the rule of law realizing the multi-party system, parliamentary democracy and a social market economy'.[2] The socialist concept of rights as operative only within the framework of socialism and on fulfilment of the citizens' obligations to the state was dropped in favour of the western concept of human rights. The word 'People's' was to disappear from the state's official title of Hungarian People's Republic. A Constitutional Court, Ombudsman and powerful legislature would provide further checks on the executive at a time when non-communists in the Round Table feared the reform communist Pozsgay might win the national vote proposed to fill the new presidency. Pozsgay himself, moreover, after orchestrating a refounding of the communist party as the Hungarian socialist party in October 1989 was ostensibly a communist no more, the first east European politician to perform what would become a familiar vanishing trick. Yet again the path to full democratization might not have been so assured without the impetus of the autumn storm elsewhere. Pozsgay's new party showed no sign of wanting to give up the communist privilege of organizing branches in the workplace and the government continued to use the security services against the new pluralist opposition. However, that storm had arguably been whipped up by a Hungarian decision in the first place. East German citizens fleeing their barracks state were crowding West German embassies in Budapest and Prague, and ranging the Hungarian–

Austrian border, where some of them were injured by the workers' militia stopping their bid for the west. The militia being a typical communist institution out of keeping with the spirit of the emerging new Hungary, the Hungarian government, worried for its reform credentials, on 11 September opened its western borders to East Germans seeking to flee their homeland for the west, a gesture for which they had a promise of West German aid to soothe sleepless nights over Hungary's hard currency debt mountain. Moscow was not consulted, in keeping with the new norms, but the Hungarians knew they were taking no risk there, from Gorbachev's previous acquiescence in their course and his refusal to offer the GDR more than perfunctory diplomatic support over the refugees. The breach with socialist 'fraternity' and Hungary's obligations to the GDR was deliberate and fateful; 'we are choosing Europe', foreign minister Horn told an anxious colleague.[3] More than any other single act it set in train the fall of the dominoes in the socialist camp.

The *Wende* in the GDR

The German Democratic Republic was the first to go. This strange creation from the Soviet-occupied zone (1949) had begun to stabilize with the institutionalization of cold war, the building of the so-called Berlin Wall along its western border (1961), and its recognition by West Germany and the rest of the non-communist world from 1970. Indeed, its success may have been too great for its own good, for it helped to shield general secretary Honecker and his colleagues from the GDR's growing economic problems, the inadequate investment and productivity, swelling hard currency debt and environmental pollution. Another factor in self-deception was no doubt age. Honecker had been born in 1912, his security chief Mielke in 1911, his prime minister Stoph in 1914. Honecker was provided with 'feel-good' statistics by his subordinates, and the manufactured 98 per cent vote for the government list in the May 1989 local elections showed his determination to keep up traditional practices. Attempts by politbureau members Krenz and Schabowski to point out weaknesses were ruled out as inappropriate by colleagues.

These two men were themselves less concerned about the East German dissidents than they were about the creaking economy's failure to satisfy the growing numbers of mainly young qualified people seeking emigration. Some 40 000 emigrated in 1988 and this figure already looked like being exceeded for 1989; the GDR authorities knew of 120 000 applications in the pipeline. The Hungarian decision of 11 September came therefore at a sensitive time. Two days earlier several East German dissident groups had joined in forming New Forum, offering a political platform for discussion of the pressing problems caused by the gulf between state and society. Other groups followed: Democracy Now, Democratic Breakthrough, the

Freedom and Human Rights Initiative and by early October a revived
Social Democratic Party. The church-based milieu from which these groups
emerged had, in the weekly prayers for peace in the Lutheran church of St
Nicholas in Leipzig, a symbolic institution of considerable force. Beginning
as early as 1981 the Leipzig prayers had inevitably taken on a political
colouring and through 1989 had been increasingly attended by would-be
departees. In September attendances doubled and trebled weekly, reaching
8000 on the 25th, who went in procession through the town, meeting the
usual police repression. By this time they included many people who
wanted to stay, thinking they could now put pressure on the regime for
change. The government's decision to allow 2500 East Germans in the
Federal German embassy in Prague to go westward strengthened dissidents'
view that it was no longer wholly master of the situation. In Leipzig the
weekly demonstration held on 9 October was seen on all sides as a test case
in the ever clearer social crisis. A plan for its prevention had been approved;
Honecker telegraphed all district heads on the 8th to follow suit; live TV
links enabled the Berlin authorities to watch what was happening in
Leipzig. But the sheer numbers involved (70 000) led them to back off;
many of the intended local forces of repression in any case stayed at home.
The fact that for the first time the demonstrators were allowed to proceed
unhindered showed the bind the regime was in. Protest movements no
longer needed the matrix of the church, and their leaders responded to the
government's pressure by calling on it to engage in dialogue with the
people. So did Gorbachev, with his famous leaked admonition to Honecker
that life punishes those who come too late, delivered during the fortieth
anniversary celebrations of the founding of the GDR on 7 October.
Honecker replied stubbornly that those pronounced dead usually live a
long time.

Honecker's intransigence had come to be seen as counter-productive even
by his colleagues and he was forced to resign as state and party leader on
18 October. His successor, Krenz, who had praised the Chinese communists' bloody repression of democracy in Tiananmen in June, was no convincing exponent of dialogue. Gorbachev barely concealed that West
Germany was more important to him, that only it could help the GDR's
economic woes and that it was up to Krenz to take the initiative in putting
his house in order. The politbureau, then the central committee, were told
for the first time the brutal truth that avoiding impending bankruptcy
would mean an immediate 25–30 per cent cut in living standards and 15
years of belt-tightening. Meanwhile, with repression relaxed, crowds continued to swell, reaching half a million in Berlin on 4 November; the chief
calls were for free elections, freedom of movement and an inquiry into
police repression. On 7 November prime minister Willi Stoph resigned and
two days later, with minimal pre-planning, the party central committee
decided to allow unconditional right of passage to the west. This was first

intended as a solution to the problem of would-be emigrants, not a general 'opening of the Berlin Wall'; but in the characteristic press of revolutionary process it was widened to include all cross-border visits, while stipulation that official permits would be issued was simply overlooked in media transmission of the decision, so that crowds at once thronged the exits, making any kind of formality impossible.[4] The central committee also legalized the new associations, endorsed free elections and adopted an action programme, calling vaguely for 'a socialist planned economy guided by market conditions'. But the Party had now lost control, its members began to desert and the Volkskammer, East Germany's previously tame parliament, abolished its leading role on 1 December. A few days later Krenz's politbureau resigned en masse, marking the effective end of the old regime. At an extraordinary congress of 8–9 December the communists reorganized themselves around the November action programme as the Socialist Unity Party – the Party of Democratic Socialism.

If the old regime was vanishing it was not clear what was going to replace it. The opposition suspected the new prime minister, the former Dresden party chief and reputed reformer Hans Modrow, of wanting to shore up the system by transferring its weight from the discredited party to the state. His programmatic statement of 17 November declared his government to be one of socialism and peace. Much play was made of genuine consultation with the four previously satellite parties, who now held 12 of the 28 cabinet posts, and of governmental responsibility to the Volkskammer. Noncommunist distaste for all this is thoroughly understandable; talk of reining-in party interference had been a cliché of communists every time their regime got into trouble since Stalin's death. In Modrow's case, however, circumstances make it unlikely he thought he was going to be able to turn back the clock. It seems he had already concluded from Hungary's opening of her frontier to the west that the Warsaw Pact was fading, yet still thought in November that a socialist East Germany was possible.[5] It may be he believed the pro-socialist message of opinion polls and statements of dissident individuals and groups in favour of East German 'renewal' as an 'alternative' to western consumerism, which could resolve the obvious tension between his talk of perestroika and the multi-party system to which, unlike Gorbachev, he was now formally committed. He claimed, too, only now to become aware of the full scale of the GDR's security service (the infamous Stasi) and the depth of bitterness it had aroused. Through December, however, the tide of events disabused him of such hopes if he had sincerely held them. Almost daily disclosures on the lifestyle of the reputedly ascetic Honecker and his colleagues behind the high walls of the elite's Wandlitz compound swept away any claim the East German state might have made to being a poorer but purer version of Germandom, and helped depress support for an autonomous state. No doubt many earlier references to socialism by non-communist activists had

been merely verbal and tactical.[6] By December, when protest had generalized itself beyond the churches and the dissident groupings such as New
Forum, the only idea which could still appeal to an aroused public was that
of union with their fellow Germans in the west. Modrow's claim that from
this time his aim was to stabilize the turbulent situation so as to prepare for
a step-by-step reunification with West Germany on the best terms possible
may be believed. He was encouraged in this by the collaboration of a
Round Table of existing parties and new opposition groups meeting for the
first time on 7 December.

Unification had been put on the agenda by the West German Chancellor
Helmut Kohl on 28 November in a ten-point programme for a confederation of the two German states. Anything diminishing the status of the GDR
challenged not only the *raison d'être* of the communists, at least as a ruling
party, but also that of the dissident groupings. Arguably, East German dissidents' desire to reform the East German state had blinded them to its fundamental inadequacy, leaving them nowhere to go when the state's
structures collapsed, except to a nebulous 'third way' which a new GDR
would somehow exemplify. In a common view, the guilt of the sensitive liberal-minded at Nazi misdeeds had turned broad swaths of an overcompen-
sating East German intelligentsia into Marxists or at least fellow-travellers.
Thus New Forum's founding statement spoke of greater individual freedom
without abandoning welfarism for an uncaring 'elbow society'. Some
50 000 attended New Forum's first state-wide conference after legalization
in mid-November but thereafter its largely intellectual membership (at
15 000 the largest of the new opposition groups) lost direction as they
debated different ways of synthesizing the best of capitalism and communism. The gobbledygook of a position paper drafted in November by two
members of Democracy Now shows why the public was turned off the original initiators of the public movement. Calling for an East German renewal
leading 'from the rigidity of administered objects in a monopolistic subject
to self-organization in a plurality of subjects', it argued more comprehen-
sibly if hardly more practicably, for 'the integration of the GDR in a global
system in an emerging world society'.[7] What made the predicament of the
dissidents worse was competition from the former satellite parties, who in
December got out from under the communists' coat-tails, dropped any reference to socialism and, using the superior resources they inherited from the
old order, mopped up the support of the anti-communist majority. The one
issue on which the dissident groups could continue to engage with the
masses was their campaign for the dismantling of the Stasi organization,
whose Leipzig and Berlin HQs were stormed on 3 December and 15
January respectively. Modrow finally conceded the disbandment of the
security police just before this second act.

By this time the GDR was in a state of near collapse. The true economic
situation was being revealed and the Modrow government was wondering

if it could provide the goods that would get its people through the winter. Modrow writes bitterly of a New Forum member of the televised Round Table who demanded the end of all subsidies, thereby precipitating a panic run on the shops for subsidized goods, which took a fortnight to control. Any hope of a lengthy time-span in which the once cocky German socialist fatherland could prepare for a union of equals faded fast. The economic factor was crucial. Chancellor Kohl's threat to withhold East Germany economic support without democratization had been an important final spur to the opening of the Berlin Wall. At Kohl's visit to Dresden on 19 December Modrow had tried to get a pledge of 15 billion DM (£6 million) of aid to tide his ailing land over 1990 alone. The implied threat of East German collapse was less and less effective as the alternative of rapid unification cohered in Kohl's mind, prompted among other things by the rapturous reception he received from East Germans. Crowds that had chanted 'Gorby! Gorby!' now shouted 'Helmut! Helmut!' and 'Deutschland! Deutschland!' The East German elections recommended by the Round Table for 6 May 1990 were brought forward to 18 March because uncertainty could no longer be prolonged. The atmosphere was already being engendered in which the ex-satellite Christian Democrats, who had declined from the start to participate in the Round Table and were drawn increasingly towards their West German counterparts, Kohl's party, were to win 42 per cent of the votes in the first and last free elections of the GDR, while the alternative alliance including New Forum which had set the remarkable process in motion won a mere 2.9 per cent.

This dramatic turnabout has shaped many somewhat dismissive judgements of the East German opposition, renewing a tradition going back to 1848 of seeing German liberals as ineffectual theoreticians. In this case a popular argument has been that the real underminers of the GDR were those who wanted to leave it, not the dissidents who were actually propping it up by calling on them to stay and work for democratization. The East German dissent produced no single striking movement or publishing ventures like Solidarity or Charter 77, and its first independent organizations emerged only in September 1989. Nonetheless, the antithesis between emigrants and reformers seems somewhat overdrawn. When a regime is weak it is vulnerable from all sides. The East German opposition numbered several thousand, and had developed networks and techniques which enabled the emigration crisis to be exploited to the full. To oppose the East German communist party was indirectly to oppose the state it ruled, while to accept the framework of that state as a basis of action rather than hanker for deliverance from the west was no more than a practical necessity at the time. The real ground of West German criticism was the reluctance of some of the East German intelligentsia to give up the ideal of a reformed GDR. Not all the dissidents were wedded to a specific East German identity. Democracy Now first emerged as a group which refused to accept the present division of Germany. It was among writers that East German loyalties beat strongest. Christa Wolf and Stefan Heym helped produce the appeal 'For Our Country' at the end of November which sought to rally support for the state's separate identity, as the cries of 'We are the People' and 'We Want to Stay' heard in Zurich on 9 October turned more and more to the 'We are One People' of the fall of the Berlin Wall, which implied pan-German feelings. For Heym this could turn next into 'Ein Volk, Ein Reich, Ein Führer', understandable over-reaction from a holocaust survivor. The intensity of feeling of a minority appears from an address of the famous novelist of moral resistance under communism, Christa Wolf, of 31 January 1990:

> In a period of a few weeks we have seen our chances of making a new start as an alternative society vanish before our eyes, and seen the very existence of our nation vanish with it. . . . Many East Germans . . . sink into depression. Others throw fits of rage and disappointment, fear, humiliation, and unacknowledged shame and self-contempt.[8]

At the time the great majority, lacking Wolf's view of the GDR as a national homeland, did not share this bleak view of the East German *Wende*'s evolution as a sell-out to alien values: the word means turnabout. The popular movement, with its use of symbolism and slogans, its burgeoning demonstrations, the communist authorities' step-by-step retreat, the initial pivotal and subsequently declining role of the intellectual opposition, set scenarios for other east European experiences, particularly the Czechoslovak. The East German opposition deserved the 'almost indescribable joy' they felt at times in their successes and if these have faded from general memory it is because of so many dramatic events yet to come which they helped to inspire.

Velvet Revolution in Czechoslovakia

Until summer 1989 the Czechoslovak dissidents were a step ahead of their East German counterparts. By August that year the number of independent organizations had grown to 39. Nonetheless, they were not planning a direct challenge to the authorities. Havel's statements stressed that the communists were on their last legs in an unprecedented situation but also noted that no alternative body existed. He was still pushing for the 'non-political' politics of moral stiffening, fearing that street demonstrations could provoke violent repression. The demonstration of 21 August 1989 against the Soviet invasion was first called for by Democratic Initiative and the Movement for Civilians' Rights, not Charter 77, whose main concern in following weeks was a demonstration to be held on International Labour Day in December. The stimulus that led to breakthrough came from students, determined to commemorate the fiftieth anniversary of the funeral of

Jan Opletál, a student victim of the Nazi occupation. The independent student bodies in existence since earlier in the year negotiated an agreed route march with the official student body, but on the day, 17 November, in what appears to have been a spontaneous act, the unprecedented crowd of 50 000 students and secondary school pupils diverted to the centre of the city; some 2000 found themselves trapped in their approach to Wenceslas Square and were subjected to a brutal assault by security police which left 592 injured. Neither Czech nor police leadership authorized this violence, though the question of possible intervention by the Soviet KGB, allegedly to discredit the anti-perestroika Czech communist leaders, remains mysterious, as does the report to an opposition leader, and through him the international media, of a student death which had not in fact taken place.

Much clearer is the outcome of 17 November. By the next day an indefinite strike had been decided on by Prague actors and students. On the 19th Václav Havel led the organization of a central body for dissident groups, Civic Forum, something which had failed two months before. Its first proclamation, calling for an enquiry into the anti-student violence, the end of censorship and dialogue of rulers and ruled became a template for proliferating resolutions and checklists of demands from meetings and organizations all over the country. With the semi-institutionalization of daily mass meetings in Wenceslas Square, Civic Forum leaders first addressed a crowd of some 200 000, from a balcony, on the 21st.[9] The call now was for a general strike on 27 November if the authorities did not respond. Previous adjuncts of communist power were crumbling. Unwilling to go on doing the regime's dirty work for it, 142 Prague judges called for the rule of law; 4800 television workers voted overwhelmingly for the opposition, part of a Havel speech being broadcast for the first time; the satellite parties of the National Front declared on the 22nd that they expected a solution to the crisis 'in a new way'. The journalist section of the official student organization supplied the independent students with badly needed equipment, while Mohorita, the communist student leader, came out in support of an inquiry into police violence. No doubt this was partly not to be left behind student opinion – student elections were due on 20 November – but the generational difference between Mohorita and the party leadership was also a factor. As to the all-important workers, the ČKD engineering plant, long regarded as the stronghold of militant communism, gave the Prague police chief Štepán a rough time (embarrassingly televised) when he sought to enlist them against Civic Forum, and the trades union central council, meeting on 26 November, felt obliged to shore up its membership by opting for secret elections to new, purportedly independent organs. Already, however, construction workers decided to join an independent trades union movement, which was to win 62 per cent of workers (as against 14 per cent for the old movement) when the option was open in December. Bitterness against the way they had been taken for granted breathed through many rank and file branch declarations complaining against non-consultation and all-pervasive corruption. Finally, the head of the security services, Colonel Lorenz, was something of a Gorbachevite. The workers' militia had no appetite for action; 17 coachloads of them from Moravia at one point arrived in Prague to relieve exhausted policemen, but given no instructions or accommodation arrangements they seem to have melted away. Only the army leadership appeared prepared to stand by the regime: defence minister general Václavík repeatedly reaffirmed 'its full support for the existing leadership of the Czechoslovak Communist Party and rejection of the protest demonstrations of the population' and continued to plan actions Wave (for seizure of media installations) and Intervention.[10]

The beleaguered government did not have the stomach for a Tiananmen-style bloodbath, however, nor was it clear the troops would fight. Prime minister Adamec and general secretary Jakeš had felt constrained to deny force would be used on the 21st and the 24th respectively. All in all, the communist party no longer disposed of any social support, making the opposition's nervous caution appear exaggerated, though only in hindsight. Civic Forum seems to have been particularly concerned about communist propaganda that the two-hour strike would damage the national economy, though it was set so as to be least disruptive, from 12 to 2pm, which for many workers in communism's economic wonderland marked the end of the official working day. Underlying anxiety, however, was uncertainty as to how far the intellectual opposition really had working-class support. Student emissaries going out to factories in the provinces had not been warmly received, until the government lost its monopoly of the provincial media around 23 November. In a strict communist state as Czechoslovakia had been, it is easy now to overlook the extent to which people withheld their views even from quite close acquaintances and had few objective means of knowing how far their dissenting opinions were more widely shared. In the event the general strike of 27 November proved a clear success. In the country as a whole, 38 per cent of workers stopped for the full two hours, 9 per cent for shorter periods and 24 per cent showed support in other ways designated by Civic Forum and its Slovak equivalent, Public against Violence.[11] The figures are perhaps not overwhelming; miners played a limited part and in some cases, like the industrial centre of Olomouc and the largest factory in the Moravian capital Brno, no strike committees were formed. Thus a twin thesis of this book was borne out. When the chips were down, the great bulk of east Europeans opposed communist repression of democracy, but they could not simply be slotted into the same framework as the mainly intellectual opposition.

The general strike confirmed communist isolation. It continued despite Jakeš's resignation on 24 November because of opposition suspicion, borne out by Adamec's attempts to qualify his acceptance of Civic Forum's dialogue programme in a Prague mass meeting held the next day. Adamec was invited to the rally of half a million people partly because Civic Forum strategy was posited on dialogue and he seemed the only likely communist partner. But as a Czechoslovak cross of Krenz and Modrow, hoping to negotiate the rapids more flexibly than his party rivals, he showed his limitations when he issued his new cabinet on 3 December, containing fifteen communists and five non-party figures, despite parliament's abolition of the communists' leading role two days earlier. A mobilized population rejected this charade of partnership and the new government resigned en masse, to be replaced by one equally balanced between the two camps. As in East Germany the skids were now clearly under the communists. Gustav Husák resigned the state presidency on 10 December, the youth leader Mohorita took over the party leadership and on 29 December Václav Havel emerged as the new Czechoslovak president. His chief potential rival Alexander Dubček, the 1968 reform communist, accepted the lesser post of chairman of the National Assembly, a suitably sentimental ending to the 'velvet revolution', which smoothed over the fact that Havel had been a strong critic of reform communism. Here lay an important difference between the East German and Czechoslovak events, namely that the vein of neo-Marxist idealism and anti-westernism that animated many of the East German opposition activists had little place in Czechoslovakia. The desire to join a wider world in Czechoslovakia could simply mean western Europe more or less as it was, rather than East German intellectuals' vision of the reconstruction of east and west.

The East German and Czechoslovak cases, however, show many close similarities: the exponential growth of mass demonstrations; the initial communist complacency turning overnight to panic and desperate attempts to stay abreast of events, the continued personal rivalries on the sinking ship, the shrinking from the use of force and the final collapse of the party's mass base amid recrimination. Demonstrations were a learning process, in which rhythms were acquired, even in such a thing as the singing of the national anthem in time by a vast crowd.[12] Humour, irony and pathos played a role among the huge, mainly good-humoured crowds, in ritual and symbolic action (candles figured in both, and jingling keys, ringing bells and blaring hooters and sirens in Czechoslovakia told communist leaders their time was up) and in the countless slogans they chanted or wrote on walls: 'Circus Krenz: the performance is over' matched in Czechoslovakia by 'the truncheon; the beating heart of the communist party'; 'intellect is invisible for those who don't have any' (directed at Štepán), 'Come and join us! After all, we're your children!' Czechoslovak slogans showed strongly the humiliation of being ruled by perceived incompetents: 'we want a government we don't have to be ashamed of!'[13] In both countries, purloined recordings of communists addressing their own were eagerly played. The moral dimension of the anti-communist struggle loomed large, the 'moral rebirth' which the student organizer Martin Klíma gave as the goal of student participation in social life in his keynote speech on 17 November.[14] Participants' sense of the moral purity of the revolutionary experience, the feeling of wholeness and cleanness of the in-group, was matched by a view of communism as the violator of the natural order that entailed its symbolic exclusion, in the mock executions of red stars that took place in Olomouc or the cardboard boxes erected around the communist party's headquarters. Ultimately, the tension between the Velvet Revolution's non-violence and the symbolic violence directed against the communists and other perceived impurities (like 'turncoats' who had come over to the opposition late in the day), was to have a decomposing effect on the initial sense of revolutionary unity and idealism, since it was a tension of which participants became aware.[15]

In this, too, the Czechoslovak experience was not so far removed from the East German, though the processes of disillusionment were subtler. Moreover, though reform communist influences were much weaker in Czechoslovakia than in the GDR, at the grass-roots level a socialist-orientated mentality appears to have been similarly strong in both societies. Thus 45 per cent of respondents preferred a socialist 'way' on 24 November (down to 41 per cent by 9 December), as against only 3 per cent each time opting for capitalism.[16] Such figures may help explain communist passivity. The collapse of communism elsewhere and denial of Soviet support, conveyed to Jakeš by the Soviet ambassador, undoubtedly speeded communist demoralization. It is interesting that dissenting movements used a more socialist language in their dealings with the authorities than they did towards their supporters, and this and the reiteration of the path of non-violence may have reassured communist leaders who may well have been frightened for their own fates.

Finally, it would be wrong to think of the whole of society as having been won to the idealistic perspective of the initiators of mass protest. A third of Prague students took no part in the events of autumn 1989 and another third only an occasional one. A December poll showed that a third of those questioned believed that Civic Forum and Public against Violence were only in it for themselves. During these heart-warming events such reservations were rarely heard by an applauding world but they were also to help shape the future.

Interlude in Hungary and Bulgaria

While the world watched the crises unfolding in East Germany and Czechoslovakia, events only relatively less dramatic were afoot in Hungary and Bulgaria. They had a common core, for in these two countries there were communists who saw the unsustainability of the old order and wanted to get on the right side of history in time. In Hungary this tendency under Pozsgay's leadership had been signalling its intentions for some time; in Bulgaria it crystallized more belatedly. Ironically, though, it was Pozsgay whose reformist ambitions were to be quashed more quickly.

These ambitions centred around his candidacy for the new, popularly elected post of president in the post-communist order predicated by the Hungarian Round Table decisions of September. Or rather, that was to have been the scenario. The fact that the Alliance of Free Democrats (AFD) refused to sign the final Round Table document did not seem very significant until its influence began to grow in October and it was able, together with the Young Democrats, to gain the 100 000 signatures necessary for a referendum on whether the new president should be chosen by the people or by parliament. A parliamentary vote would deprive Pozsgay of his greatest strength, the fact that he was the only candidate widely known to the public. In the event, the Hungarian Democratic Forum (HDF), having supported a popularly elected presidency in the Round Table, abstained in the referendum, which the Pozsgay camp lost by just 6000 votes. This was the beginning of the slide of Pozsgay's new Hungarian Socialist Party. From a poll rating of 35 per cent at the turn of October/November, it had fallen to 16 per cent by December, while the AFD and particularly the Democratic Forum advanced. There was a logic to this. Pozsgay was right that a left-wing party which threw off the communist label could do well, as the 1990s were to demonstrate, but he was wrong over the timing. For the bulk of the public there had to be some more signal break with the bad old communist past than just repackaging a party. Pozsgay had overlooked the moral factor mentioned in the first part of this book, the sense of revulsion that for the time being tarnished everything of communist provenance. The revelation at the end of the year that the security services were still monitoring opposition politicians' phones reinforced this feeling, though they were probably acting more from habit than a plan to reverse the changes. The fortunes of the other major groupings also showed analogies with elsewhere. The AFD of urban, liberal intellectuals made the early running, paralleling the upsurge of alternative, left-liberal influence in the initial phases of the 1989 revolutions. The HDF moved to the centre-right, closing up to the so-called populist constituency which suspected intellectuals and inclined to nationalism, and won the first free elections of March–April 1990 fairly comfortably. The theme of a divergence between dissidents pursuing a liberal civil rights agenda and a wider, less liberal majority was repeated.

In the Bulgarian case the reform communists retained the initiative longer. The background was the damage done to the country's international image by the exodus of nearly a third of the persecuted Turkish-speaking minority from June 1989 and rough handling of Bulgarian ecological protesters during an international environmental conference in Sofia in October. The foreign minister, Mladenov, gained Gorbachev's approval and made his move, getting a majority of the party politbureau to turn against party chief Zhivkov, who resigned on 10 November. The new power wielders then renounced the party's leading role and promised free elections, hoping to take advantage of an opposition not yet well organized enough to win. This time the tactic of catching the opposition on the hop, which had been tried unsuccessfully by Jaruzelski and Pozsgay, bore more fruit. While public opinion welled up against the former dictator it did not rapidly coalesce against the would-be reform communists, who were able to hold off Round Table talks with the opposition until the new year and eventually win the free elections of June 1990. For now, Bulgarian politics saw the men of 10 November maintaining an uneasy control in a volatile situation: Mladenov, who replaced Zhivkov as head of state, Lukanov, the new leader of the redubbed socialist party, and Lilov, the prime minister.

Bloody revolution in Romania

In Romania too the events of late 1989 had a backdrop earlier in the year, in the March letter of six protesting at Ceauşescu's policies. Two sets of harvest statistics later found in a presidential palace (one false, one true) suggest that the ageing diabetic was not unaware of the declining situation, though much bad news seems to have been kept from him by his anxious wife. However, the 'Danube of Thought' had no intention of changing course, except to urge stronger collective action against dissidence by Warsaw Pact members he had once kept at arm's length. There was no organized intellectual dissent, and subsequent claims for the emergence of a Military Revolutionary Committee towards the middle of the year appear overstated. The spark needed to mobilize the mass discontent undoubtedly felt came from a tangential source, the charismatic Hungarian Calvinist pastor László Tőkés and his courageous defiance of the authorities' attempt to transfer him from his Timişoara parish to a rural backwater. What was remarkable about the events of 16 December was that Tőkés's parishioners were joined by hundreds of Romanians in a protest which by the next day had swelled into a major demonstration calling for free elections and democracy. On a direct order from Bucharest the army turned to violence and on the 17th about 70 protesters lost their lives. On 20 December protests resumed, however; a 100 000-strong crowd gathered in Timişoara city centre and the army withdrew to barracks. Major disturbances took place in some other Transylvanian centres (Cluj, Arad, Sibiu, Tirgu Mureş) and Ceauşescu ordered a rally in the centre of Bucharest for the following day. His look of incredulity when the commandered crowd turned against him at the 21 December rally offered devastating insight into the mentality of authoritarian rule. That evening crowds remained in the city centre and clashed with army and Securitate forces. The same day, about 25 people were shot dead in Sibiu, where Nicu Ceauşescu, the dictator's son, was party secretary.

The turning point was 22 December. As crowds converged before the party central committee building, the defence minister, General Milea, refused

Ceauşescu's command to order security forces to fire and committed suicide. It seems to have been news of his death that produced a spontaneous decision by troops of the 1st Armoured Division, the main army units involved (alongside militia and ministry of interior troops), to return to barracks. Crowds then stormed the building, from whose roof the two Ceauşescus took flight by helicopter. The pilot found a pretext to land and the fleeing couple hijacked a car, only to be captured some 50 miles north-west of Bucharest. Meanwhile fighting continued in Bucharest and other towns between pro- and anti-Ceauşescu elements. Ceauşescu had paid Securitate officers better than their army equivalents but the line-up of forces was not clear-cut. The army came on to the side of the revolution only on 22 December and some army units may have sided with the outgoing regime as late as the 24th; on the other hand, only the presidential protection force and parts of the Securitate's five directorates seem to have resisted the popular movement. Doubts about Securitate loyalties, however, and fears that the Ceauşescus might be spirited from captivity helped spur the new authorities' decision to put them on trial for treason on Christmas Day in a dubious charade which ended in their immediate execution. This had the intended effect of restoring order. Altogether official figures reported 1033 dead and 2383 wounded in the revolutionary events, about a quarter of them soldiers.

In Romania the shift from idealism to pragmatism observable elsewhere occurred with such speed that the largely youthful cohorts who braved the violence spoke of their revolution having been stolen. The idealism took various forms: the willingness of the young on the streets to risk death in an act of moral cleansing; the deployment by the courageous Tőkés of the anti-tyranny resources of the Christian lexicon in sermons on texts like 'Perfect love casts out fear';[17] the passion of the poet Mircea Dinescu, under surveillance since his anti-Ceauşescu interview in the Paris *Libération* in March, who appeared first on national television to announce the tyrant's overthrow. Dinescu records, however, that the generals who came over to the revolution on 22 December were wary of consorting with a poet. Here the National Salvation Front suddenly emerging that afternoon played a canalizing role. Once-leading communists like Ion Ionescu and General Nicolae Militaru squared the generals and speeded to the radio station before convoking a small group of dissident communists in the central committee building and giving it the above high-sounding name. By the end of the day they had published a communique offering free elections, pluralism, human and minority rights, and economic reform; very soon they also set up a nominally ruling Council for the Front, naming first, without consulting them, leading non-communist dissidents like Dinescu, Tőkés and the literary critic Doina Cornea.

It was the communist past and to an extent techniques of the new rulers which quickly attracted criticism. How far back did Iliescu's dissident credentials really reach: to 1971 when he allegedly disapproved of the influence on Ceauşescu of the megalomanic North Korean leader Kim-il-Sung; to 1984 when he lost his central committee post; or only to 1987, when he made his first oblique public criticism in an article advocating perestroika? Militaru had likewise been a central committee member until 1984 and Sylviu Brucan, a prominent Front member, had joined the party in the same year as Iliescu, 1944. As to General Victor Stanculescu, who succeeded Militaru as defence minister in February 1990, he had changed sides only on 22 December and had apparently not been approached by discontented communists in the 1980s because he was considered 'Ceauşescu's man'.[18] Militaru's fall from grace pointed to jockeyings for position in the new power order in a system which bore analogies to communist organization, in that the NSF Council was an over-large body meeting occasionally, like the old party central committee, while real power lay with an Executive Council of 11 members, similar to the politbureau. In a joint interview of 23 August 1990, Militaru and Brucan added their voices to allegations of a history of plotting against the Ceauşescu regime, which threatened to turn December 1989 into a coup rather than a popular uprising. They depicted themselves and some 20 generals of an alleged Military Resistance Council as the neglected architects of the new order. The elusive truth appears to be that Militaru and Brucan had their own motives for exaggerating plot theories, and that the manoeuvrings of high-ranking communists critical of Ceauşescu from the 1970s were neither well organized nor reached far into party, as opposed to military ranks.[19] They would have achieved nothing without the impetus and bravery of December's mass crowds, though the speed of Iliescu's response shows that some former apparatchiks had a strategy in place. In the event this at best reform communist figure was able to win 85 per cent of the presidential vote in June 1990 against more authentically democratic candidates. Taken with Bulgarian developments evidence was growing of a divergent path between the northern and southern tier of what had been the communist bloc which will continue to be of interest in future chapters.

Assessment

The upheavals of 1989 were very distinctive revolutions, so much so that the very name has often been denied them. Is 'revolution' an appropriate term here? Why did hardly anyone predict what was about to happen? How real was the sense of unity and clarity of purpose which are the essence of the revolutionary experience for its participants?

Debates about terms are valuable if they push behind stereotypes to examine the unspoken associations underlying the concepts at issue. The association of revolution with violence is what leads commentators to doubt the revolutionary nature of some of the peaceful transitions of 1989. Yet in its core meaning of turnabout, fundamental change of direction, the use of revolution in a peaceful context is established most famously in the

'Glorious Revolution' of 1688 in Britain, although of course the threat of violence was present. Plainly there was a fundamental change of direction in East Germany and Czechoslovakia in 1989. This would seem true of Poland and Hungary as well, though the tumultuousness of the mass demonstrations of Leipzig, Berlin and Prague was absent there. It is the Round Table process in these countries which has been invoked as undermining the notion of revolutionary change because negotiated settlements were reached by which communists retained a role on the stage, indeed, arguably a leading role. Such interpretations commonly reflect disappointment at the outcome of 1989 and the sense that guilty men did not pay fully for their crimes. In the context of 1989 itself they are anachronistic. The collapse of communist regimes was not on the agenda when the Round Tables were held; a tougher line by the non-communist participants would have sabotaged the whole reform process. But the absence of a formal rite of passage from authoritarianism to freedom has given rise to a set of terms expressing the distinctiveness of what took place. Timothy Garton Ash has coined the word 'refolution' for Poland and Hungary; the East Germans spoke of a *Wende*, or turnabout, a word that has been taken over by some Bulgarians to describe their own transition.[20] The Hungarian conservative successor regime of the Democratic Forum preferred *rendszerváltozás* (system change) to *rendszerváltás* (exchange of systems), so as to emphasize the gradualist and consensual nature of the Hungarian transition.

These distinctions seem in order but should not invalidate the revolutionary nature of the changes that took place in 1989. First, even if the turnabout was non-confrontational in form, in ideological substance it was total. The Hungarian Round Table was more about the mechanism than the principle of transformation; Polish communists at first were less prepared to throw in the towel than Hungarian ones, but the 4 June elections provided the classic revolutionary turning point which upended what had gone before. Though Civic Forum did look for a partner with which to parley, there was no real negotiation because communist institutions simply collapsed. Second, the issue of force so often linked with revolution was initially pervasive, though fully realized only in Bucharest. Leipzig on 9 October and Prague on 17 November were charged with violence or the threat of it; later the Stasi HQs in Leipzig and Berlin were to be attacked in December and January respectively. Third, above all, the autumn events showed the dizzying pace of events characteristic of revolutionary process, when acceleration becomes a leitmotif in itself and consciousness, unable to operate by normal criteria, is transformed, constantly expanding the bounds of the possible to create ever new scenarios. When experienced commentators opined in October 1989 that by 1995 not only Hungary but perhaps even Czechoslovakia (but not Poland) might have joined Austrians and Swiss in neutrality, or in December that 'the two German states might yet come closer together' through some extended European community of the future, but this was 'a long way off', the now tame predictions only show how the speed of change beggared the imagination.[21]

The French experience has inevitably influenced the connotations of what is understood by revolution. The events of 1989 exemplified the first of the French revolutionaries' famous goals, liberty. Perhaps their most remarkable feature was the crumbling of power in the face of demonstrating crowds, evoking the storming of the Paris Bastille or the March Days of 1848. The effect was all the greater because, by contrast to the authoritarian regimes of 1789 and 1848, communist regimes disposed of vast police apparatuses, whose ineffectiveness bolstered optimistic views of the human condition. Of its nature, the role of the security forces in 1989 remains obscure in places, encouraging conspiracy theories. What happened in East Germany suggests something about the nature of the system, however. The Stasi was designed for supervision and manipulation of individuals and small groups, so as to nip disaffection in the bud. Shooting on vast crowds transcended its modus operandi and ideological remit, as the failure to act in Leipzig on 9 October shows. Similarly if, as seems likely, KGB elements had their own plan to use the 17 November student demonstration to destabilize the hard-line Prague regime in the interests of perestroika, the outcome only confirms that such undercover tactics cannot control mass movements. What was involved in Czechoslovakia was the difficulty of ensuring unity in the repressive apparatus itself; this is true also of Romania, the other country where conspiracy theories about 1989 have been strongest. Part of the Securitate went over to the opposition generals despite Ceauşescu's deliberate bid to favour them over the army.

Yet in 1789 liberty was twinned with equality, lending subsequent notions of revolution a left-wing twist. Did 1989's rejection of communism mean a disavowal of the further development of the revolutionary idea towards equality in the 'progressive' scenario? Was the 'grand narrative' of the left now played out, as Francis Fukuyama implied when he wrote in 1990 of 'the end of history', with mankind henceforth oscillating in ever more stable cycles around the station called 'liberal democracy'?[22] Pro-socialist slogans early in the East German and Czechoslovak demonstrations in autumn 1989 might suggest that people hoped to reconcile the liberty ideal of the cold war west with the equality ideal of the cold war east, the much-mentioned synthesis of the 'third way'. This would be a logical enough extension of the thesis of the first section of this book, that east Europeans opposed the totalitarian aspects of communism but went along with socialist principles of egalitarianism and a provident state. The experiences recorded in this chapter, however, suggest that the third way turned out to be as elusive as reform communism. Post-communism, it seemed, faced its subjects with a choice of either/or. The swing of East Germans from the idea of an alternative German society to unification with the west, of a section of Solidarity headed by Lech Wałęsa towards the market, of the Hungarian Democratic Forum from a questing third wayism to orthodox national democracy: all this indicated the pressures towards an opposite, rightist choice this time round. In 1978 the Czechoslovak dissident Šimečka had envisaged that communism's creation of a homogenous society augured well for 'the implementation of bold social reforms' once the dictatorship went, as there would be no special interest groups concerned to resist them.[23] Nothing could be further from the truth. What communism had done was to inoculate people from any desire for more social experimentation. In this sense, its effect had been profoundly conservative.

On the other hand, 1989 was eminently about fraternity, the third of the French Revolution's slogans. This came out both in the togetherness of demonstrating crowds and the extended sense of national solidarity. The direct option of East Germans for German unification, the invocation of previous national events (in the names of many new groupings, anniversaries celebrated, past aspirations), the Polish Round Table participants' appeal to their common Polishness, Pozsgay's sense that communists had neglected the mobilizing power of nationhood: all this was somewhat overlooked at the time in favour of the liberty theme. It reflected the deep-seated nationality factor running through the history of the region and present in previous explosions, in 1956, 1968 and 1980–81.

But why did autumn 1989 take the world so much by surprise? A detail posterity may overlook is the tendency of contemporary intellectual assumption, more Marxist-influenced than is now recalled, to see struggle and violence as the likely outcome in historical imbroglios, rather than peaceful change; this applied also to apartheid South Africa. More generally, economic downturns and dissident activities from 1987 on outpaced contemporary observers and can be fully appreciated only in hindsight; besides, the absolute figures of those involved were still very low. Fear that the masses were ensnared in the tangles of consumerism ran deep and dampened too much optimism about a speedy exit from the system. The present writer was told by a leading Hungarian dissident in 1988 that when he had broached the issue of constitutionalism in a public rally on the Hungarian national day, the previous 15 March, he had no idea whether the crowd would cheer or jeer him. Hence the delight at the huge popular participation in the events of 1989. But did it mean that the people of eastern Europe had been on the dissidents' wavelength all along? Or is the bald statement of an East German participant that there were two waves, an intellectual movement outnumbered later by those whose motives were 'quite obviously based on material interests', nearer the mark?[24] Such antitheses are somewhat overdrawn. People are capable of multi-faceted responses and of being lifted from the rut of conventional assumption. There is too much evidence of the exhilaration of the 1989 crowds, and their sense of uplift and purification, to doubt that this occurred. Moreover, the liberal ideology increasingly in the air tended to blur any tension between ideals on the one hand and material prosperity on the other, because classical liberalism notoriously claims that political freedom is the essential precondition of wealth creation. One of the greatest works of liberal historiography, T.B. Macaulay's account of the Glorious Revolution of 1688, seeks precisely to demonstrate through this event 'how, from the auspicious union of order and freedom sprang a prosperity of which the annals of human affairs had furnished no example'.[25] Thus many demonstrators in 1989 will have seen private enterprise as a benign force rewarding personal effort, based on their experience in the 1980s, when it appeared in the form of much-needed small businesses filling in gaps in socialist welfare. Capitalism as a great impersonal force swathing through state industries and throwing thousands into redundancy irrespective of their merits was a mere abstraction, remote from people's experience up to that time. It is quite probable, therefore, that large crowds rejoiced in their growing strength and looked forward to a future in which political, economic and national freedom went together. Yet the hopes of enthralled observers that this mood presaged some permanent, benign shift in outlook were pithily set in perspective by Kołakowski's ironic comment: 'Euphoria is always brief, whatever causes it'.[26] The popular mood in autumn 1989 is no real guide to what people felt a year before or to what they would feel a year later, hence the difficulty of prediction. Another of Kołakowski's *aperçus* is apposite, when he quoted the saying 'Nobody is so old that he cannot live for one more year.' How could one tell before the event that eastern Europe had reached the critical degree of abnormality when the acts even of individuals (a László Tőkés, say) could have the powerful ripple effects chaos theory tells us a butterfly's wings in Mongolia may exert on the British weather?

A fairer criticism of contemporary commentators is that they might have looked harder at the communist leadership in eastern Europe. The increasing failures of the system and its growing cynicism were noted but with rarely a hint that these might affect communists' will to go on. But even in a country like Romania the defence minister Milea's alleged remark before his death on 22 December, that he had read through the army manual and not found anything in it about the army firing on its own people, only makes sense if there were people around who assumed that communist populism was not just a charade. Published records of Soviet politbureau meetings and memoirs of communist inner circles suggest that in private many top leaders used much the same kind of stale communist formulas they did in public, so that their political monopoly was based on conventional complacency as much as Orwellian lust for power. Just below them, however, communist belief was being hollowed out, so that the party structures folded when put under pressure in 1989. Thus the Czechoslovak Institute for Economic Forecasting turned out to be a nest of unbelievers, including none other than the high priest of Czech economic Thatcherism and post-communist prime minister, Václav Klaus. In these circumstances observers overestimated the system's power of resistance, just as they underestimated the public's capacity for protest.

There was certainly some overestimation of Mikhail Gorbachev. The Russian leader was evidence of a bad system's capacity to throw up humane leaders, but an intrigued world was too ready to assume that perestroika was a linked-up strategy instead of a tactical gift for turning Soviet weaknesses into apparent strength. People simply did not imagine that the accomplished Gorbachev would preside over the collapse of his country's superpower position, which they plausibly linked with its satellite empire, while he and his fellow reformers had an interest in appearing to be in control. In January 1990 the Soviet foreign minister Shevardnadze told a Supreme Soviet critical of the 'loss' of eastern Europe that he and Gorbachev had always anticipated the outcome of their policy of relaxation there. This is unlikely. It seems Gorbachev first overestimated the capacity of reform communists to hold their ground in the region and then turned a resolute blind eye to any possible negative consequences, making it difficult to judge what he would finally do if his optimism proved misplaced. Thus he dismissed as rubbish the idea that Hungarian communists' acceptance of multipartyism in February 1989 could be relevant to the Soviet Union[27] and he still presupposed a Europe of two social systems in his speech to the Council of Europe in July. Meanwhile, doubts grew. The head of KGB foreign intelligence from January 1989 recalls that the first major assessment he read stated that the Warsaw Pact regimes had small chances of survival; foreign minister Shevardnadze's advisers after the Polish elections in June concluded that eastern Europe would probably 'go'.[28]

Gorbachev's attitude to eastern Europe may have had some parallels to Roosevelt's in 1945, about which historians surmise that he was ultimately willing to sacrifice the region in the interests of a wider settlement but may have hoped for a better deal there. The fact is that by autumn 1989 the Soviet Union could not have switched to suppression without undermining its whole domestic and international strategy of the past four years; the problematic consent of the Supreme Soviet would have been needed, for example, while the military problem of action on several fronts would have been formidable. As it was, American leaders rubbed Soviet noses in their own rhetoric, with Bush in Warsaw in July citing Gorbachev on the necessity of freedom of choice and saying that a common home was all fine, provided one could move from room to room.[29] There was little alternative to the reaffirmation of the non-intervention line by Gorbachev in Paris after the Polish elections and in Rome after the fall of the Berlin Wall, by the Soviet ambassador in East Germany closer to the latter event and again at a meeting of the European Conference on Cooperation and Security (CSCE) in Helsinki in November 1989. A *Pravda* article of 23 March 1990 reaffirmed the optimistic perspective, arguing that the end of 'coercive custody' of the Soviet Union's neighbours was 'a victory for common sense, a victory for our long-term strategic interests, and a victory for democracy'.[30] By this time the Soviet party too had renounced its leading role. Some historians have likewise given Gorbachev the credit for rational decisions,[31] but quite apart from the question of his original intentions the ignominious way in which Soviet hegemony ended could not but damage hopes of stabilizing perestroika in the Soviet Union.

Gorbachev was simply overtaken by the pace of events, no more so than in the case of Germany. In November 1989 Moscow responded with irritation to the first talk of a confederation of West and East Germany. When Chancellor Kohl pushed further, Gorbachev seems to have thought at first that Polish, French and British opposition to German unification would do his own work for him. When these countries yielded to the democratic inevitability, he resigned himself in February 1990 to unification but as a neutral state. Eventually, in July he accepted a united Germany's membership of NATO but on the assumption that NATO troops would not be stationed beyond the old East German frontier. The successive retreats were doubtless eased for Gorbachev by dollops of West German aid but more powerfully by the prospect he clung to of his country's final admittance into the wider civilized world and a reorganized Europe of 'the common home', where its former enemies would help fund its much-needed modernization. His policy placed great emphasis on the CSCE machinery which had emerged from the Helsinki détente process of 1975 rather than on instruments of the old blocks like NATO and the Warsaw Pact. There was much illusion here. The CSCE remained a talking shop. In place of the continental and global reorganization on the basis of high principle which Gorbachev liked to invoke as the framework of his concessions, what actually took place was a step-by-step expansion of one power bloc at the expense of a defeated one. The economic quid pro quo he looked for did not materialize as his diminished realm sank deeper into poverty, disinclining western governments from sinking money into a black hole. Gorbachev's self-confident optimism and faith in his personal wager on democracy and a new world order allowed him to be sucked unwittingly into a process he could not control, but they had meantime projected a figure to the world who was punching above his declining country's weight, a persuasive figure more redolent of reform than – as proved to be the case – collapse.

Something of the Gorbachev syndrome may help explain why the east European opposition did not expect an abrupt breakdown of Soviet hegemony. Sharing his rationalist assumptions, they linked such a momentous event to the emergence of an alternative order, a new civilizational norm, which they aspired to but knew they were not yet in a position to bring about. They said much about their peoples' moral health as a systemic problem but little about the economic aspects of system change. They sought dialogue, not power. Hence the prevalence of 'Round Tables' for negotiation with a communist 'other' in 1989 and the emphasis on rational discussion implied in the ubiquitous term 'forum' among opposition organizations. The rational instinct is to expect power only when one feels fully ready for it. Even Lenin wrote that he might never see revolution in Russia, just months before February 1917.

History, however, is rarely tidy. It is its unpredictability that casts doubt on some of the more ambitious attempts by political scientists to locate 1989 in a 'third wave' of democratization, of which the third began with the demise of authoritarianism in Portugal and Spain in 1974–75. The comparison is worth attempting. Adam Michnik for one became interested in the Spanish case and urged it as a model for the Polish transition to democracy in a book published in 1990. The Round Table techniques of 1989 were arguably anticipated in the negotiations between old regime elements and democratic forces in the Iberian peninsula and certain Latin American countries in the 1970s. Yet only Hungary followed these examples at all closely in that the old and emerging elites there bargained over a transition; elsewhere the group in power either still did not really envisage such a transition to a new regime (Poland) or was fatally crippled by mass action which had already taken place (East Germany, Czechoslovakia). Moreover, unlike in the Iberian and Latin American cases the military were not a distinctive party to negotiations, while an external factor, the Soviet Union, did provide a third force. Political science specialists of eastern Europe have themselves made these points, noting too that it was now not just the political but also the economic system which had to be changed.[32] This was crucial because the economic system was responsible for the deformation in people's attitude to work and for the corruption and materialist/consumerist fixations which made dissidents fear for their peoples' moral health. The moral dimension in east European national revivals, spearheaded as they were by writers and artists, gave such concerns special importance. There seem too many distinctive features in the east European experience leading up to and in 1989 for it to be usefully slotted into a purported global process of democratization.

Yet the instinct to desire tidiness in human affairs swayed not just scholars but Gorbachev and east European dissidents to envisage that great events could not take place without an overarching framework to receive them. Gorbachev dreamed of the common European home and a bloc-free world order; the dissidents dreamed of the maturation of a civil society hollowing out the communist distopia. What happened was untidy. Masses demonstrated who wanted western freedoms without giving up eastern securities, the free market but not unemployment. The Soviet hegemony was overthrown without prior arrangement over the economic ties that had developed in Comecon over the previous 40 years. The revolutionary upsurge of late 1989 was truly an upsurge of the human spirit and a historic turning point, as it was seen at the time, but like all such events it did not come neatly packaged but entangled in a thousand webs in ways which only revealed themselves in the aftermath. The next two chapters will take the story further along the road.

6

System change
The liberal moment in east-central Europe

It is hard from the aspect of the eastern Europe of the present, with more than its fair share of the greyness of real life, to appreciate the heady hopes and apocalyptic fears infecting views of the region's future in the immediate aftermath of 1989. On the one hand were visions of countries taking their rightful place within a matter of years as full participants in an unprecedently free and prosperous 'Europe'. On the other were voices pointing Cassandra-like to dire consequences for a region unfamiliar with democracy. 'Any fool could have foreseen that the consequences of the almost overnight removal of repressive regimes would mean serious disorder verging on anarchy and chaos,' wrote the ex-Labour MP Robert Kilroy-Silk in February 1990; 'Gorbachev has let loose the dogs of war, as we shall see in the next few months and years in Eastern Europe.'[1] The historian Orlando Figes uttered a more qualified warning: 'If on the other hand social democracy fails to hold things together in eastern Europe, then it will not be replaced by some genteel Bohemian version of a conservative party. Instead, racism and extremism will raise their ugly head.'[2] Amid euphoria, commentators were aware that the harder battles were yet to come.

One shadow hanging over the region receded quickly: that of a Soviet backlash. The collapse of its military and economic ties with the Soviet Union had not been part of Gorbachev's script. Briefly, east Europeans forebore to embarrass him on this score. Then the Poles first called for Soviet troop withdrawal and became embroiled in undignified claim and counter-claim over compensation for Soviet-built military facilities and environmental damage due to Soviet occupation troops. Eventually, Hungary also plucked up courage. The resignation of Gorbachev's reformist foreign minister Shevardnadze in protest against a conservative backlash in the Soviet Union (December 1990) strengthened east Europeans' desire to rid themselves of remaining Soviet troops. When Gorbachev proposed the reorganization of the Warsaw Pact into a political arrangement, his neighbours only responded to the part of his démarche renouncing a military role. Gorbachev now agreed to dissolve the pact almost immediately (by April 1991) in advance of the Visegrád states' goal of the start of 1992. The last troops left Polish soil in 1994. Meanwhile, Comecon held its final meeting in February 1991. The webs which tied eastern Europe into the Soviet bloc were broken faster than most people had foreseen.[3]

As the external problems diminished, internal ones multiplied. Politically, how were atomized populations, where differentiated social structures and sophisticated interest groups had been eroded by authoritarian rule, to build pluralist democracies? Economically, how could profit-orientated market economies be established in a zone which had imploded in large part because it was bankrupt, and what would meanwhile happen to the vast numbers currently dependent on the discredited state enterprises? Socially, would resources be available to reshape policies on totally new principles, given that the unemployment, drugs, pornography, pollution and delinquency which had gone unrecognized or been treated in a hole-in-the-corner fashion in the old system were likely to grow in a more open society? Psychologically, could the mentality necessary for civil society be created in societies where so few – 30 per cent in the Czech lands, for example – believed people could be trusted?[4]

These problems in various forms have continued to engage the region to this day. The distinctions of some social science theories between stages of transition and consolidation appear glib in the light of many economists' view that even transition is not yet over. In a noted work of early 1990 Ralf Dahrendorf prophesied that the politics of transition would take six months, the economics six years and the attainment of a fully civil society sixty. Yet some kind of periodization is clearly helpful. This chapter is concerned with the second stage of the revolutionary process, when the basic institutions were set in place to fill the vacuum left by communist collapse. It will deal with the fundamentals of system change: the devising of electoral and judicial procedures appropriate for a liberal democracy, the launching of schemes to dismantle the command economy, the beginnings of a new social policy, the first confronting of questions of retribution and compensation for communist misdeeds. The absence of a comprehensive model of post-communist society on dissidents' part left the field open for concepts of sweeping change, often advocated by spokespersons of the patently victorious west. More completely than even the brief aftermath of 1918, western liberalism became hegemonic in the region. As a result, western advisers and social scientists exerted a powerful influence on the process of transition and how it was conceptualized. 'Democratization studies', 'big bang' or gradualist models for the reintroduction of capitalism, questions of the optimum 'sequencing' of reforms and arguments over the validity of comparisons with other post-authoritarian societies became points of reference for the region's intellectuals as well as outside observers. This very centrality of liberal policies, together with the controversies to which they gave rise, may be seen as a defining feature of the process of system change, in which the post-communist order in east-central Europe first took recognizable shape. It is so understood in this account.

Hence the first breach of the liberal ascendancy, with the election of ex-communist parties in Poland and Hungary in 1993–94, marks an approximate end point for the subject matter of this chapter. The further evolution of the institutions created in the early 1990s will be treated in the last section of the book. The emphasis given to liberalism as a defining characteristic of the period of system change also explains this chapter's concentration on the northern zone of the region, the countries of east-central Europe as opposed to the Balkans. It is the greater strength of liberalism in the former rather than the latter zone which best explains the different fortunes of the two areas and makes it desirable to treat them separately from 1989. The distinctive experience of the Balkan lands will be the subject of Chapter 6.

The triumph of liberalism

Why did liberalism so rapidly emerge as the overarching ideological framework for post-communist reconstruction, in historically stony soil? Three inter-related factors help explain its rapid rise. The strongest factor was no doubt a negative one, the discrediting of the left. After both world wars the vision of the left had seemed the untried next step in the historical process unleashed by 1789. Now with the failure of communism, which claimed to be the highest stage in that process, the wheel had come full circle. The anti-communist tide swept with it even vaguely left-wing ideas of social interventionism. When the influential economist Jeffrey Sachs called Lenin's victory 'one of the great disasters of the twentieth century' the reason he adduced, namely the 'false and dangerous presumption that human society can be arranged, rather than simply allowed to evolve', would have damned most liberal reformers.[5] The temperamentally far from conservative Václav Havel showed the distrust communism had created of any social engineering, when he held that totalitarianism was bound up with western rationalism and people's belief that through control of nature they could improve their lives.[6] Perhaps the best-known east European economist, János Kornai, turned his harsh criticisms of the command economy also against the 'grotesque absurdity' of reform communist attempts to 'simulate' the market and all such halfway houses.[7] Another weighty figure, the Anglo-German political scientist Ralf Dahrendorf assailed the illusion of a 'third way' between the 'closed society' and the 'open society' which eastern Europe now had to embrace.[8] 'Liberalism offers the most radical form of escape from the totalitarian system, for it is its exact opposite,' wrote a Polish journalist in 1991.[9] So strong was the revulsion at left-wing traditions that the entire edifice of

Czech history and the national self-image as a left-leaning neo-Hussite people was called in question by Czech historians. While the historical essays of the severest critic of 'President Liberator' Tomáš Masaryk, the conservative Austrophile Josef Pekař, were re-published in large numbers, regrets were expressed that the Czechs had not had a patriotic aristocracy like the Poles and Hungarians, and calls were made for a 'full-blooded' history of Czech Catholic Christianity as a priority of national historiography.[10]

The second factor in the appeal of liberalism was that the recipe was available. Liberal democracy and the market economy, it was held, were tested formulae which had brought the west to its enviable heights. Sachs made the comparison with Spain, a country which had been on the same level as Poland in 1950 and now had four times its per capita income. From early on commentators noted the absence of original thinking in eastern Europe after the spectacular events of 1989, which was quite different from the explosion of new ideas after 1789 and 1848. The prestige of the west seemed to make questioning irrelevant. This was a time when the European idea was at its apogee, before the controversies surrounding the European Union's Maastricht treaty and its ineffectual Balkan policy opened an era of greater scepticism. Western experts on constitutional and economic reform descended on the region, to sell their nostrums and bask in the admiring glow. Slogans like civil society and the free market acquired an almost incantatory quality, as if their mere repetition would bring benefit in itself.

Third, the more sophisticated advocates of liberal solutions pressed for their rapid adoption because they knew the problems they entailed and reckoned it was wise to strike while the iron was hot and the public still ready for sacrifices. For the aspect of liberalism which seemed most immediately germane was economic liberalism: laissez-faire. The centralized economy could be overcome only by the most determined and ideologically committed assault, during which large numbers of people might lose jobs in defunct state industries, prices would rise with the abolition of subsidies and wealth disparities would grow. Reformers saw a window of opportunity to expose a momentarily biddable population to these trials, with the promise of pain now, followed by gain down the road.

One should not assume that liberalism became the creed of all east European non-communist intellectuals. Everywhere liberals were coteries, operating alongside social democrat, populist, nationalist and Christian strands of thought. It is true, too, that there was often a theoretical mismatch between talk of civil society and the individualistic bent of the kind of anti-leftist liberalism soon in vogue. East European notions of civil society as they emerged in the last phase of communist rule had been designed to inculcate the moral solidarity of society against the state, as most famously in the Polish movement of that name. They had therefore a collectivist, moralistic thrust, not fully attuned to the rational, impersonal goals posited by laissez-faire liberalism. That said, for the reasons given above, government policies reflected mainly the liberals' priorities. Nor should one exaggerate the artificiality of the adoption of liberalism in east-central Europe in 1990. Issues of personal freedom and of freedom of association, assembly, press and religious conscience were very meaningful for populations which had lived under an intrusive, inept authoritarianism, and they could be given a resonance from earlier struggles in the region's patriotic past. Thus the election programme of the Young Democrats in Hungary in April 1990 set side by side the 12 points demanded by liberal revolutionaries in 1848 and their own; the resemblances were remarkable. For a spell, liberal nostrums appealed well beyond the circles of liberal intellectuals.

The political framework

Establishing popularly elected governments was everywhere the first priority. In the interests of stability the East German elections were brought forward from May to March 1990. The Hungarian general election took place in April, and the Czechoslovak in June. Poland did not follow suit until October 1991, since Solidarity was bound by the 1989 Round Table agreement with the communists which provided for the partially free elections of June that year; communists remained the largest single block in the Sejm.

Political observers feared that, in the absence of the differentiated social structures of advanced democracies, parties would be either catch-all vehicles for anti-communism or fiefdoms of individual personalities lacking broader appeal. The ethos of anti-communist dissidence was not an ideal preparation for 'procedural democracy', or commitment to the impersonal rule of law. Dissidents themselves had operated in groups united by bonds of personal trust, as intellectual coteries rather than representatives of social interests. The very popularity of political labels like Forum, Solidarity, Alliance, Union hinted at a certain unease at the idea of parties as interest groups and a preference for the moral unanimity the struggle against communism had evoked. Alongside a handful of charismatic figures, the new politicians were often men of technocratic bent who had kept their heads under the parapets in the communist years. While aged figures emerged to represent the parties the communists had suppressed after 1945, party political continuities had been broken far more than in 1918 and 1945 after the two world wars. A striking feature of the first set of elections in 1990 was the total eclipse of almost all 'traditional' parties at the polls. New groupings lacked the legitimacy of tradition; revived parties lacked credibility. It was through a sense of weakness as much as democratic principle that nearly all groups supported proportional representation, thinking it would guarantee them at least some voice. Proportional representation was mathematically complete only in Czechoslovakia, as before the war.

Elsewhere, there was either a pattern of multi-member constituencies or a mix between single-member seat and national and regional lists. Except in Poland, a threshhold of 4 per cent or 5 per cent prevented too great a proliferation of minor parties in parliament.

The results indeed cast doubts on the chances of strong parties emerging in the region as instruments of the new politics. In East Germany none of the native bodies, with the partial exception of the ex-communist party of the Democratic Left, were rooted enough to compete with imported machines of West German parties. New Forum took only 2.9 per cent of the vote in an election won convincingly by Kohl's conservative Christian Democrats over the Social Democrats. Particularly unnerving were successive scandals forcing the resignation of democratic politicians as alleged collaborators of the Stasi: the first and last post-communist East German prime minister, the Christian Democrat De Maizière, and the vice-president of the East German Social Democrats were only the most prominent examples. Meanwhile, the two most successful parties in the first Hungarian contest, the Hungarian Democratic Forum (25 per cent) and the Alliance of Free Democrats (21 per cent), were both creations of the dissident intelligentsia of the later 1980s, well ahead of parties which did have a social base, like the Independent Smallholders or Pozsgay's ex-communist Hungarian Socialist Party, at around 11 per cent each. The Social Democrats failed to clear the threshhold hurdle into parliament at all. After the comprehensive defeat of the left, the Smallholders and the Christian Democrats entered a conservative-orientated coalition led by the Democratic Forum. Yet the lack of public enthusiasm was shown by the heavy losses the Forum suffered in nationwide local polls only two months later, in which just 42 per cent of the electorate voted. By 1993 the six parties elected to parliament in 1990 had become some twenty separate groups; no fewer than fifty MPs had left or been expelled from their original homes, the Smallholders proving particularly fissiparous.[11] Pozsgay's departure from the Socialists into a new, unsuccessful movement was an ironic comment on his dream of leading a post-communist Hungary under the aegis of a broad-based reformed party of the left. Hungary was now led by prime minister József Antall, medical historian and austere son of a pre-war civil servant, conservative-minded enough to make several visits to the grave of Admiral Horthy, interwar Hungary's none-too-democratic Regent.

Czechoslovakia showed parallels to both countries, with the communists outdoing the threshold-failing Social Democrats, as in Hungary, and Civic Forum proving even more effective than the German Christian Democrats in creaming off the anti-communist vote, with 53 per cent of the ballots. It was, however, essentially an umbrella organization, in which splits soon became apparent between laissez-faire and more libertarian versions of liberalism. The abrasive Václav Klaus, representing the former wing (against Havel) was already pushing in autumn 1990 for an orthodox political party with a strong laissez-faire orientation. By January Civic Forum had split. Indeed, in the general election of 1992 its old partners stood in at least four camps, with the more conservative Civil Democratic Party of Klaus the best attuned to the continued right-wing spirit of the times. With allies it gained nearly 30 per cent of the poll. The extent of party permutations, alliances, divorces and regroupings was bewildering. Only three of the chief Czech parties of 1993 had even existed in 1990, while only the rootedly unfashionable communists retained roughly the same level of support in the elections of 1990 and 1992. Slovak politics (there were three governments and sets of election, federal, Czech and Slovak) took the process a stage further. The equivalent there of Civic Forum, the Public against Violence, collapsed altogether in 1992 under the weight of the national question, bequeathing its supporters mainly to the new Movement for a Democratic Slovakia which emerged with 37 per cent of the poll. The MDS was led by a demagogue, Vladimír Mečiar, an ex-boxer and political bruiser who exploited Slovak resentment both of perceived Czech superciliousness and the Hungarian minority. The restored Czechoslovak democracy proved insufficiently flexible to defuse Slovaks' sense of being patronized little brothers. The long dispute on the very name of the state gave the game away. First it was to be a hyphenated Czecho-Slovakia in Slovakia but unhyphenated in the Czech lands and abroad; then it became the Czech and Slovak Federal Republic. The victory of the equally uncompromising Klaus and Mečiar in the 1992 elections paved the way for the break-up of the common state at the start of 1993.

The instability of the movements which had brought liberation was still more dramatically illustrated in Poland. There rifts began to appear almost immediately between the mercurial Wałęsa and the first non-communist prime minister Mazowiecki and other Solidarity intellectuals. Wałęsa assumed the role of protector of worker interests and forced a presidential contest to replace Jaruzelski in which he and Mazowiecki stood against each other. The real loser in this election (November 1990) was not just Mazowiecki, a ruling prime minister who won only 18 per cent of the vote, but Polish politics: Wałęsa was forced into an embarrassing second-round run-off against an eccentric Polish-Canadian business man, Tyminski, who played on the naïvety and disillusionment of the electorate with promises of economic quick fixes. By the time of the first full Polish parliamentary elections in October 1991, Wałęsa, Mazowiecki and the arch-economic liberal Bielecki all led separate parties hived off from the abandoned Solidarity fold, while there was also a left-wing ex-Solidarity Labour Union. Twenty-nine electoral lists gained representation in the Sejm, making Mazowiecki's Democratic Union the largest party with a mere 12.3 per cent of the vote. By 1993 Poland was on its sixth post-communist government, and quarrelling politicians came up against Lech Wałęsa's ambitions in ways that for some commentators recalled Piłsudski's role in undermining Polish democracy at that time.

The rapidity with which the new democratic politicians came to be widely seen as 'them' must seem surprising until the circumstances of the demise of communism are remembered. For the masses there had been no educative campaign over principles; communism collapsed and from its ruins emerged figures little better known to the wider public than communist leaders had been in 1945. This is the strongest argument for non-'revoutionary' interpretations of 1989. Several of the new politicians were previously politically passive professionals, chiefly economists or lawyers, like the new finance ministers in Poland and Czechoslovakia, Leszek Balcerowicz and Václav Klaus respectively. Early middle-aged economic graduates who had moved straight into the communist state's economic administration, they were able, energetic men influenced by youthful studies in the west, who now saw their chance. Many others did have dissident records, if unspectacular, like the brief internment of the legal Catholic journalist Tadeusz Mazowiecki in 1982, or at a remove in the past, like the post-communist Hungarian president, Árpád Göncz, imprisoned after the 1956 revolution, or the prime minister József Antall, director of the Semmelweiss Medical Museum in Budapest. Sometimes previously non-political figures could prove more charismatic than those who did have a record. This was true of Mečiar, a legal adviser to a glass factory as opposed to his successor as Slovak prime minister, the Christian Democratic leader and persecuted legal defender of dissidents, Jan Čarnogursky. Even the few famous names of anti-communist protest (some more so in the west than at home) could be diminished in the new circumstances. Lech Wałęsa, shielding himself from perceived political rivals with an ill-assorted clique which came to include his chauffeur, alienated many who expected a different style in the presidency. Havel as Czechoslovak president saw his popularity leap ahead, but partly because he was contrasted with those who really did exercise power. It became apparent that 'We, the people', the slogan by which Timothy Garton Ash captured the mood of 1989, was an inspiration for resistance but not for government.

Party and personality uncertainties made the organization of the structures of power all the more important. Should a parliamentary or a presidential model be adopted, and should the president be elected by the people or by parliament? How might the new order be constitutionally guaranteed? These questions were variously answered in the region but there were common threads. The reaction to an authoritarian past, sharpened for Solidarity intellectuals by unease at Wałęsa's ambitions, was one. The prestige of the postwar West German model was another. These inclined the region to a prime ministerial rather than a presidential model, though the Polish president was to be elected by universal suffrage which potentially strengthened his legitimacy. Predictably Wałęsa chafed at his limitations and proposed a series of reforms to break what he called the 'Bermuda triangle' of tussles between premier, Sejm and president. The 'Little Constitution' of autumn 1992 brought him only limited gains. He could veto legislation, unless a two-thirds parliamentary majority overruled him, initiate legislation and dissolve a parliament that failed to pass a budget in time; but he failed to increase his influence over the composition of the government. Havel's requests of March 1991 for emergency powers and the right to dissolve deadlocked parliaments and order elections were rejected by MPs, for all the popularity of his weekly broadcasts with the public and his extensive presidential staff, which numbered 630 in 1991.[12] His calls for a referendum on the issue of Slovak separatism (which he thought would bury it), his preference for the setting up of a constitutional court and his unease at Klaus's free market policies were also passed over. President Göncz in Hungary, ostensibly a less significant figure, actually had more influence. Though he did not succeed in increasing his powers over the choice of ministers, he used his right to refer the government's decisions to the constitutional court to check its accumulation of power, as in its control over the media.

All-in-all the region's new presidents were determined not to be ciphers. If they did not gain all they wanted, this seems to have been due to a wide feeling in the new political class in favour of a division of powers. Hence arrangements like proportional representation everywhere, the deal struck in Hungary between Antall's Democratic Forum and the largest opposition party by which president Göncz came from the latter party, and the strengthening of the judiciary alongside the legislative and executive branches, by devices like the Polish and Hungarian constitutional courts. The Hungarian court was particularly active, tending to side with Göncz's criticism of an overmighty government. Acceptance of its verdicts helped to bed down the spirit of respect for the rule of law that liberal democrats wished to inculcate.[13] Politically, the chief problems remained the shallow roots of fragmented party systems and an abiding sense of a legacy of contamination from the previous regime. The East German problem of trust, of not knowing which post-communist politicians might have compromised pasts, existed more widely; it was particularly strong in Poland where commentators suspected ex-communist security personnel still held potential powers of blackmail over shaky regimes, or at the least, power over networks and resources weak states did not yet have. Political uncertainties were all the more unwelcome because the region was in the grip of an economic downturn which magnified discontents and gave plausibility to Cassandra-like prophecies of destabilization and faltering of renewal.

The jump to a market economy

The economy was the crucial test for the new governments. Here the communists had bequeathed them a poisoned chalice – how could the dead weight of more or less bankrupt state enterprises be integrated into the desired system of democratic choice and market profitability without subverting it and creating an interregnum of dislocation and hardship? Moving from communism to capitalism was compared to unscrambling an egg.

This is where the economic liberals had their trump-card. They saw the problem as a historic opportunity to vindicate their principles by seizing the bull by the horns. Already heavily engaged with democratizing regimes in Latin America, people like the trouble-shooting Harvard economist Jeffrey Sachs responded eagerly to Solidarity's overtures for experts who would save them from being outwitted by the communists in Poland's dawning pluralism. He saw prime minister Mazowiecki in 1989 even before the latter had appointed his cabinet. The programme he and József Kornai, based in Budapest and Harvard, advocated (there were nuances in approach) stressed the need to tackle the economic transition simultaneously through interlocking measures on many fronts.[14] The quicker the reform process, the shorter the painful interregnum referred to above. Technically, the crucial problem was to maintain macroeconomic stability during the transition, that is, to balance the budget and repress inflation – already raging at an annualized rate of 17 000 per cent in Poland by autumn 1989. While this was due immediately to Polish wage inflation, there was a problem of monetary 'overhang' throughout the region because people had money they could not spend on the inadequate supply of goods. The solution proposed by liberal economists was to let existing artificially low prices rise to market levels at a stroke (the famous 'Big Bang') so as to soak up the overhang, while holding down wages, slashing subsidies and keeping interest rates high to squeeze out inflation. This of course meant cutting people's living standards, but they would bear the pain if they were convinced that it would do the trick. Firms would get the message that the gravy train of state support ('soft budget constraints') was over. To counter the excess profits that firms would make through the higher prices, currencies should be made convertible and barriers to foreign imports removed so as to expose native industry to foreign competition and begin the improvement of standards. A social safety net, targeted according to need, should meanwhile alleviate the problems of inevitable unemployment. Alongside 'stabilization' but over a longer timespan, economic 'reconstruction' should proceed, transforming state firms as rapidly as possible into private businesses and encouraging the development of new ones.

Economic reform on these lines was the creed of coteries in east-central Europe: around a Balcerowicz in Poland, a Klaus in Czechoslovakia, a Kornai in Hungary. It was the situation and need for action that helped it become the operative doctrine, together with its knack of the vivid phrase: Big Bang, Shock Therapy and Sachs' clutch of hard-hitting analogies, 'you cannot cross a chasm in two jumps' being his favourite. Generalized approval was reiterated from early on: in the Mazowiecki government's programmatic statement of autumn 1989, the Czechoslovak parliament's support in April 1990, repeated in September, and the Hungarian government's Programme of the same month. Exact implementation varied. In Czechoslovakia Klaus faced opposition from the ex-reform communist Komárek, head of the old regime's institute of economic forecasting, who estimated that immediate marketization would destroy a third of production. President Havel was also a sceptic, seeing economic reform pragmatically as a means to an end rather than an article of faith. Klaus himself was often more cautious than his radical free-market rhetoric, which had led him to rebuke a western questioner who asked him what he *planned* for the economy for not understanding what a market economy was.[15] The Hungarian economist Kornai, a believer in a big bang approach to price reform and 'stabilization', warned against any over-impetuous attempt to dismantle the state sector; Hungary would have to live with a dual economy for another 20 years.[16] This left Poland as the best terrain for the most radical implementation of Sachs' ideas, for no significant figure or movement opposed them apart from the declining left wing of Solidarity, which did not have Wałęsa's support.

Thus the Big Bang had its baptism of fire in the region with Polish price liberalization on 1 January 1990. Czechoslovak food prices were raised by 20 per cent in July 1990, after a legitimizing election, and the great bulk of prices were freed on 1 January 1991. Hungary completed price liberalization, more or less, only by 1992. Whether reforms came earlier or later, however, the results by the end of 1992 were similar in all three countries. Liberated prices shot up far more than reformers had calculated – by 80 per cent in the first fortnight in Poland. Real wages plummeted accordingly, by about a third throughout the region. Inflation remained obstinately higher than expected and industrial production collapsed, by two-fifths on average. Unemployment rose as a result, to 15.2 per cent in Poland by July 1993 and 11.4 per cent in Hungary by September 1992. If Czechoslovakia as a whole seemed to do better here, the incidence of unemployment was far higher in Slovakia, an area which had been industrialized only lately on the communist model of the massive production plant; it was one of the factors driving the two nations apart. Overall, state finances fell into a parlous state because though the share of subsidies in budgets declined, tax revenue collapsed with production, while the new private businesses to a large extent avoided paying taxes altogether. The currency union of East and West Germany (July 1990) had equivalent disastrous consequences for ex-GDR industry, as sudden exposure to western competition drove unit production costs to 172 per cent of western levels, while productivity stood at only 40 per cent, with corresponding collapse.

Could a stable transition from communism survive such shocks? The haste of the architects of reform was due to a fear that unless the nasty medicine was taken in one gulp early on, the answer would be no. Sachs said somewhat vaingloriously in his 1991 lectures that the economics of the reform was easy; it was the politics that were hard. Nonetheless, the unpredicted severity of the recession produced a spate of sceptical commentary, from anxious to angry. It was the free marketeer Kornai who wrote pensively that output had fallen by more than under the Depression, noting also that it had risen slightly in the 1980s.[17] He reflected a common view which located the major source in the collapse of the supply lines between state enterprises, which left them without requisite materials. The collapse of Comecon in 1991 was a body blow; the Soviet Union, for example, was the major export market of the giant Hungarian tractor firm Ursus. The free market romanticism which supposed that the energies of the people only needed to be released from communist chains was subjected to some ridicule. Total laissez-faire led only to chaos, markets had to be made; it was not a matter of the flea markets implied by Sachs' starry-eyed view of farmers bringing in their produce to the streets of Warsaw, bypassing the state distribution system. Kornai by 1993 admitted he had dropped his earlier distrust of any state role and acknowledged the need for an industrial policy in the priority task of the raising of output. Other commentators saw a design flaw in the reformers' excessive credit squeeze to counter inflation. In economies like Hungary and Czechoslovakia, which unlike Poland in 1989–90 were not at the hyperinflation stage, the effect of higher energy prices and high interest rates was actually to create a cost-driven inflation in place of the demand-driven inflation which had been diagnosed. Not only dead wood state enterprises were killed off in the process but healthy ones, as well as new private firms it was desired to foster. The monetarist assumption that price changes did not affect output was wrong.

One of the main criticisms of economic reform as carried out was that it prompted a depreciation of national wealth. Firms expecting to be privatized had no incentive to obey the discipline of the old planners or the new market. They could vegetate on at the cost of gradually running down capital assets, or their communist-appointed managers could exploit their position to hive off the most profitable parts into mushroom companies and become new-born capitalists. The nomenklatura lived again, just as the aristocracy survived its formal abolition as a class in bourgeois revolutions. The reform assisted this development, since the price liberalization of the Big Bang preceded privatization, enabling the old bosses to cream off inflated profits. Critics argued that since privatization would inevitably take time, it should have been regularly preceded by commercialization, whereby firms to be privatized were turned into joint stock companies or transferred to holding companies to be run efficiently before final transfer.

As mentioned above, the reformers' way round the problem of windfall profits for old apparatchik managers was to expose them to foreign competition through trade and currency liberalization. Yet the foreign factor did not work out quite as intended. Foreign direct investment fell well short of expectations. The postwar Marshall Plan had transferred 1 per cent of annual American GNP to western Europe; only some 0.02 per cent of OECD GNP now went to eastern Europe in grant form.[18] Yet east Europeans long expected aid on Marshall Plan lines and free market optimism envisaged risk-taking western capitalists homing in on new opportunities in the liberated zone. In practice, western investors showed themselves markedly cautious in investing in an area where the legal and psychological supports of a capitalist society were not yet in place. At the most basic level, property rights in state enterprises could be disputed between workforce, managers, municipalities and previous owners claiming restitution of businesses or premises taken off them by the communists over the previous decades. Real western capitalists wanted easy profits at low risk and preferred to cherry-pick east European assets rather than make the strategic investments eastern Europe required. The involvement of the United States took place largely through poorly coordinated agencies, primarily large accountancy firms, whose determination only to work through private enterprise channels limited their influence to small networks of English-speaking easterners taken to represent 'public opinion'. 'You pretend to help us and we pretend to be helped' was one ironic depiction of this process.[19]

West Europeans were no more helpful in practice. The efficacy of the conventional wisdom of export-led growth was undermined by the fact that the east-central European countries all did increase their trade to OECD countries very substantially in the most depressed years up to 1992. Some east European economists came to think that the region had been too quick in embracing trade deregulation, leaving itself nothing to bargain with when a downturn began in western Europe in 1992–93. Certainly the 1991 trade agreements the European Union (EU) concluded with the east were far from generous, as import quotas were not abandoned on some of the east's most important exports and wide let-out clauses were included that were soon used. Thus in 1992–93 the EU imposed a sanitary ban in agriculture and closed steel markets, opened only five months previously, on grounds of alleged dumping. One commentator called it all but a mockery that the EU should have adduced low eastern wages as unfair competition when these had been recommended to the region as a competitive advantage.[20] Kornai thought there could be a case for the protection of infant industries. Yet there could be more fundamental criticisms, whereby foreign investors, far from diffusing new technology, remained islands in the host economy and were seen as exploiting its cheap labour before moving on to yet more accommodating locations. In such analyses the economic reform strategy had presupposed an outdated concept of industrialization, as if there were a series of models one could take off the peg. In an increasingly complex world, however, technologies had all the more to be adapted to circumstances and there was a place for state industrial policy in providing the levels of skill and infrastructure needed. Success depended on these skills rather than low wages to attract investment.[21]

How did those most associated with the reform process deal with these criticisms, none of which came from people opposed to reform on principle? In his commentary on the Polish case Jeffrey Sachs argued that many indices exaggerated the extent of decline. Communist production figures inflated results, whereas post-communist statistics were likely to understate those of the private sector, not least for tax reasons. Similarly, the fall in real wages was exaggerated; under communism people had had to struggle with queues to spend their money; now the shops were well stocked with higher-quality goods. Consumption statistics showed a negligible drop, about 4 per cent. The positive side of Sachs' message was of a dramatic shift in economic patterns. In the two and a half years since the start of the reforms 700 000 businesses had been registered and more than half the working population were employed in the private sector. This shift in the structure of the east European economy was indeed striking, outpacing the imagination of many specialists just as did its socialization 40 years before. Of course, Sachs' figures presupposed that privatization was a good in itself, necessarily leading to more efficient management. Not everyone could be so doctrinaire. His argument from private-sector growth said more about his premises than about real outcomes. On the latter score, however, the argument was that recession had bottomed out and expansion had already begun again in 1992, and an export boom to the west was under way. Indeed, the fact that Poland resumed upward growth before her neighbours was taken as proof of the success of the Big Bang and a sign that regional economic difficulties were due to failure to avoid half measures. In milder versions of this view the region lacked the knowledge and resources for a really consistent implementation of 'shock therapy', which could thus not be seen as the cause of undoubtedly disappointing results.[22]

As the post-communist depression continued scepticism grew on the identification of efficiency and private ownership posited by privatization theory. Privatization became the focal point of attack and defence of the radical free market position. The whole long-drawn-out debate showed how complicated the economic transition was. Not all aspects of privatization were so fraught. The so-called 'small privatization' process involving shops, restaurants and the like went forward relatively quickly by means of sale or auction. It was substantially completed in Poland by the end of 1991, if more sluggishly in Hungary; a time of falling real incomes was not the best one for buying a retail business, after all, and the Hungarian authorities wanted to avoid appearing to sell off assets too cheaply. The real problem was the privatization of the state enterprises characteristic of communism, the industrial monoliths which in Czechoslovakia averaged 3000 workers on the eve of 1989. Britain had privatized some 22 companies in the 1980s. How long on that basis would it take to transfer several thousand state businesses to the private sector? In fact, the east European problem was greater than this. Communist records simply did not provide the information which could enable valuation of assets of firms to be privatized according to western criteria, making the valuation process arbitrary, expensive (especially when western experts were used) and likely to be undermined by inflation and conflicting claims. These last included not only those of former pre-communist owners but the complex of interests set up by the extension of market and managerial elements in the last years of communist Hungary and Poland, beneath a formal state umbrella. Besides, east Europeans did not have the capital for purchase and sale only to foreigners raised awkward questions. The result of all these factors was lengthy confused debates between alternatives: western-style valuation and sale; commercialization, or transformation of state firms into joint stock or limited liability companies; transfer of ownership to workers or municipalities; or mass privatization, whereby shares in former state property would be distributed among citizens as a whole. Debate also raged as to 'top-down' or 'bottom-up' approaches, the former emphasizing the organizing role of a central body, like the Hungarian State Privatization Agency, the latter so-called 'spontaneous' privatization brought about as a result of a hiving-off or leasing of enterprise resources into joint stock or limited liability companies run by former managers. In practice all these methods were to be found and received sanction in the various privatization laws passed, though emphases varied. Spontaneous privatization was associated by some with the enrichment of ex-communist nomenklatura, yet it also reflected the grass roots which the new capitalism was supposed to encourage and the need to break up the giants of the old system. It had its roots in late reform communist legislation like the Hungarian Company and Liquidation Laws of 1989–90. The campaign for worker-orientated privatization was strong in Hungary but particularly in Poland, because of Solidarity and the influence which workers' councils had acquired there in the 1980s; free marketeers blamed it for the arguments which held up movement forward on privatization in 1990 and 1991. By the end of 1992 privatization of one kind or another had been initiated for something over a quarter of the 8454 Polish state enterprises involved and two-fifths of 2201 Hungarian enterprises.[23] Privatization in the sense of direct sale to a domestic or foreign buyer was relatively rare, though often headline grabbing: the transfer of Hungary's flagship company Tungsram, producer of 8 per cent of the world's lightbulbs, to America's General Electric for $150 million helped feed native fears of rip-offs at foreign hands. Meanwhile, only just over half the job-creation investment contracted for through the East German privatization Trust Agency had actually been delivered by mid-1993.

Slow progress led to calls for 'acceleration' but the privatization process could hardly be anything but bitty and protracted. This was what gave celebrity to the dramatic stroke by which Václav Klaus sought to cut through the Gordian knot in Czechoslovakia. His voucher programme was a form of mass privatization whereby each citizen was to acquire a thousand crowns' worth of vouchers for a nominal fee, which could be used to buy shares in companies remaining to be privatized. The trick was to avoid problems of initial valuation by selling these shares in successive rounds, in each of which prices were adjusted according to supply and demand until all had been sold. The arrival on the scene of private investment funds offering to take over citizens' vouchers on favourable terms sparked a remarkable burst of enthusiasm from a previously apathetic public; eventually more than half the population took part in the bidding, and the two stages of voucher sale were completed in 1993–94. This very popular way of speeding the process was imitated with modifications by Poland in the Mass Privatization Programme of 1993 but the programme was only partially implemented. The Hungarians had always set their face against giving away national assets as opposed to selling them because with their huge debt they needed the money – Poland had been more successful in negotiating debt reduction.

Klaus made his reputation as a financial wizard with voucher privatization. Many, however, were sceptical. Was this really popular capitalism or a form of finance capital, whereby a few among the hundreds of investment funds, linked to leading banks, would engross the shares of millions of people? The investment companies were imperfectly monitored; Klaus was so anxious to speed privatization that he took too much red tape to savour of communist bureaucracy. In the event, a young opportunist, Viktor Kozeny, got away with billions of Czech crowns from 800 000 small investors and proceeded to live it up at fabulous expense in exile in London. The pursuit of privatization had become an end in itself. Just as countries had competed in the 1950s as to which had nationalized the most, so now journals like *The Economist* ranked them in league tables according to the proportion of the workforce in the private sector and the extent of deregulation. Moreover, political considerations were not absent. With an election looming even the Hungarian Democratic Forum produced a 1993 scheme for the give-away of $250 million of shares.

It is difficult for non-economists to opine on highly technical matters like these. It is open to them, however, to apply normal tests on the consistency and tone of arguments. On this basis it seems plausible to hazard that some of the drive behind the economic liberalization programme derived from a triumphalist enthusiasm rather impatient of means to the goal. Though Sachs rejected the charge that he showed the same doctrinaire zeal as the advocates of the command economy in their time, a sense of historical vindication breathes through his and other reformers' work as compared to earlier, no doubt too indulgent judgements, of communist economics. In 1985 a well-known American economic textbook on comparative economic systems had said that differences in growth rates within systems were more important than differences between them;[24] World Bank figures had regularly given communist Czechoslovakia a per capita GNP not far short of Britain's. Now Dahrendorf wrote indignantly that East Germany's per capita income was not some half West Germany's as previously thought, but more like a fifth or even a seventh.[25] The communist experience was dismissed with crushing severity and denied achievement in any field, though in almost the same breath Sachs was saying that his policies had more chance in eastern Europe than in Latin America because of the region's high level of literacy, low infant mortality and even distribution of income.[26] Some western writers were disquieting in their ideological zeal. A book recommended by the IMF said it had been 'demonstrated' that 'big leaps' only occurred in the aftermath of 'catastrophic destructions', and eastern Europe had a 'historic opportunity' to avoid the mistake of unnamed west European countries 'whose oligarchic and inward-looking politico-institutional framework has not had the chance of being dynamited away'. The degree of western help would be proportionate to the determination with which east Europeans pursued the implied path of creative destruction.[27]

The element of arrogance in such cavalier attitudes rubbed off on western dealings with the region. At one point extra-judicial status was demanded for western aid organizations. Anyone who lived through the period will recall the patronizing manner of many western would-be advisers towards easterners and their 'Mickey Mouse money'. In their turn many east Europeans developed a paranoia about western rip-offs and a squandering of assets. Sachs may have had a point in arguing on the likely undervaluing of the Polish złoty in the reform that the priority had to be a rate which would not have to be suddenly abandoned. Inevitably his sanguine view of Poland's emergence from crisis by 1993 provoked mixed feelings when linked to his report that Polish per capita GDP was one-tenth Germany's. If, as Sachs and his school had never denied, privatization, the creation of a modern banking system and the bedding down of a legal framework and respect for the rule of law were necessarily longer-term projects, what, their critics asked, did the Big Bang slogan mean except to justify an ill-considered dogmatism which could be wasteful of current assets to a point of no return? Even if east European economic recovery did eventually follow, it is easy to see the force of the comment in 1993 that it would begin at a position 20 per cent worse than before.[28] By this time the almost unchallenged hegemony of radical market liberalism had yielded to acrimonious controversy and the very idea of transition, with its presumption of a successful outcome, was in doubt.

Society in transition

These uncertainties are widely reflected in contemporary comment on the region's social scene. Dark prophecies of street action, right-wing extremism, a descent into chaos if the fall in living standards continued, colour many accounts. The proportion of Polish employee housholds in poverty rose from 7.6 per cent to 30 per cent; from spending 45 per cent of their budget on necessities, Poles now spent 75 per cent.[29] Cinema attendances and book publishing plummeted; as an extreme form of belt-tightening births in East Germany fell by 65 per cent. The most vulnerable were the most affected. Everywhere except Czechoslovakia, the majority of the unemployed were women. Of Polish youth, 26 per cent had no work. Homelessness made its appearance as did crime, the latter increasing by 64 per cent in Bohemia in 1990; it did not help that the youth and culture services characteristic of communist regimes were being run down. Services already highly stretched could hardly survive savage funding cuts impelled by the fall in state revenues. The Polish education budget was slashed by a third in real terms in 1991; health care funding then stood at a tenth of EC levels. The crisis in drug supply is an object lesson. Since the great bulk of drugs used in Poland were imported or made from imported materials, which had previously been bought at low rate of currency exchange, currency convertability made their price rocket sky high; special funds were allocated to this, but only at the cost of other parts of the health budget; the problem was worsened when the pharmacies were privatized, contributing to the rapid lurch to a two-tier system for health care.[30] The problem was not just the sharp rise in poverty but perhaps even more significantly the thrusting of great swaths of middle-earners into positions of near poverty, not sufficient to qualify them for special aid. Funds for culture and scientific research were cut most of all; junior university lecturers got 60 per cent of the average wage. The social crisis took the most wide-ranging and unpredictable forms; art thefts for foreign markets shot up throughout the region. Not everyone, of course suffered; the sudden growth of income disparities disconcerted populations used to a high degree of equality, even if at relatively low levels. Suddenly the provident paternalism that made contributions towards two-thirds of people's holidays in Poland in 1983 was ceasing to be; in 1991 the figure was down to 21 per cent.

Post-communist governments had no ready response to these problems. No searching debate of social welfare matters took place, partly because of the host of other pressing problems, partly because the new principles presupposed the answers. Just as the communists after 1945 assumed that with the abolition of capitalism social problems were also banished, so their successors trusted that the abolition of communism would unfetter social energies. Voluntary associations, charities, foundations and, in more conservative visions, family and church would take over functions the state had vacated. Most aspects of welfare, like health care, old age and unemployment, would be organized on an insurance principle through autonomous institutions rather than from the state budget. Labour exchanges and retraining schemes would shield society from the new phenomenon of unemployment. Subsidies for food, housing, transport, heating and the like should be gradually dismantled. Thus the Polish Solidarity government held in prospect the total cessation of housing subsidies by 1993.

The difficulty was the transition period. In fact, no one thought the state could simply abandon its social role. Mazowiecki declared the *social* market economy as his country's goal in February 1990; the revision of the Hungarian constitution in October 1989 committed the state to the principle of social justice. The free market Czechoslovak Scenario for Economic Reform (September 1990) was flanked by a Scenario for Social Reform in obvious counter-balance. Opinion polls showed people still expected the state to provide. Although Hungary had 17 000 NGOs (non-governmental organizations) by 1991 many of these may have been set up for private people to profit from the associated tax advantages; besides, the British figure was some 172 000 charities and 350 000 other NGOs. Meanwhile, the services which had been provided by state socialist enterprises were often discontinued by new owners. In practice, the policy followed by the new regimes was to offer a safety net at a basic level through minimum household incomes and minimum wage, unemployment and pension benefits, with state aid in further hardship cases on a targeted, means-tested basis. As the Polish minimum wage corresponded to 35 per cent of the already very low average wage and Hungarian legislation presupposed that the minimum wage would be undercut, the safety net was hardly secure. A Hungarian expert saw a contradiction between the new regimes' preference for a new politics and economics based on impersonal, regular procedures and the 'assymetric paternalism' maintained in the social sphere.[31] Meanwhile, individual initiatives touted by the new authorities, like a re-orientation of the Polish medical service towards GPs instead of the hospital-based specialists favoured under communism, and the introduction of 'managed competition' in health care, made no progress because of lack of resources, though they consumed the time of hard-pressed officials. Indeed, this was a feature of western-influenced reform proposals which outran the personnel and level of training available. One barbed comment was that what was being attempted was privatization rather than modernization.[32]

The most essential safety net concerned unemployment. The original terms offered were soon everywhere scaled down, the period covered reduced, employee contributions increased and benefits cut back due to fiscal pressure: the initial Hungarian Act of 1991 had been calculated to fund an unemployment rate of 4 per cent, which was soon exceeded. Pension systems threatened to buckle as falling numbers employed had to sustain swollen numbers retired prematurely or put on invalidity benefit in a declining labour market. Hungary met the problem by cutting benefits, Poland by almost doubling the proportion of GDP spent on pensions, up to 16 per cent by 1994. The healthier Czech employment figures enabled them to avoid this bind.[33] Pensioners came off worst: 20–30 per cent of Hungarian pensioners wanted home care but only 4 per cent could be funded. Families with children were the next most vulnerable group, for whom family allowances made up a substantial part of overall income. These the new governments tried to maintain, but inadequate or non-existent indexing of benefits lessened their efficacy in a time of inflation. Only 58 per cent of Polish rural children were having three meals a day in 1991 and where kindergarten meals cost 15 per cent of an average salary the imposition of charges was a strong incentive to withdraw.[34]

Of course, most people in the region approved the principle being held before them of modern professional service in place of a run-down paternalism. The atmosphere of freedom also compensated for much. Patience eventually began to wear thin, however, and with it some of the unquestioning faith in the new model. Between 1990 and 1992 confidence in the Polish government fell from 82 per cent to 25 per cent. Shock therapy was turning out to be more shock than therapy.

Calling communism to account

Contributing to foreboding in the first flush of transition was the fact that the problems of the new were being experienced when a final accounting with the old had not yet taken place. Long-suppressed bitterness at communist crimes and usurpations now sought outlet, feelings which could clash with liberal emphasis on due process and the rule of law. What should be done about the deaths on the Berlin Wall and in 1956, or the massive security apparatuses of communist rule and the corrosive legacy of decades of state-sponsored snooping and denunciation among fellow citizens? Could properties seized nearly half a century before be returned to their former owners? The sting in these questions was heightened by the success of many members of the former nomenklatura in transmogrifying into new entrepreneurs, even, like the Polish communist spokesman of martial law Jerzy Urban, becoming editor of a scandalous satirical weekly, *Nie*, which outsold all Solidarity journals. Suspicion that many of the old security personnel were either still in place or kept a hold on potentially explosive means of blackmail further poisoned the atmosphere.

Transitions to democracy in other regions – Latin America, South Africa – had mainly aimed to minimize recriminations. This was the course Tito had followed with regard to wartime crimes in Yugoslavia. It was implicit in the negotiated transition followed in Poland and Hungary. But the pressures from an exasperated public made it a policy difficult to implement. In East Germany, where the old state had ceased to exist and repression had been sharpest, the toughest line was adopted. Even before reunification the GDR's parliament laid charges against Honecker and his octogenarian police chief Mielke. It was not easy for such charges to stick, however, without the dubious step of making their acts retrospectively illegal. The spy chief Wolf ridiculed his six-year sentence for treason, asking what country he was supposed to have betrayed when he was serving the interests of the GDR. In the event Honecker was finally released as too ill to stand trial in January 1993 and was allowed to go to Chile to die; Mielke received a six-and-a-half-year sentence but for his role in the murder of a policeman in 1931! Protracted and in part contrived cases like these showed the limitations of attempts to master the past through the courts. Of greater practical significance were procedures to weed out compromised figures from public life. Immediately after the Volkskammer elections of March 1990 about a hundred judicial officials responded to presssure to withdraw before they were pushed; in June a special vetting commission was set up. The key issue was the secret police under the Ministry of the Interior, the notorious Stasi, with its 108 000 employees and several hundred thousand informers. A law of December 1991 set a model which would eventually be followed by other central European states. Their Stasi files would be open to all who requested to see them, prepared by a commission under an east German Lutheran clergyman, Joachim Gauck. By mid-1992 1.2 million requests to see personal files had been received. With six million files in a state of sixteen million people, plus two million on West Germans, the GDR stood condemned for mind-boggling waste of its army of snooper citizens' time – most informers' reports were risibly pedantic and trivial.[35]

One of the problems with secret police files was their reliability. They could appear to incriminate people who had no idea they were in contact with agents or informers. They also lent themselves to politically motivated manipulation. Such considerations made new regimes outside the former GDR slower to systematize their use, which however only fed controversy the more. A televised Czechoslovak parliamentary debate of March 1991, in which names from files were revealed, caused an uproar but did not stop a law being passed that September which imposed 'lustration', or vetting, for a wide range of posts in the civil service, government, parliament, army and media. Right-wing parties even pressed unavailingly for 1968 reform communists like Dubček to be banned. The allegations made against the well-known dissident Jan Kavan, from which he was not fully exonerated until 1996, showed the slippery nature of the terrain. Václav Havel himself protested unavailingly against the law, with less success than President Göncz in Hungary, whose referral of a similar law to the Constitutional Court ended in its quashing.

Outside Germany, Poland was the main battlefield. The issue of reprisals against former communists became for a time the chief political divide, as Wałęsa fought it out with his former Solidarity allies in the broadly liberal intelligentsia. The latter wished on the whole to draw a line beneath the past. Sensitive to popular disillusionment Wałęsa promised to accelerate the revolution, code for a stronger anti-communist campaign. The conservative-minded Sejm, elected in November 1991, instructed the government to reveal collaboration with the communist secret services, but the reading out of 64 names of parliamentarians (May 1992) caused commotion and led to the Olszewski government's fall. Attempts to pass a Polish lustration law became bogged down in party infighting as to who would conduct the inquiries and how openly, how wide the categories of incriminated activity under communism should be, what would be the sanctions and the like.[36] That Olszewski, who was already at daggers drawn with Wałęsa, should have thought he had evidence compromising the charismatic president himself shows the legal and moral morass in which the communist dictatorships engulfed their successor regimes.

Intercutting issues of lustration and privatization was the restitution of private property seized under communist rule. How thorny this could be appeared from the ten million court cases brought in the former GDR. Other countries sought to avoid this fate, which envenomed privatization by casting doubt on the title of new owners. The Czechoslovak laws of 1990–91 were fairly restrictive: only resident Czechoslovak citizens could apply and that within six months, so as not to drag out the privatization process. In practice this meant injustice to surviving Jewish owners who had been dispossessed by the Nazis and were domiciled abroad. The initial assumption in the region was that the land of agricultural cooperatives would not be returned but compensation paid, yet this was challenged by the Hungarian Independent Smallholders' Party, whose leader left the government coalition on this score. In the event the great bulk of cooperatives remained but with their members gaining full property rights in their contribution; many peasants had lost the variety of skills necessary for independent farming and were in any case an ageing breed. Czech peasants halved in numbers in a few years after 1989.

In 1993 the Polish economy recorded growth for the first time since the regime change. Hungary followed in 1994. It was too late to save the governments made unpopular by recession, which lost general elections to the ex-communists in 1993 and 1994 respectively. The success of the Democratic Left in Poland was particularly piquant because it was aided to government by a coalition with the United Peasant Party, which had been a satellite party of People's Poland and had brought Solidarity to power in 1989 by switching horses. For frustrated pioneers of the liberal revolution this was only proof of the corrosive impact of the communist system on their peoples' spirit of freedom and enterprise. Actually, the influence of the communist legacy appears to have been subtler than this. It was not so much a matter of totalitarianism inculcating a slave spirit vis-à-vis the state as of concrete interests fostered by the communist system which the free market threatened. Private Polish peasants had lived in a regulated framework which had isolated them from the market. Intellectuals had depended on 'soft budget' constraints for a supply of subsidized culture and cheap classics. The private enterprise which had grown up in the 1980s had been posited upon the shortages of the centralized economy and reliant on the state sector for much of its market.[37] The free market reforms posited an abstract high Stalinist model as the enemy and overlooked the peculiar hybrid nature of this late communist society, including advantages it offered which were lost under the reforms – hence many of their shortcomings. The very Polish private peasants who were supposed to benefit from increased credit facilities in a free market system found the bureaucracy associated with it too complex and inconsistent to use, while to be sure of tiding over difficulties of transition the new authorities themselves turned to the old state supply and marketing organs, at the expense of fledgling private ones.[38]

Yet if the liberal vision had proved flawed, the jeremiahs also had not been fully borne out. The descent to populist demagoguery often held in prospect happened only to a limited degree. In Hungary a right-wing group split away from the Hungarian Democratic Forum, whose leader István Csurka mouthed nationalistic slogans about the holiness of the national interest and accused President Göncz of being manipulated from Paris, New York and Tel Aviv.[39] His significance was his link to the Forum's mainstream, not shared by the nationalistic Republicans in the Czech lands or the Movement for an Independent Poland. Vladimír Mečiar in Slovakia was actually in power, a rather unsavoury populist who was perhaps marginally less disturbing than Csurka because his nationalist demagoguery seemed more narrowly opportunistic and self-seeking. The possibility of a return of the left to power had not figured in alarmist prophecies in the early 1990s, which left them only an authoritarian right as the legatee of disillusion. Yet in the light of the distinction made in this book between socialism as rationalist modernization and socialism as totalitarian utopia, it is not so hard to see, in hindsight, why the ex-communists could divest themselves of dogmas in which they mostly no longer believed and benefit from the failures of their successors. For despite their criticisms of the excesses of privatization, neither Polish nor Hungarian socialist parties in power intended to reverse the capitalist course, which in many ways they had themselves initiated while still formally communist. In Hungary the Hungarian Socialist Party entered power with the Alliance of Free Democrats, the party of the economically free market, socially liberal intelligentsia. The Free Democrats held the finance ministry. Thus the sort of strategy Pozsgay had envisaged had proved possible after all but not, as he had hoped, without an initial humiliation and rejection of the left. To this extent, the turnabout in Hungary and Poland had had to be more than a reform from above.

The course of the northern tier lands discussed in this chapter was certainly bumpy. Optimistic prophecies which saw them as resuming their national European destinies after the communist aberration tacitly presupposed communism's modernizing socio-economic role, so that all that was necessary was to end its political yoke and everything would be well. This oversimplified the complex, deep-seated nature of the communist impact and the flawed nature of communist modernization. On the other hand, since the war living standards *had* risen to the point where the economic downturn of the early 1990s for the majority was cutting away at the fat (vacations, consumer expectations and the like) rather than restoring the indigence large parts of the region had traditionally known. The result was a less unstable evolution than some pessimists feared, explained as well by trades union splits and weaknesses, and a growing willingness of the authorities to consult labour within a semi-corporatist framework. The countries discussed showed many post-communist similarities. They themselves recognized this in the meetings of their leaders in the Hungarian border town of Visegrád on the Danube, which gave the east-central European countries a convenient journalistic label. Before 1945 and certainly 1918 the 'Visegrád' lands had seen little in common between themselves and the Balkan peoples with whom they had then been lumped together in 'communist eastern Europe'. How and why they now began to diverge again will be the theme of the next chapter on the Balkan countries in the aftermath of 1989.

7

Balkan vicissitudes

The year 1989 looks set to become one of modern history's most recognizable dates. Yet when it ended the event with which it is associated, the collapse of communism in eastern Europe, had still not occurred in half the region. Yugoslavia and Albania remained ostensibly untouched; would-be reform communists were still in control of Bulgaria and in Romania ex-nomenklatura elements dominated the shadowy National Salvation Front. The historic division between east-central Europe and the Balkans, largely effaced since 1945, was re-emerging. While the 1989 slogans of democracy and the free market soon became nearly as pervasive as to the north, the size of the gap between rhetoric and reality was far greater and ex-communist parties stronger, bitterly contested though their influence was. To the economic and social upheavals of post-communism was thus added political turmoil, which in former Yugoslavia burst into war and massacre. By 1995–97 something of a turning point can be seen in the Balkan lands, but many of the hopes then raised proved premature. The diverging fortunes of the Višegrad and Balkan states gave rise to a variety of theories, the best known being Samuel Huntington's on the civilizational divide between western Catholic and eastern Orthodox worlds. After tracing the troubled course of system change in the Balkans this chapter will attempt to assess such ideas.

Romania – how clean a break?

The events of 1989 in central Europe had been characterized by a near consensus of public opinion, articulated by the dissidents, that the area should reclaim its European heritage and adopt the pattern of civil society that had been so successful in the west. By contrast, the men who seized control in Romania were reform communists of apparatchik background. Iliescu barely sought to conceal his distrust of western liberalism. Multi-partyism was passé, he declared in January 1990, adding that democracy should not be identified with political pluralism and a market economy led to extremes of wealth and poverty.[1] At both Christmas 1990 and 1991 he urged Romanians not to dismiss everything that had been achieved in the communist period. Given these premises, the cooptation of so much of the old administrative apparatus into the new order is unsurprising, other than its sheer speed. Within little more than a month of Ceauşescu's death, the dissident intellectuals initially courted by the new regime found themselves discounted, the Front had gone back on its original promise not to stand in the forthcoming elections and the ethnic peace declared between Romanians and the Hungarian Transylvanian minority was close to breakdown. Iliescu spoke as early as 25 January 1990 of Hungarian separatism and appeared initially to blame the Hungarians for ethnic rioting that flared up in the mixed city of Tirgu Mureş in March, though the likelihood is that Romanian peasants had been bussed into this Hungarian stronghold before the Hungarians replied in kind.[2] It was the techniques used, smearing, manipulation, exploiting ethnic issues and the like, that led to the rapid escalation of distrust on the part of mainly youthful radicals, the assault of 20000 on the NSF headquarters in Bucharest on 28 January and the Timişoara declaration in March that the popular movement had not acted in order to replace one set of the communist nomenklatura by another.

This forceful line showed that the NSF and Iliescu were not going to engineer their own kind of transition unchallenged. About a hundred radicals began a hunger strike in a self-proclaimed 'communist-free zone' in Bucharest's University Square and numbers occupying it swelled daily. A Committee for Democracy in the Army exerted pressure for the army's freedom from political manipulation and succeeded in forcing General Militaru's resignation as defence minister, though his successor was perhaps even more compromised by links with the old regime. The withdrawal of the army from a role as coercer for the state, however, increased the problem of public order at a time of great uncertainty. The executive's jumpiness is not wholly surprising. The outspoken intellectual dissident Doina Cornea hardly breathed a spirit of cooperation when as early as 26 December 1989 she called the NSF leadership 'dubious elements, profiteers, lackeys and liars'.[3] The University Square demonstrations had the passionate commitment characteristic of student youth. Yet a wider social base for democratic opposition was lacking. In the general election of May 1990 the NSF and Iliescu were able to obtain sweeping victories, with two-thirds of the party vote going to the Front and 85 per cent of the presidential vote to Iliescu. Two sets of factors were important here and proved relevant elsewhere in the Balkans. One was the NSF's media control, vastly greater resources (drawn in all likelihood from old communist funds) and ability to position itself both as instrument of the December revolution, opening the way for foreign capital and peasant acquisition of land, and as shield against alleged threats posed to welfare benefits by its opponents' free market policies. The other was these opponents' weaknesses. In the characteristic splurge of weakly organized groupings, over 80 in all, the Front's chief rivals were Romania's 'historic parties', the National Peasant and National Liberal throwbacks to the interwar years. Their leaders were in their seventies and had spent the communist years either abroad or serving lengthy prison terms. The peasantist presidential candidate Ion Ratiu, a bow-tied British-based millionaire, won 4 per cent of the vote, as against his party's meagre 2.6 per cent in the parliamentary election. The National Liberals did better, but were still third behind the party of the Hungarian minority, the HDUR, which polled 7.2 per cent.

A feature of Balkan elections to be matched elsewhere was that even an electoral mandate too decisive to have been fixed had no impact on intransigent opposition protest. The University Square demonstrations continued until broken up by Jiu valley coal miners brought into the city by connivance of the authorities on 13 June, to be followed by two days of rioting which left several dead. This thuggish tactic more than anything tarnished the international image of Iliescu's administration, but the development of anti-Hungarian nationalism also contributed. A self-styled patriotic cultural organization called *Vatra românească* (Romanian Homeland) became the scourge of the Hungarian minority, encouraging the view that any concessions to Hungarian language or individuality meant sowing the seeds of potential separatism. In the local elections of spring 1992, its most charismatic figure, Gheorghe Funar, won the mayoralty of the Transylvanian capital Cluj, aggressively supported by the regional military commander. Outside Transylvania nationalism took off in the Great Romania movement led by two of Ceauşescu's leading journalists, Corneliu Tudor and Eugen Barbu, whose Greater Romania Party joined the new government coalition after the 1992 elections. Romania had undergone a worse cultural holocaust than the Jews, its organ proclaimed, and Jews had been prominent culprits in this process.

The Iliescu government did not want to maintain the failed communist economic model, but its legislation kept a strong role for the state in the restructuring programme. Bills for land reform and privatization of industry were passed in February and August 1991 respectively. The former limited the plot a peasant could acquire privately to 10 hectares (about 24 acres), envisaging the restructuring of the old collectives along cooperative lines rather than their disappearance. Considerable swaths of the economy were not envisaged for privatization; of those that were, 30 per cent was to go to the 16 million adult Romanians in the form of certificates administered initially by Private Ownership Funds (PFOs); the remaining 70 per cent were to be subject to a State Ownership Fund charged to sell them off within seven years. Critics alleged that the initiative for privatization was to come from above through the State Privatization Agency (without an initiative role from firm managers, as in Hungary, or employees, as in Poland); that free distribution of certificates contradicted the ethos of the market; that the ostensibly private POFs were made subject in many respects to governmental fiat; and that their managers had little incentive to administer assets effectively which they did not own.[4] Some of these criticisms for 'etatism' could also be made of Václav Klaus's Czech scheme of mass voucher privatization, but characteristic of the ideological nature of the whole privatization issue in eastern Europe was that *The Economist*, of London, a free market champion, did not make this point either of Klaus or the early Romanian reforms. The ideological battle required heroes and villains. In the Romanian case, Iliescu was *The Economist*'s crypto-communist baddie and his prime minister, Petre Roman, engineer and technocrat, the free market goodie. In fact economic etatism had been a feature of east European governance from the start of nineteenth-century modernization and the rivalry that developed between president and prime minister was mainly personal. When miners again rioted in Bucharest in September 1991 Iliescu used his links to the miners' leader to direct the protest against Roman and force his removal from power, enhancing his Machiavellian reputation.

Pre-1939 features could be seen in this tolerance of nationalism and anti-semitism, the leading party's intertwining with the state, the prevalence of unscrupulous manoeuvring and slander. Pluralism was not an empty word, however. The regime kept control of television, but not the largely critical press – even if the sharp rise of newspaper prices depressed circulation figures, as elsewhere. Opposition parties and pro-democracy groups (including the Group of Social Dialogue, 22 December, 16–21 December) came together in a Democratic Convention in autumn 1990 which won 20 per cent of the vote in the general election of 1992, against the 28 per cent and 10 per cent of Iliescu's and Roman's cohorts respectively. The outcome was a coalition of pro-Iliescu MPs and the nationalists. Romanian distrust of the Magyar minority was not quite groundless. It was lamentable that László Tőkés, now a Calvinist Bishop, was not invited to the fifth anniversary of the Timişoara drama of December 1989, yet in view of his denunciations of the regime, including a threatened hunger strike, this was not really surprising.[5] The Hungarian prime minister Antall's self-designation as prime minister of all Hungarians in August 1990 and the leaning of Hungarian minority activists towards notions of *corporate* cultural autonomy as a solution to European ethnic problems everywhere, vigorously canvassed in international forums, though never adopted by the minority's political wing, the HDUR, gave paranoia something on which to feed.

It seems the regime wanted to move towards 'Europe' but on its own terms. Early hopes of emulating semi-authoritarian South Korea's path to development quickly showed themselves to be illusory, however: GDP fell 30 per cent in the first four years of reform; the consumer price index reached 363 per cent for October 1993 over the previous year's last quarter and unemployment soared. Only 54 large companies had been privatized by March 1995.[6] In 1994 the economic decline began to bottom out, but Romania's evident need for a European helping hand came to influence regime discourse. Iliescu's 1994 speech to the Council of Europe on the anniversary of Romania's admittance shows him suavely pressing the appropriate buttons: the strengthening of the 'law-governed state', the signing of European conventions on human rights, on local autonomy, on the prevention of torture, and of the European Social Charter, legislation *en train* facilitating foreign investment and broaching large-scale privatization; minorities as bridges rather than sources of discord.[7] The west, however, remained largely sceptical.

In 1992 Martin Rady had written that the day of reckoning for Romania might not be far off, when a choice would have to be made between reform of Iliescu's 'Carolist' regime (an allusion to the ultimately bankrupt personal rule of King Carol II in the 1930s) or increasingly brutal repression.[8] The outcome was not quite so apocalyptic. Polls showed growing support for strongman rule, though this remained a minority preference over all. The democratic opposition could be as chauvinist as the nationalists; the Liberal leader Campeanu split his party by withdrawing from the Democratic Convention as long as it contained the Hungarian HDUR in 1993. Yet though Iliescu supped with elements to whom a western leader would have shown the door, he did not necessarily share their xenophobic views. Support for a more overtly democratic alternative grew sufficiently to offer an alternative. Iliescu lost the presidential election of November 1996 to the Democratic Convention candidate, Professor Constantinescu, and departed without fuss. The parliamentary vote enabled a coalition of the DC (30 per cent), Petre Roman's Social Democratic Union (13 per cent) and the HDUR to give the new president backing. The change of leader also took on something of the aura of a new course. Constantinescu's Contract with Romania – the borrowed term indicated western leanings – embodied several of the points which critics of the Iliescu regime had been making: greater stress on agriculture as the motor of economic recovery; clearer definition of private property; bigger efforts to encourage a genuine capital market and foreign investment; foreigners' right to buy land. The new government might prove inadequate to its task, like Romania's only previous democratic change of regime, the National Peasant Party government of 1928–30, but the fact of its election marked a turning point of sorts.

Deadlock in Bulgaria

The controversy in Romania about the Iliescu regime's origins was otiose in Bulgaria, where until 1997 the direct descendants of the old communist party remained the dominant force. The Bulgarian experience contained a double paradox. If, as a Bulgarian academician wrote, Bulgaria contained 'no significant social or political forces . . . that opposed the fundamental values of modern western democracy',[9] what was an ex-communist party doing in command? On the other hand, if there was this degree of consensus, why was Bulgarian politics from 1989 to 1997 as envenomed as it was? Bulgaria posed the clearest case of the Balkan difference, unclouded by Iliescu's sleight of hand or the Yugoslav national problem.

Bulgarian politics had already begun to move in autumn 1989. The anti-Zhivkov coup engineered by foreign minister Mladenov on 11 October was intended to pre-empt the anti-communist shift apparent to the north and achieve what Pozsgay was still hoping to do in Hungary: a transition under a reformed communist party. What brought the Bulgarian communists closer to this goal? First, communism had long had a popular base in egalitarian Bulgaria; and since 1891 when Blagoev had founded the Bulgarian Social Democratic Party, Bulgaria had exemplified the backward agrarian land whose students abroad imbibed the most radical foreign doctrines. The communists were the second strongest party in the general election of 1919. Second, Bulgaria's modernization was more self-evidently a product of communism than that of more developed east European states, swelling the urban population of 23 per cent in 1939 to 67 per cent by 1989. In one calculation for 1980, Bulgaria was the only east European country which had improved its economic position relative to western Europe compared to the years 1928–34.[10] This reinforced the fact that to Bulgarians, traditionally Orthodox and Russophile, Soviet patronage was not the alien force it was to Poles or Hungarians. Third, the more personalized, patriarchal society handicapped the maintenance of dissident networks – anyway ruthlessly suppressed after 1945 – and their development was insignificant. When ideological fervour waned, the tendency for the most able and ambitious to enter the communist party for career reasons continued. It thus contained a high proportion of the intelligentsia which had traditionally taken the place of the middle class in developing countries, and the combination of expertise, habituation to power and privileged lifestyle made the communists a formidable interest group with strong motives for cohesion. Zhivkov's tactical alignment with perestroika from his 'July Concept' of 1987 had begun a process of nomenklatura appropriation of the country's economic assets. In the event, the ex-communists in the 1990s retained the support of talented youth leaders and still acted as an umbrella for women's groups and even some ecologists, not to speak of the category of communistic nationalist increasingly prominent throughout the region. With its financial resources and control of the media, it provided a plausible base for the Mladenov strategy of autumn 1989.

The rather weak Bulgarian dissident bodies appearing in 1988–89 included the independent trades union Podkrepa, the ecological group Ecoglasnost and associations for the protection of human rights, religious freedoms and glasnost and perestroika. The only one with anything resembling a popular base was Ecoglasnost, set up in April 1989 and building on earlier protests against chemical pollution in the Danube town of Ruse and hydro-electric projects in the Mesta valley. However, once the issue of genuine openness had been put on the agenda by the Mladenov coup, even more by his promise of free elections in a state where there was still legally only one party (17 October 1989), the powerful resentments of earlier victims of communism or their kin began to flow the opposition's way. The first demonstrations of Ecoglasnost and of opposition as a whole in November pursued this anomaly to press for the abolition of the communist party's leading role, which Mladenov promised in a broadcast of 11 December. At the same time the United Democratic Front (UDF) emerged, out of initially nine opposition groups; on 27 December the communists yielded to pressure for a Round Table procedure such as Poland and Hungary had followed, in which, in a pattern reminiscent of Poland, the communists' puppet agrarian allies broke away and established themselves as independent participants (January to March). In February, the Front's organ, *Democracy*, began publication as the first opposition daily, highlighting abuses in the concentration camps of the 1950s and 1960s. Meanwhile, the communists reformed themselves as the Bulgarian Socialist Party (BSP), a name change accepted by 86 per cent of the membership in a remarkable display of party discipline. As elsewhere, the procedure envisaged by the Round Table was consensus-orientated, with a compromise between proportional and majoritarian electoral principles, a parliamentary system and constitutional court to provide a check to parliamentary sovereignty. Each side's fear of domination by the other spurred this consensus approach rather than inner reconciliation, for many in the UDF felt passionately that only the total eradication of the communist heritage could provide the moral cleansing essential to further progress. The battle of 'reds' and 'blues' threatened to become an all-absorbing feud admitting of no compromise, when non-aligned expert specialists were too few to constitute the mediating centre consensus politics implied. In the first elections, the only third party to pass the 4 per cent threshhold, of some 40 parties and coalitions contesting, was the Turkish-based Movement of Rights and Freedoms (MRF).

The June general election was a surprise, at least for the opposition UDF. As elsewhere in the Balkans, the ex-communists ironically performed best in the countryside, where peasants feared for their pension rights and those who had been landless before communism feared the consequences of land restitution. As elsewhere, too, the outraged democrats did not accept ex-communist electoral legitimacy. Demonstrations and strikes organized by Podkrepa continued and the UDF rebuffed all offers of a coalition government, calling for new elections or even a straight transfer of the governmental mandate to themselves. It was in the BSP's interest to share responsibility for managing the difficult transition, particularly when old TV footage of Mladenov calling for tanks against demonstrators forced him to resign the presidency. His successor was the UDF intellectual Zhelyev. In the face of a general strike the BSP prime minister Lukanov resigned in November, having ostensibly welcomed the free market recommendations of a right-wing Republican American think-tank he had himself commissioned. In his place came a politically independent former judge, Dimitri Popov, with a mainly socialist ministry.

In hindsight, the Popov government performed competently in implementing the price rises pressed for by the IMF without major disruption, despite a 54 per cent fall in real wages in three months. Laws were passed for land and urban restitution, privatization and foreign investment. In particular, a new constitution was drafted which endorsed political pluralism and the rights of property, while rather sharply limiting presidential powers. It also prevented foreigners from owning land, declared Bulgaria a social state obligated to provide welfare and free medical care to all, and qualified the rights given in ways recalling communist constitutions; thus associations were forbidden which worked against state sovereignty or national unity. The UDF launched a bitter campaign against ratification of this constitution, involving a hunger strike by some MPs. After it nonetheless passed parliament in July 1991, the democratic camp split into left, centre and right wings which greatly reduced the anti-socialist majority in ensuing elections and gave the balance of power in the new UDF government to the fundamentalist right. You could make a communist out of a human being but not a human being out of a communist was one view of the more intransigent 'blues'.[11] This did not help matters. The government's seeming preoccupation with restoring old property rights, particularly urban ones, led it to neglect the formidable problems of economic modernization, ironically making it easier for the old nomenklatura to burrow its way into the new economic dispensation. As many as 77 per cent of the business elite in 1994 openly declared a past or present allegiance to the BSP.[12] In July 1992 the former BSP prime minister Lukanov was deprived of his parliamentary immunity and arrested; it says something for the Balkan post-communist experience that he later turned to business and was murdered in 1996 by a Russo-Ukrainian hitman paid for by another businessman. President Zhelyev, despite his role in the creation of the UDF, rebuked the UDF government for its confrontational course. Eventually, the government fell because of the withdrawal of Turkish minority support, many Turkish peasants fearing potential landlessness as a result of restitution policies.

Only under the next government, effectively a coalition of the socialists and Turkish leaders, was a serious start made to implement privatization. It became embroiled in some of the usual difficulties: the practicality of mass privatization, the valuation of enterprises to be sold off, whether a start should be made with failing or successful firms, and the role of banks in the process who might be creditors of firms in question. Meanwhile, a large majority of the population came to believe that privatization would benefit only the rich and had no relevance to themselves. Attitudes to the free market were much less positive than in Romania or Albania; unemployment reached 16.2 per cent in July 1993. The decline of the faith in individualism of the early transition and return to older notions favoured the BSP, which comfortably won the election of December 1994 under a former youth leader, the 35-year-old Videnov. Under him ex-nomenklatura elements tightened their exploitation of state property, while the problem of internal bad debts as insolvent state enterprises ignored the huge sums they owed each other was disregarded. It helped provoke currency crises in 1994 and 1996, in the second of which the IMF refused to release its stand-by credit. The result was a massive collapse of the value of the lev, bringing monthly wages down to $25 in February 1997 compared to $127 at the end of 1995; the proportion of state-regulated prices had gone up again from 18 per cent to 45 per cent between 1991–92 and mid-1996. This was not transition, but its failure. In the event, though, the economic crisis had a positive political effect. Street demonstrations by students and impoverished professionals helped force fresh elections and a crushing defeat of the BSP. Only 58 per cent voted as opposed to 91 per cent in the heady days of 1990. However, the ignominious expulsion of the socialists has been seen as the end of the beginning by Bulgarians – their *Wende* or turnabout, in the German phrase.

Why should a society which is relatively homogenous both socially and nationally have found it so difficult to reach an equilibrium? (The Turkish minority question was actually well handled in the 1990s.) Bulgaria exemplified the problem anticipated by observers at the start of post-communist transition in eastern Europe, as to how societies atomized under communism could produce the interest group bases for political pluralism. The enervating dog-fight between the socialists and their opponents can be seen as the contest of two elites, both claiming the mantle of national intelligentsia and disposed by the arrogance implicit in this tradition to identify their own interest with the national one, to the neglect of concrete issues of reform. While socialist rationalizations included the plausibility of gradualism, the desirability of the 'social state' against an unheeding free market and the congeniality of these views to Bulgarian people and tradition, democrats denounced the evils of moral relativism in dealing with the communist legacy and backed this up by oversimple assumptions about the workings of the western alternative. The learned and scrupulous American director of the New Initiative Foundation in Sofia, for instance, endorsed inter alia such views as that unemployment was really no more than people's unwillingness to work for low wages and tax revenues could be stimulated by lowering taxes, as if the dynamic response to incentive to which he appealed could be duplicated in Bulgaria's circumstances.[13]

While rival abstractions negated each other, Bulgarian society made some but not much progress in restructuring. The great bulk of people accurately described themselves as poor or middling economically. By 1993, 7 per cent ran their own business, against 0.8 per cent in 1986. By 1995, 59 per cent of agricultural land had been restituted, but very rarely in the form of private farms. Most peasants went along with the BSP policy of voluntary cooperatives, which could often be very little different from the old collectives, because farmers still had to rely on the state for marketing services. Indeed, democrats' hostility to cooperatives and neglect of peasants helped ensure this class's majority support for the ex-communists, which is further explained by the fact that under communism many villagers had drawn closer to urban workers, using a secondary line in farmwork for subsistence or as a source of additional consumer income; with higher input prices this was no longer possible.[14] 'In Bulgaria economic and political conditions for the creation and development of a rural middle class do not exist' was one bald comment.[15] Two-thirds of peasants were already over 55 in 1986. The demographic situation rapidly declined thereafter, with the national death rate three-quarters higher than the birth rate in 1996.[16] Since the fall of communism 600000 people, mainly young, had left the country. Youth had been hard hit by unemployment and the decline of the social–sporting infrastructure the old regime had shaped for them. Socio-cultural life in general was hardly a priority of the struggling new order. The National Assemby's budget, through inflation, increased 12 times between 1991 and 1993, the Academy of Science's 3.6 times and the National Research Fund's only 1.5 times.[17] Theatre audiences halved as state subsidies were cut drastically. Ironically, many ex-weightlifters, perhaps Bulgaria's best-known achievers, entered the mafia while crime-fighting professionals retired in despair. In the absence of legislation on insurance, cars carried stick-on mafia notices which meant they enjoyed protection from vandalism.

One poll figure may help explain why, despite these tribulations, instability was not much worse. Well into the crisis slightly more than half those questioned said that they were better off than their parents had been at a similar age. What the fall of the lev meant for impoverished professionals was an inability to eat out, take holidays or buy a new house. People retained their home, furnishings, colour TV, washing machine, often a car. The sharp rise in postwar national wealth shown by communist statistics was not all eyewash. People had more fat to lose. Ex-professionals were often prominent among the petty traders who formed the bottom rung of a new commercial class, the top level being filled largely by former nomenklatura figures. The rationalist temper of the long-obligatory Marxist discourse and awareness of the unprecedented nature of the transition may, too, have had some effect compared to earlier times. Among Bulgarian academics there was much sober analysis and resignation to the long haul. As with Romania just before, the electoral victory of ostensible democrats in

1997 was a better outcome of crisis than in some predictions but the crisis of transition continued with no end in sight.

Albanian anarchy

The Albanian experience proved still more divisive than the Bulgarian in a climate of growing lawlessness and despair. This is not surprising. Albania was historically the most backward society in Europe, boasting a mere kilometre of railway in 1938. Under Enver Hoxha, who died in 1985, it had had no truck with reform communism or globalization, making the very contraction of foreign debts unconstitutional. The result was a growth rate which by the 1980s limped behind the rise of the population, nearly two-thirds of whom lived on the land. The Bulgarian ingredients were present in terms of an official intelligentsia arrogantly convinced of their right to manage the inevitable transition, disparate elements determined to unseat them and an economy foundering amid their disputes. The mix, however, was more explosive.

Hoxha's successor as leader of the Party of Labour of Albania (PLA), Ramiz Alia, had shown mild signs of pragmatism; in 1987 the party drew a theoretical distinction between the fundamentals and the inessential features of socialism. Albania's leading novelist, Ismail Kadare, living out of harm's way in Paris, was published in his native land. Yet the country remained so isolated that (true) reports of riots in the second city of Shkoder in January 1990 appeared in the western press as speculative rumours. Alia's response was belatedly to move closer to previously scorned perestroika positions, telling the party daily that participation in European cooperation and security was 'a demand of the time and meets our own interests'.[18] The PLA's tenth plenum in April re-legalized religion, allowed people to apply for passports and permitted collective peasants private plots. The economic reforms proposed mimicked those long tried in the Soviet bloc: more enterprise control over their own finance, which would, however, allow heavy industry combines still greater power to maintain a lop-sided economy. As in Bulgaria, if more slowly because dissident organizations had not existed, public protest broke through communist plans. In July 1990 thousands of Albanians besieged foreign embassies in Tirana in a bid to leave the country. Alia forced out hard-liners in his party. When students began to murmur in the autumn – intellectuals were still cautious – he sent the Paris-educated cardiologist Berisha to talk them round. Instead Berisha became the organizer of an opposition grouping, the Democratic Party (December 1990). His difference from the Bulgarian opposition leader and later moderate president Zhelyev shows something of the rougher Albanian climate, for Zhelyev had a dissident's pedigree (his book implying criticism of left-wing totalitarianism had been banned in 1981), while Berisha went from hard communist until 1990 to anti-communist demagogue thereafter.

From autumn 1990 order broke down successively with the unravelling of the centralized economy and distribution system. Initially it was largely a matter of bands operating at night rather than the mass demonstrations elsewhere in eastern Europe, which presupposed organizational networks. But in December Alia accepted the need for elections; in March 100 000 demonstrators in Tirana's main square tore down Enver Hoxha's statue. As in Bulgaria, though, peasants fearful of privatization voted for the party in power, the Democrats winning overwhelmingly in Tirana but gaining seats in only 9 of the 25 districts in the country as a whole. Again as in Bulgaria, the opposition did not recognize the result. Strikes resumed; the trades unions had already separated from the PLA. While the ruling party tried to cajole the opposition to join them in a national government and passed privatization laws characteristic of transition, the country sank deeper into the morass. Industrial production and exports in 1991 were 40 per cent below their 1990 levels; vast numbers of workers in state enterprises were idle yet still receiving 80 per cent of their pay. The 1991 budget deficit amounted to 34 per cent of GDP and only the international Pelican food aid programme, to the tune of $200 million, averted worse. As it was, 1991 saw more than 40 000 people try to reach Italy, often on unseaworthy vessels. In a plausible IMF view of the PLA's purported gradualism the regime's transformation measures had been slow, uncoordinated and poorly heralded.[19]

Any hope the PLA had of maintaining an essentially socialist system faded amid these tensions. It accepted the opposition's call for another election, winning only 28 per cent of the votes to the Democrats' 62 per cent (May 1992), renamed itself the Socialist Party of Albania and expelled Enver Hoxha's widow. Democrat rule in Albania under President Berisha was to be more disappointing still than in Bulgaria, however. The international aid Berisha had promised in the event of his victory was not forthcoming and he suppressed the consequent disaffection ruthlessly, often making use of his regional affiliations in Albania's traditionally tribal Gheg north. Alia and most of his colleagues had come from the more urban and urbane south, land of the Tosks. Berisha's rival in the party, the respected economist Gramoz Pashko, was expelled, Alia put under house arrest, then tried and sentenced to nine years' jail. Berisha's press spokesman was a hard-line former editor of the PLA daily. While local elections and opinion polls showed a clear fall-off in the government's majority, the first concrete blow to this course was the defeat of Berisha's referendum proposals for a stronger presidency in autumn 1994; they would have enabled him largely to dispense with parliamentary supervision, besides making public meetings dependent on government permission. Undeterred, he went on to legislate to disenfranchise many of his political opponents and won the May 1996 elections on a patently fraudulent ticket. He was long shielded from question, however, from a prevalent western view of his regime as a haven of stability amid the Yugoslav woes, even as the initiator of a free market mir-

acle. The American ambassador went so far as to speak on the Democrats'
election platform. Other commentators have written rather of a 'veneer of
commercialism' and 'anarchocapitalism'.[20] Berisha's Albania was another
example of the west's need to hail devotees in former enemy territory. The
country remained in a precarious condition. Only 2 per cent owned cars;
20 per cent were in receipt of the social security dispensed to impoverished
families, usually those unemployed after the year of unemployment pay had
ended. According to a 1996 estimate, 60 000 were engaged in blood feuds.
It was a society unsophisticated enough to fall for a gigantic pyramid-
selling scandal on which the Berisha government chose the line of least
resistance. The pricking of the bubble at the turn of 1996–97 nipped in the
bud what economic recovery there had been and turned the socialist-
inclined south of the country to armed mutiny against the regime. In July
1997 Berisha resigned.

It was unlikely that the PLA would achieve a smooth perestroika where
the likes of Gorbachev, Jaruzelski, Pozsgay and Mladenov had failed.
Ramiz Alia knew the stakes and was probably not bluffing when early in
the transition he tried to portray it as a choice between his course and anarchy. In 1995 he was to call his successors 'provincial amateurs',[21] convey-
ing the bottom line of the Marxist project in such countries as Albania – the
hauteur of Platonic elites self-charged to implant the Idea in stubborn soil.
It was good but not sufficient that people rose up to thwart such calculations, for the goal of a civil society required that some of its seeds should
already have been planted.

Turmoil in Yugoslavia

This was the paradox of Yugoslavia. Of all communist countries it was the
one where there had been most experience of economic decentralization
and freedom of expression. Why was the failure of post-communist transition here the most calamitous? The intractable national question cannot be
a full explanation: heightened nationalism was as much consequence as
cause of socialist Yugoslavia's decomposition. It seems that the very length
of the Yugoslav experiment in liberalization had given most of its citizens
time for disenchantment with 'socialist self-management', which like the
Stalinism it replaced was oversold as the unique answer to all problems,
national and economic included. When these problems patently worsened
the effect was to discredit the overarching ideology. By the late 1980s
Yugoslavia was a society seething with frustrations and resentments, its
nerves frayed by the ongoing economic crisis and by inter-ethnic polemics
reopening the scars of the Second World War. It was fertile soil for myth-
laden alternatives to the failed rationalist utopia.

The key victim of disillusionment was the Yugoslav idea itself, despite the
fact that it offered the most rational solution to the national dreams that

now came to the fore. Notions of the unity of all Serbs or all Croats in one state could only be achieved in Yugoslavia without vast displacement of minorities living interspersed among their neighbours. That this obvious fact was so quickly overlaid by the view of Yugoslavia as a 'prison of peoples' testifies to a certain wilful myopia which now occurred. The Serbs inveighed against the rise of Albanian and Muslim consciousnesses as once the Habsburgs had against the Serbs. Croats, with the traditions of the nineteenth-century pro-Yugoslav bishop Strossmayer and his rival Starčević to choose from, chose the gloomy Starčević in whose solipsistic view Serbs did not exist at all, and certainly not in Croatia or, for that matter, in Bosnia.

The least attractive forms of the respective national traditions on display got the leaders they deserved. While being more interested in power than patriotism himself, Slobodan Milošević, dominant in Serbia from 1987, openly took the Serbs' side against the Albanians in Kosovo. Since this violated the communist taboo of 'brotherhood and unity', it could appear to an uncritical Serb public to be part of a refreshing breaking of the mould, trumpeted as the 'anti-bureaucratic revolution'. Milošević's special skill was to appeal to raw nationalism while retaining the shell of the old socialist language of rationalism, progress and proud independence. The choice lay between going forwards to peace and prosperity or backwards to war, underdevelopment and dependency, as he put it in the Serbian election of November 1990; 'with us there is no uncertainty' ran the slogan.[22] Socialist society, not civic society was needed; Serbs would go into Europe as their 'socialist selves' – a claim of November 1989.[23] Milošević appealed here to the same instincts as ex-communist leaders elsewhere in the Balkans: distrust of a western civic tradition unfamiliar to rural voters, fear of free market capitalism, yet the desire to see oneself as part of a modern project which had achieved something, not just a failed backwater. The self-isolation from wider reality can be seen in Milošević's dismissal of the 1989 revolutions as no more than Yugoslavia had achieved in breaking with Stalin in 1948.[24] The official Serbian press put reports on provincial towns' award of honorary citizenship to him ahead of the fall of the Berlin Wall. Differently combined, a related mix of the rational and irrational can be seen in the historian who became president of Croatia in 1990, Franjo Tuđman. Still marked by the rationalist mind-set of his communist past, the anti-communist Tuđman went to turgid lengths to demonstrate the ubiquity of the human trait inclining men to genocide against the alien, as witness the universal aversion to the Jews. Tuđman's agenda was to counter Serbian charges of Croatian genocide against them in the Second World War and to challenge the historical role of the Serb minority in Croatia.[25] The work of national polemicists was replete with claims for the scientificity and objectivity of their procedures, a feature going back to the ethnic disputations of the nineteenth century and suggestive of how Balkan communism functioned as a further stage in the area's aspirations towards the perceived norms of an enlightened Europe. Yet alongside ethnic-orientated politicians like Milošević and Tuđman the Yugoslav federal government under the Bosnian Croat Ante Marković struck out on its own course of economic reform in 1989, effectively replacing workers' control by managerialism and a mixed pattern of firm ownership, and opening the way to privatization. Yugoslav economists confident in their country's reform credentials assured the present writer in 1990 that the Marković programme would inevitably win out over nationalist shibboleths in the nitty-gritty of real politics.

Under Milošević the suppression of Kosovo's autonomy within Serbia (1989–90) rightly filled Croats and Slovenes with foreboding. Slovenes, recalling their central European heritage in the climate of the later 1980s and alienated by the heavy-handed role of the Yugoslav armed forces (the JNA), were the first to seize on the revolutions of 1989 as offering a way out of the Yugoslav quagmire. Their communist party, whose liberal wing had come to the fore in 1986, walked out of the last congress of a united Yugoslav League of Communists in January 1990, leaving it inquorate. Since 1988 Slovenia had gone in parallel with central European countries in developing a network of independent associations which after the legalization of political associations (December 1989) now appeared as political parties. Other republics followed and multi-party elections were held in Yugoslavia's constituent republics in 1990. As elsewhere the emerging political process was characterized by an enormous splurge of political organization (from 60 to over 200 parties during the year) and the mutation of communists into socialists or social democrats. But the characteristic Balkan division between democrats and ex-communists here took on an ethnic form, with victories for the former in Slovenia and Croatia (where in April Tuđman's Croatian Democratic Union took 42 per cent of the votes and two-thirds of the seats) and for the latter in Serbia and Montenegro (December). One of the more significant features of the year was the electoral failure of federal premier Marković's supranational Alliance of Reform Forces. Marković's only card, his temporary success in stabilizing the economy, was then snatched away from him by the Serbian government's unilateral increase of the money supply – a blatant defiance of federal authority.[26]

Ostensibly, Yugoslavia's problem after the 1990 elections was how to reinvent the constitution to accommodate political pluralism. In fact, the issue was not pluralism but nationalism. The talks of republican leaders which took place in the early months of 1991 could not succeed because none of the chief players, Serbs, Croats and Slovenes, had any intention of compromising national goals. The Serb position was for continued federalism and, if this was refused and Yugoslavia broke up, a redrawing of boundaries along ethnic lines, not the old republican borders. The reason was the 600 000 Serbs in Croatia and nearly 1 400 000 in Bosnia. Neither federalism nor redrawing of boundaries was acceptable for non-Serbs, for whom as in 1918 the freedom aspired to revealed itself to be a national freedom. The counter-proposals for confederalism were likewise a non-starter, when the proposers were unwilling to concede any concrete powers to the central authority. On the ground Yugoslavia's constituent republics were creating faits accomplis as, starting with Slovenia, they affirmed their sovereignty and the precedence of their own law over federal law, and mandated referenda to decide on the question of independence. Constitutional court wranglings over these matters were irrelevant, but not so the attempts of the federal army, the JNA, to disarm Slovene and Croat territorial units, or secret Croatian attempts to get arms from Hungary. The minority question became acute when Serb-majority areas of western Croatia, collectively known as the Krajina, held their own referendum (August 1990), which led on to successive shifts towards a declaration for union with Serbia. The Krajina question showed how ethnic conflicts fed on each other at the grass roots, so that it became all but impossible to say who started a particular chain of escalation. Symbolic acts of renaming and choice of flag by Tudman's Croatian government seemed to Croatian Serbs to rehabilitate the Second World War ustasha fascist state installed by Hitler, while they felt downgraded by the new constitution declaring Croatia a national state of the Croatian people. On the other hand, the JNA was giving active support to Croatian Serbs, impelling the withdrawal of Croatian police from their areas. Nonetheless, when Croats and Slovenes declared their independence on 25 June 1991, they probably expected a lengthy period of bargaining, as had followed Lithuania's statement of independence from the Soviet Union. Instead, the JNA acted to reassert federal control in Slovenia by force.

Here the mixed signals of the international community played a role. Before 25 June Milošević was encouraged not to compromise by statements of international support for the maintenance of Yugoslavia, while the Croats and Slovenes reckoned that when push came to shove the democratic world could not oppose the right to self-determination. The European Community mediation which helped to end the JNA's conflict with Slovenia switched outside emphases by putting the presumption on secession. The independence declarations were to be put on hold pending three months' further negotiation – which gave the non-Serbs more reason to sit tight than to seek a compromise. When the three months had elapsed, with the JNA backing Serb seizures of about a third of Croatian territory, an International Commission for Yugoslavia set up at the Hague moved towards another deal, finalized in January 1992. Slovene and Croat independence was recognized but the Serb-occupied parts of Croatia were to remain de facto under Serb administration, and a ceasefire was to be supervised by lightly armed UN observers, the so-called 'blue helmets'. This beginning of the dismemberment of Yugoslavia brought the fate of the republics of Bosnia-Herzegovina and Macedonia on the agenda. Would they remain in a smaller Yugoslavia or secede and take independence in their turn? In 1990–91 they had preferred 'assymetric federalism' (Slovenia and Croatia in confederation with a federation of the other four republics); independence threatened to split multi-national Bosnia and leave tiny Macedonia prey to potentially hostile neighbours. But faced with Serb dominance without any shield from Zagreb they applied for international approval of their independence, via the Badinter Commission set up by the Hague process to monitor such claims.

The Badinter Commission reported against Bosnian independence without an internal settlement between Bosnian Muslims, Serbs and Croats; Serbs had threatened violent resistance to an independent Bosnia in which they feared the hegemony of the relative Muslim majority (44 per cent to their 31 per cent; Croats were the third force). European-sponsored discussions at Lisbon envisaged a complex cantonal arrangement, allowing for local majorities of the three national groups. The Muslim leader, Alija Izetbegović, on return from Lisbon withdrew his reluctant agreement to this breach of the unitary civic Bosnia his party preferred and held a referendum on independence (29 February–2 March 1992) in which the Croats (most of them for tactical reasons) supported the Muslims, giving a 63 per cent vote in favour. Bosnian independence was promptly declared and recognized by the European Commission some weeks later, whereupon Bosnian Serbs with Belgrade and JNA backing rose against the new state, beginning a brutal process of ethnic cleansing of Muslims from eastern Bosnia, adjacent to the Serbian border. This was the start of a three-and-a-half-year war, both desultory and sanguinary, in which the outside world's failure to stop the violence became a major international issue. The international community was accused of recognizing a Bosnian state but not allowing it the means to defend itself. This was true, but it begged the question of whether the recognition of Bosnia, against the advice of the Badinter Commission, was precipitate. The referendum, boycotted by Bosnian Serbs, gave a more ambiguous endorsement to Bosnian statehood than at first appears because much of the Croatian vote in favour was tactical. Most Bosnian Croat leaders were as suspicious of Muslims as Serbs were, and the more nationalist of them envisaged either a Bosnia that was an adjunct of Croatia or even a part of it, as Croatian 'state right' doctrine said it was. If multi-nationalism had broken down at the Yugoslav level, the sad fact is that it was only a little more likely to work at the Bosnian one.[27]

The Bosnian war is significant for its negative impact on former Yugoslavia's democratic transition and for showing how difficult that transition intrinsically was. There was the enormous problem of finding constitutional formulae for a new order and then creating the civic spirit to apply them. Thus Croatia legislated for minority rights for its Serbs, but even more than Iliescu's regime it acted under international pressure. Tudman's own commitment to the Starčević idea, identifying the Croatian state and nation, made the extent of his tolerance doubtful in practice. However, the problem was not just guaranteeing civil rights in a new state framework but what the framework should be, since there was no agreement on borders. In Bosnia most non-Muslims would not accept a unitary state, yet the three nations lived so intermingled that attempts to find some territorial basis for minority protection, as in cantonalization at Lisbon or in the later Vance-Owen Plan (1993) became implausibly complex. The JNA represented the integral Yugoslavism of a still surviving communist partisan tradition; it became increasingly indistinguishable from Serb hegemonic schemes before it was dissolved in spring 1992. It was compromised by association with the paramilitary groups that sprang up, associated with gangster-style leaders and often intertwined with the corruption and extortion rackets that accompanied collapsing economies and – in the Serbian case – international sanctions. This was Albania writ large. In these circumstances talk of economic reform was a mirage. All the Yugoslav successor states passed their own privatization laws which significantly broadened the state role and reduced that of employee share ownership, as compared to the federal law of 1990. Thus over 50 per cent of capital of what under self-management had been called 'social property' was renationalized in Croatia.[28] The lingering socialist ethos in Milošević's Serbia specified that social property could remain an ownership option. Successively upgraded international sanctions contributed to the return of hyper-inflation in Serbia in 1993, to a higher level than that reached in Weimar Germany.[29] Unemployment rose from 20 per cent to over 50 per cent, sanctions-busting enhanced the prospects for criminal businessmen, and private banks, some organized on a pyramid principle and with shady government links, flourished temporarily before inevitable collapse.

That such a regime could survive is usually put down to the irrationality of a population of lately urbanized peasants whose existing confusion of values made them ready prey for nationalist propaganda. This explanation no doubt goes a long way, perhaps even too far. Not everyone was carried away by regime propaganda, after all, as Slavenka Drakulić's satire of the Tuđman cult in Croatia shows. In the Serbian presidential election of December 1992 an emigré businessman back from America won 32 per cent of the vote to Milošević's 53 per cent, while turbulent public opinion in Belgrade was on balance anti-Milošević. Authoritarian rule had become subtler than under communism. Independent media were periodically harrassed, and limited to the capital, rather than forbidden altogether. The Serbian opposition, too, was divided; part of it, far from posing a civic alternative, was more nationalistic than the government (Šešelj's Radicals in particular) and the ostensibly liberal Democrats were divided (Koštunica/Djindjić) more often than not. Yet the bewildering splits, quarrels and short-lived reconciliations of Milošević's opponents need not always be put down to egoism or muddle-headedness. The situation was immensely difficult; even a civic-minded democrat like Djindjić could hardly be indifferent to the fate of so large a group as the Bosnian Serbs. The demonization of 'the other', particularly of allegedly alien Muslims, is not just a device of nationalism but reflected a fairly universal capacity for self-righteousness. The most interesting feature of this demonization is not its alleged roots in ancient hatreds so much as what links it with the modernizing tradition of the Balkans – the claim to Europeanness. It was this which created a gradient of contempt, shown by a Bosnian Croat spokesman when he urged that it was necessary 'to pay attention to the essentially different mental make-up and value system of the creator of the Islamic Declaration [Alija Izetbegović] and his followers from those of the European-oriented Christians, even if they [i.e. Serbs] are on the margins of civilization'.[30]

The decision of the United States to back Croatia militarily and bomb the Bosnian Serbs, but also to accept a de facto partition of Bosnia for the medium term, brought an end to the Bosnian conflict in 1995. Milošević greeted the Dayton Accord as a chance to resume his rhetoric as the modernizing statesman even as his henchmen forced out the governor of the Serbian National Bank for proposing a classic post-communist reform package: devaluation, privatization and making Serbia attractive to foreign investment. President Tuđman also saw himself vindicated by Dayton and continued his pressure against the opposition newspapers which criticized him. Both figures within a year would defy the verdict of local electors who had voted in the opposition in their respective capital cities. The Kosovo question ignored at Dayton began to bubble. The temporary mood of optimism engendered by the 1995 Bosnian settlement was thus no substitute for a real turning to democracy in the former Yugoslavia.

Assessment

Leaving this discussion of the post-communist Balkans in the uncertain limbo of 1996–97 is premised mainly on an implied comparison with the northern tier of east-central European states. There in 1993–94 the renewal of economic growth, the velvet divorce in former Czechoslovakia and the change of governments in Poland and Hungary, bringing to power ex-communist parties pledged to continue pro-market policies, all marked a clear enough stage in the process of transition. Not for some years later could meaningful watersheds be found in Balkan scenarios and then they could hardly be given as positive a spin as in the other cases. The final departure of the ex-communists in Bulgaria and the change of regime in Albania were both precipitated by economic disaster which wiped out what economic improvement had latterly taken place. In Yugoslavia the regime of Milošević and for that matter Tuđman remained in place. The northern states by this time were being considered for entry into NATO and for the next round of European Union expansion. The Balkans, except for Slovenia, were left in the cold. Bulgaria was a total failure, the forgotten state which nobody wanted, commented a Bulgarian newspaper on NATO's studied neglect in 1995.[31] In a gloomy Balkan perspective the area had had a tougher transition course than its northern neighbours without even finishing it.

The Balkan experience contained most of the same elements as that of the northern tier: the pullulation of political parties; the privatization laws and free market protestations; the disputes on restitution and de-communization, the economic crisis, confusion of values, rise in crime and ethnic hostilities. They were, however, differently balanced in the Balkan zone. Even less progress was made towards the privatization of large enterprises, though here it is often difficult to distinguish between deliberate obstruction and the huge difficulties involved, not to speak of the Yugoslav wars. Official links with corruption and organized rackets, alleged in Poland, were pretty patent in Serbia and Albania. The controversy elsewhere about government–media relations and about the growth of racism, the anti-Roma intransigence of the 10 per cent of Czech far-right voters, the whiff of anti-Semitism even in parts of the Polish and Hungarian mainstream, was small beer against the systematic inculcation of demeaning ethnic abuse on Serbian and Croatian media.

Two kinds of explanation for the travails of Balkan post-communism were prominently touted. One had an ideological colouring, mirroring the line of advocates of shock therapy against gradualism. Equating democracy, the free market and prosperity, it located the Balkan problem in the strength of ex-communist forces in the area, which had disguised their hostility to any real democratic transformation behind slogans about the social state and the dangers of unregulated capitalism. The difficulty with this approach was that economic reform as prescribed did not necessarily correspond with economic success, and views of what constituted success fluctuated disconcertingly, with east European countries succeeding each other as flavour of the moment in western eyes. A Bulgarian comment by 1997 denied that one could interpret what was happening any more in terms of (artificial) categories like 'democrat', 'communist', 'reform' or 'change of system'.[32] Political scientists themselves complained of the fickleness of the numerical weightings by which research institutes sought to rank cohorts of states in democratization progress reports, but in their straining for the scientificity of theory construction they still seemed reluctant to admit the subjectivism, and remoteness from reality on the ground, of the computed scores from which they hoped to coax their generalizations. Philip Roeder noted, too, the difficulty of deciding the respective importance of starting points or outcomes for analysing democratization processes, when many political scientists had abandoned the late communist period to historians and were starting their courses from 1989 or 1992.[33] The whole attempt to measure progress towards democracy by ticking off items of liberal capitalism introduced in the 1990s appears flawed.

Against an approach which seems too mired in the present was one which sought explanation in the span of centuries. Robert Kaplan's book *Balkan Ghosts* (1993) rooted the Yugoslav war in an age-old pathology of ethnic violence. It was both influential and widely condemned, on grounds that it employed crude ethnic stereotyping. Some of this criticism can go too far, as if pointing out genuine group tensions is tantamount to justifying ethnic cleansing. However, on the main issue, it may well be argued that the most influential tradition in the area over the 150 years prior to the Yugoslav wars, however contested, was not exclusive nationalism but Yugoslav fraternity. More academically regarded than Kaplan's thesis was that of the political scientist Samuel Huntington, who posited that after communism's demise the east–west split would be replaced by civilizational divides with a religious base. One of these potentially confronted the western world and Islam; another was that between eastern and western Christianity, an old distinction now revived between a west shaped by Renaissance and Reformation and a more authoritarian Orthodox world.[34] In cutting through the Balkans, it implied the inclusion of Catholic Slovenia and Croatia in the culture sphere of the Visegrád states, more apt for democratization. The fact that these two Yugoslav republics had voted anti-communist in 1990, unlike the traditionally Orthodox Serbs, therefore received the authority of a thousand years' religious separation. Yet if the first explanation of transition fortunes offered above seems too narrow, this second, cultural approach is too broad. Croats themselves naturally supported the view that they voted anti-communist in 1990 because they belonged historically to the west, unlike 'Byzantine' Serbs, but there is a simpler reason. They associated the communist regime with Belgrade and Serbian dominance; many Serbs, having the mentality of a majority nation, were still not so alienated from the communist federation. True, Croats had a higher average standard of living than Serbs – by about 20 per cent – but in the medium span of the past both peoples had been overwhelmingly illiterate peasant societies (80 per cent of Croats in 1867) of similar lifestyle and folk culture. Tuđman was little less of an authoritarian than Milošević.

By contrast to these short-term and long-term views, it is in the medium perspective that the traumas of the post-communist Balkans are best understood: that of backward communities' struggle to modernize from the nineteenth century on, during which Serbs, Croats, Muslim Slavs and Albanians often followed rival state trajectories. Communism cut across these, giving the region a lifestyle and, in Yugoslavia's case, a status closer to the European norm than they had had for centuries, while suppressing the rivalries. As Yugoslavia broke up, reviving state rivalries could fuse with religious intolerance, particularly of Serbs towards Muslims, and with material and psychic strains of breakneck urbanization. Balkan societies by 1989 were faced, in hindsight, with a tragic situation, because communism could no longer meet expectations, yet had reinforced traditional authoritarian traits inimical to smooth transition to an individualistic civil society. Moreover, communism had not come in much of the Balkans just through Soviet arms but through civil war in Yugoslavia and Albania, and enormous bloodletting in Bulgaria. The personal and familial aspect of the Balkan strife of the 1990s must be appreciated. Chuck Sudetic has shown vividly through family history how the pattern of flight and massacre between Serbs and Muslims in eastern Bosnia reprised events from the Second World War and before.[35] Though propagandists milked these events for all they were worth, real revulsion and foreboding existed at the licence given to ustashi returnees by the new Tuđman government, just as for Croats and Bosnian Muslims Serbs became again chetniks. The visceral enmity between ex-communists and the UDF in Bulgaria often went back to personal histories. It is interesting that in 1981 the break-up between Hoxha and Shehu had been heralded by Shehu's son marrying into a family who had been on the other side in the Second World War. The JNA chief of staff Kadijević, the military leader of the Bosnian Serbs Mladić and the influential Bosnian Serb historian Ekmečić had all suffered grievous family losses at ustashi hands. Even in the Vojvodina in northern Serbia, barely mentioned in accounts of the Yugoslav affrays, Hungarian spokesmen claimed the right to commemorate the slaughter of allegedly 40 000 Magyars in this multi-national province in 1944. This is the background to the uncompromising politics of the Balkans in the 1990s. The stakes were higher than to the north. Decommunization involved not just economic and political overhaul but reconstruction at the state–national level, just as the added ethnic factor made liberal revolution more fateful in Germany and the Habsburg Monarchy in 1848 than in western Europe. Even in relatively homogenous countries like Bulgaria and Albania, however, the harsher historical background contributed to the inter-party intransigence which had the negative consequences described above. Padraig Kenney's book on 1989 in central Europe has taken 'Carnival' as its title in tribute to the spirit of events there, sparked off in part by the creativity of individual dissidents who refused to let a stale, repressive bureaucracy stifle their power to imagine something better. There was little carnival in the Balkans.

Even in central Europe the implementation of the anti-communist revolutions of 1989 was a messy, often disillusioning affair which incidentally left many of Kenney's book's protagonists as alienated as before. But the basic tasks of 'system change' were accomplished by the mid-1990s. Parliamentary regimes and market economies operated, institutions like the constitutional courts worked in a reasonably consensual spirit and procedures for dealing with the legacy of communist misdeeds were gradually being put in place. None of this was yet true of the Balkans. This section has shown how difficult it becomes to plot the demise of east European communism within a common narrative.

Yet what is common to all parts of the region is the clash of values which system change provoked. Advocates of change sought to depict this as a simple opposition between modernity and a clinging to the past, whether from backwardness or bad motives. This has always been so; Robespierre explained resistance to the Jacobins through the malign influence of the *ancien régime*. Yet such criticisms reflect oversimplified views of the process of system change, presenting transition as an unproblematic movement from an erroneous past to a successful future, which can be opposed only for negative reasons. In reality, reformers rarely have all the answers, and there are always unanticipated consequences of their reforms. To be sure, it was vital for eastern Europe to have an alternative ideology to put in place of the failed communist experiment, for otherwise the post-1989 years would have been even more traumatic than they were, resembling the 'times of troubles' that have often dogged interregnums in the past. But while the relative political stability outside Yugoslavia owed much to the framework provided by the new liberal individualism, in its highly theoretical economic form, particularly privatization, it ran up against a dense network of overlapping claims of use or ownership and also against ingrained values, communist and pre-communist. The encounter produced situations that existed in their own right and could not be labelled strictly communist, capitalist or merely 'transitional' and thus destined to disappear. Support for ex-communist parties could be a way of responding to these existing situations rather than nostalgia for the old communist order. In such circumstances, the brash tendency to associate modernity and rationality with, say, the culture of the salesman trained in western management techniques and contrast it with the inflexibility of unskilled shopfloor workers mired in socialist backwardness was neither wholly convincing nor calculated to wean voters away from ex-socialist parties.[36]

The malaise of former Yugoslavia may be seen as an extension of this problem of disentangling overlapping rights into the ethnic sphere. Torn from the cocoon of 'socialist self-management', a marvel of obfuscation of where power and responsibility really lay, the interspersed components of this multi-national state confronted each other naked in a battle for the inheritance. In 1991 the western media often called for the break-up of a state 'whose time has gone' as if oblivious of the likely consequences. It was an extreme case of the liberal optimism underlying the 1989 events, that people unshackled from authoritarian constraints would find their way to a reorganized life in order, freedom and harmony. Elsewhere, for all the problems of carrying through the revolutionary process begun in autumn 1989, one might describe what had been achieved by the mid-1990s as two steps forward, one step back. In much of the Balkans it was at best a matter of one step forward, two steps back.

III

CONSEQUENCES

Towards a new eastern Europe

8

The internal dimension
An end to transition?

The Chinese communist leader Dzou-En-Lai, asked his opinion on the significance of the French Revolution, is said to have answered that it was too early to tell. This is a salutary warning for anyone attempting to summarize the impact of communism's demise in eastern Europe. The transition is not yet over. As the immediate processes of the dismantling of communism merge into history, however, it becomes easier to answer some of the questions observers asked at the outset of system change, and even to hazard some generalizations about the role of this great episode in a still wider context. Interrelated as they are, internal and external aspects of the legacy of 1989 will be separated out for purposes of discussion in this final section. This chapter looks at the outcome in the political, socio-economic and cultural spheres, after a brief overview of events taking the story on from the mid-1990s, when the chequered pattern of pluses, minuses and regional variation shows no fundamental change from that of the earlier post-1989 years discussed above.

Put schematically, events in eastern Europe since the initiation of system change have seen political stabilization in the Visegrád states and moves towards it in former Yugoslavia. The electoral pendulum has swung twice more in Poland and Hungary, bringing back right-wing governments in 1997–98 and then ex-communists in 2001–02. The somewhat bumptious rule of Václav Klaus ended in the Czech Republic in 1997 in favour of the left, and the more objectionable rule of Mečiar in Slovakia in favour of a somewhat unstable centre–right coalition. Alongside signs of consolidating political pluralism, however, is the continued disappointment of the hope for sustained economic recovery. The Czech Republic, vaunted in the mid-1990s, suffered a series of disastrous bank failures in 1996 which absorbed 8 per cent of GNP, exposing Klaus to the charge of mishandling the mass privatization scheme and forgetting that a free market needed regulation.

The tenth anniversary of 1989 passed with open admission of disappoint-ment at what had been achieved. Poland, whose shock therapy tactics made it the darling of free marketeers in the early 1990s and whose strong growth in the late 1990s was held to have been vindication, ground to a halt from 2000, with minimal growth and unemployment rising to 16 per cent. Former East Germany, despite having 5 per cent of West German GNP pumped into it annually remains economically blighted, while the whole process has contributed to the slowing down of the German econ-omy overall. The disruption caused by property restitution matters was finally coming to an end, however; by autumn 1999, 92 per cent of such cases had been resolved. Elsewhere, action by the Hungarian and Czech constitutional courts went some way towards restoring property rights of Jews expropriated by the Nazis. Yet the expulsion of Sudeten Germans from Czechoslovakia after 1945 still cast a cloud over Czech–German relations.

In the Balkans the hope offered by the 1995 Dayton agreement and the displacement of ex-communists in Romania and Bulgaria has borne partial fruit. The most promising turning point has been the overthrow of Slobodan Milošević by popular protest in October 2000, less than a year after Franjo Tuđman died and his authoritarian Croatian Democratic Union was defeated by a left-centre coalition. Milošević is now on trial for war crimes in The Hague. Yet the politics of rump Yugoslavia remain fraught, with tension between the two chief figures of the former anti-Milošević opposition, Vojislav Koštunica and the recently murdered Zoran Djindjić, while its economic situation has hardly emerged from the trough of the 1990s which saw the halving of its GNP. In Kosovo, whose liberation by a NATO campaign in 1999 helped to precipitate Milošević's fall, some Albanian groups by 2002 were declaring NATO's rule to be as oppressive as Serbia's, and the province's lawlessness and Slav–Albanian strife had spread to nearby Macedonia. Most Romanians early in the new millennium were reported to be worse off than in 1989, with monthly incomes of little more than $100 a month. The run-off presidential race in December 2000, between Ceauşescu's former court poet, the arch-nationalist Corneliu Tudor and a comeback Iliescu, was described by one Romanian newspaper as a choice between AIDS and cancer[1] – but the democratic coalition in power since 1997 had completely discredited itself. Bulgaria under the Kostov government fared better economically, but the electorate was still sufficiently disillusioned with both the major parties of the transition to vote in the totally untried Simeon II National Movement, just formed by its ex-king, exiled since the age of nine, with a thumping majority (June 2001). In Bosnia a virtual NATO protectorate of indefinite duration con-tinues, in which some progress is being made in slackening the grip of nationalist parties on the population, but through the spread of demoraliza-tion at powerlessness and poverty as much as the attractions of democracy.

A clear-cut victory for Albania's ex-communists in the relatively uncontroversial 2000 elections was soon followed by personal infighting amongst them.

Below, an attempt will be made to put flesh on these bones. It is not easy to describe so complex an aftermath. But it is harder still to pin down exactly what it is the aftermath of. The most tantalizing question of the demise of communism is how to assess the relative weight in post-communist societies of three different legacies: that of the communist epoch, the pre-1945 inheritance and post-communist policies themselves.

Party politics and the communist legacy

A widely shared fear in 1990 was that atomized east European societies would not provide the social or psychological basis for a multi-party pluralism of large, coherent, competing interest groups. This fear did not prove groundless, for much post-communist politics has shown a baffling pullulation of minor parties often serving as vehicles for personal ambition; in fact, this was remarkably similar to the complex patterns of interwar elections, which were the reflection of disjointed, undeveloped social structures. Nonetheless, relatively stable patterns have emerged since 1989 which are distinct from the pre-communist era, characterized by swings between left and right, and a strong left, a divided right and a weak centre. Here it is the strong left which is the substantive novelty, for which the communist era paved the way. In majority peasant interwar societies socialists (anyway badly split between social democrats and communists) never came within a whiff of power outside participation in Czechoslovak and, more rarely, Polish coalitions. Plainly the shift in social structures effected by communist urbanization has been a crucial factor, creating a large working-class base for the ex-communist parties of the 1990s. Yet the communist legacy is wider than urbanization alone, because in the Balkans parties of this type, including the Romanian NSF, initially gained relatively more support from collectivized peasants. The success of the left in contemporary eastern Europe needs to be explained not just by communist industrialization, but by the entire communist package of a state-centred economy and a secularizing ideology which affected the countryside as well.

As usual, a distinction must be made between the Balkans and the northern tier. In the former area, the resource of a large working class was often supplemented in the formation of left-wing parties by a dose of nationalism, while in the Visegrád countries socialism tapped into liberalism. Hence the Socialist–Free Democrat alliance in Hungary and the evident support which ex-communist President Kwaśniewski has enjoyed from many old Solidarity intellectuals. It is this socialist–liberal alliance, open or tacit, which has underpinned the stability of the northern states, tending towards the kind of pragmatic left often to be seen in power in western countries. The northern–southern distinction is only approximately valid, for Milošević's leftist nationalism was parallelled in Slovakia under Mečiar, while most Bulgarian and Albanian ex-communists fairly quickly followed their Hungarian and Polish counterparts in adopting the style of western social democratic parties, accepting the market and pluralism but differing from their right-wing opponents on the speed of privatization and the scope of safety nets, above all on attitudes to ex-communists and the communist past. Here they condemned witch hunts and urged the need to look to the future.

In societies where many have uneasy consciences about collaboration under communism this line was quite attractive, and ex-communist parties were to regain and maintain support by a mix of factors. These included the resources they managed to keep from the communist period; habits of solidarity and discipline sharpened by the threat of persecution, and the genuine appeal of the programme for those who were neither religious, nationalistic nor free marketeers. Thus ex-communist parties kept old leaders from the time when communists had a monopoly on political experience and expertise, like former Hungarian prime minister Gyula Horn and the Polish prime minister Leszek Miller. But they also kept a younger generation of members, like the ex-youth leaders Kwaśniewski and Mohorita; the 35-year-old Bulgarian prime minister of the mid-1990s, Videnov; the Albanians Nano and Meta; and the East German Gysi. Above all, there was a parallelism of practical interest between the masses of people whose living standards free-market policies were shredding and former elites out to salvage their situation as best they could; 'in Poland there are people feeding off rubbish dumps', Miller remarked indignantly before the socialists' return to power in 2001.[2] The rise in unemployment, the plight of pensioners, the decline of public services and wage levels still vastly below western levels allowed the new socialist parties to retain much working-class support, as a whole, even as they adopted pragmatic policies calculated towards the new dominant capitalist paradigm. There are shades of New Labour here. Certainly, the left had the support of many young technocrats: one-third of Nano's 1997 Albanian government were economists; the real rulers of Macedonia, one source reported, were ex-communist socialists in their thirties.[3] The popularity of ex-communist parties after 1989 bears out a major theme of this book, that what east Europeans disliked in communism was not the egalitarian, welfarist 'nanny state' so hated by free-market liberals, but economic stagnation and the repression of individual and national freedom.

Thus parties of the left have regularly been the largest single parties in much of the region, though ruling through alliance with a variety of other forces, a peasant party in Poland, the Turkish minority party in Bulgaria or liberal centrists in Hungary and Albania. Ex-communists and Liberals also make up the major part of the six-party coalition which has succeeded

Tudman's conservative regime. There is a historical dimension to many of these alignments. Centre-left coalitions like those in Croatia and Hungary were eased by the fact that both the ex-communists and most liberals share a common communist past in countries where communism liberalized relatively early. By contrast, in Poland the oft-expected coalition between the ex-communists and the liberal Freedom Union has not come about because of the bitterness many Polish liberals still feel towards their left-wing enemies from the time of martial law. Even the socialist–peasantist alliance in Poland has a historical trace, as the Polish Peasant Party was a puppet ally of the communists throughout the communist era. The fact that only in the Czech Republic is the dominant force on the left a social democratic party goes back to the country's strong left-wing and industrial traditions, which can support two substantial parties of the left (socialist and communist), with roughly the same relative electoral share as they had between the wars. The SD's rise from 7 per cent to 32 per cent of the vote between 1992 and 1998 shows that the forces making for left-wing success in the region cannot be explained only by ex-communists' exploitation of old nomenklatura privilege.

If a strong left usually correlates with a degree of modernization and urbanization, a strong democratic right is a surer sign still of political maturity. The exemplar is England where democratic conservatism has been underpinned by a large property-owning class, a fulfilled national tradition and centuries of stability – rare conditions indeed. The interwar eastern European right could offer by contrast only the embattled flags of faith and fatherland, increasingly spiced by a flavour of imported fascism. Communism removed the impoverished peasantry to which fascism could appeal (though note the 16 per cent vote of the fascistoid Greater Romania Party in 2000) but obviously could not nurture the basis for a mature property-owning democratic conservatism. The failures of the Bulgarian and Albanian democrats have shown that anti-communism alone cannot create this phenomenon. Thus the only party which has approached the democratic conservative model is Václav Klaus's Civil Democratic Party, which has fairly consistently won some 30 per cent of the poll in the historically most advanced bourgeois society of the area. In the absence of such traditions, establishing a strong profile for the political right means trying to combine different and often opposed strands, one bourgeois liberal, the other clerical/national. Poland has shown the difficulties of such a project, for the two strands easily come apart on matters like abortion and church influence in education and morals. This see-saw relationship between liberal and clerical wings split Solidarity in 1990 and contributed to disastrous electoral results for the right in 1993 and 2001, in the first of which the clerical-national wing and in the second both main elements of the governing anti-socialist coalition won no seats at all. The insufficiency of bourgeois liberalism alone for a successful right-wing party in the region is further shown by the evolution of the Young Democrats (Fidesz) in Hungary. Starting off as a youth movement confined to the under-35s and exemplifying the fresh irreverence that so delighted foreign observers of 1989, it not only moved towards mainstream conservatism and power in 1998 but its leader Viktor Orbán became increasingly nationalistic and its Smallholder allies even more so. In this it followed the course of the right-wing governing party of the early 1990s which it had displaced, the Hungarian Democratic Forum, which by 1998 had fallen to 3 per cent of the poll. The divisions and fissiparousness of the right pose a possible question mark against the final success of stabilization in the region.

It is the region's swing of the pendulum which constrains thinking along left–right lines, and this swing is itself a positive factor, for all the sardonic view that no government has been elected twice running because every one has failed. The left–right pattern has led to a remarkable vogue for party alliances, in which the individual units are often confederations to start off with. The Solidarity Electoral Alliance which was the major force in the 1997 Polish government was composed of over 30 parties and blocs. The advantage of large groupings and the accompanying swing of the pendulum is to create less amorphous parliamentary structures than those of interwar eastern Europe, when peasant and ethnic minority parties occupied vast swaths of the middle ground, now vacated after communist urbanization and the reduction of minorities in the population exchanges/ethnic cleansing of the 1940s. Of the great Bulgarian, Croatian and Romanian peasant parties between the wars, only the last-named has played a significant role, along with the Hungarian Smallholders and the Polish PSL. The disadvantages of a weak centre are that eventually the electorate might be disenchanted with the democratic process by successive failures of left and right, and also that 'moderates' with expertise are electorally under-represented. The first of these dangers has been for the moment averted in Bulgaria by the path-breaking Simeon II Movement, where the prestige of a royal name ushered in an untried centre following the electorate's disillusion with both 'reds' and 'blues'. The second has been made good in large part by the strong representation of 'moderates' at presidential level, through men of the liberal left like Václav Havel (1989–2003), Zhelyu Zhelyev in Bulgaria (1990–97) and Árpád Göncz in Hungary (1990–2000). Ironically, ex-king Simeon only became prime minister because he was prevented by lack of residency from standing for president.

Eastern Europe's political systems, at least in its northern tier, have been one of the more successful features of post-communism. Three regimes have been changed by mass demonstrations (Bulgaria and Albania in 1997, and Serbia in 2000) but the kind of breakdown represented by the interwar coups in Poland (1926) and Yugoslavia (1929) has been avoided. The safety valve of regular swings of the pendulum tending to generalize itself in western Europe by the 1980s has been paralleled, if the mechanism is still not quite as stable given the flux thus far of the east European right. Both communist and post-communist legacies have helped produce this favourable result. The former brought changes in social structure and improved educational levels, which reduced the yawning differences in electoral mentalities, the great exception being the national problem in former Yugoslavia. The latter contributed 'the liberal moment' of early transition, the judicious preference for consensus over confrontation, which found institutional expression in the round tables, the prevailing balance between presidential and parliamentary power, and the general acceptance of the successful innovation of the constitutional court. Increasingly, governments were able to broach institutional reform of health and welfare provision, requiring both administrative skill and democratic accountability. As far as politics is concerned, we may conclude by adapting Timothy Garton Ash's pithy summary, that central Europe emerged from communism better than was dreamed in 1989, Yugoslavia worse than the worst nightmares.[4]

Post-communist society

What does the post-communist political map suggest about the underlying social forces in the region? The relative stability of democratically alternating governments reflects something similar to western political process–electoral switches are accompanied by tit-for-tat policy changes on what are symbolic issues for right or left: 'lustration' legislation for the left, abortion or property restitution for the right. Meanwhile, the main lines of adaptation to a market economy and civil society have been pursued by both sides. This kind of stability presupposes elements of a socially dominant consensus. One of the most interesting issues of post-communist society is how far a new ruling class has emerged in eastern Europe since 1989. Old communist era theses of the communist intelligentsia's rise to power were given a boost by the apparent success post-1989 of the old nomenklatura, in which the revival of ex-communist parties, nomenklatura exploitation of 'spontaneous privatization' and the whole Round Table strategy of 'refolutionary' transition could be linked together to point to the rise of a nomenklatura-based elite. Sociological research has extended this theory of nomenklatura survival only to its *economic* wing of technocrats and managers. In Iván Szelényi's claim these groups triumphed over the communist *bureaucracy* in 1989, sharing their victory with ex-dissidents who had become converts to the need for a strong state and expertise. By contrast, the political nomenklatura (bureaucracy) succeeded in turning their political power into economic power only if they also possessed 'cultural capital' (essentially, higher education), which in this view provided the post-communist route to power, as 'political capital' had bred power under communism. The argument, which rested on surveys of high-ranking managers in post-communist firms, also stressed the failure of 1980s 'second economy' businessmen to break through in the 1990s; this was explained by the interdependence of this second economy with the now defunct state sector. Szelényi thus reaffirmed much of the substance of his 1970s' theory of the rise of the intelligentsia to class power, producing an east European 'capitalism without capitalists'. Though he himself advised that this paradoxical thesis should be taken 'with a pinch of salt'[5] – an attractive confession in a discipline somewhat fond of theorizing – he remained true to his communist-era view that eastern Europe would not simply reproduce western patterns: in this case, its capitalism would be distinctive. This approach challenged evolutionary theories of 'rational choice', whereby the failure of communism would be followed by the adoption of the western capitalist alternative. It was closer to 'path-dependency' theses which held that post-communist developments would be shaped by their starting point, a position that allowed a bigger role to inherited local factors. Of course, the survival of ex-nomenklatura elements did not mean the survival of communism, though victims of communism and western hawks often saw it that way.

This thesis of a technocrat–dissident alliance at the core of the post-1989 transformation has been quite widely accepted. Though modelled on the socialist–Free Democrat government which emerged from the 1994 Hungarian election, and not followed in such terms in Poland – where ex-Solidarity liberal politicians have not yet brought themselves to cohabitation with ex-communists – it reflects the kind of pragmatic shift towards free market democracy of both intellectuals and former regime technocrats which underpinned nearly all ruling strategies in the region. Developments since the original research of Szelényi's team in 1993–94, some acknowledged by them, have given somewhat more weight to the growth of a western-style, private property-based capitalism in eastern Europe.[6] Another potentially future-pointing factor was the growing role of foreign ownership. By the late 1990s, 70 per cent, 30 per cent and 35 per cent of Hungarian, Czech and Polish industry respectively was foreign owned, and 70 per cent, 25 per cent and 50 per cent of bank capital,[7] reflecting lack of domestic funds – not just for great projects but also for supermarkets, petrol stations, hotels and on down the line. If anything, these figures recall the interwar situation of foreign dependency. The situation is still fluid and research lags behind events. Perhaps all that should be said is that the ultimate shape of the region's socio-economic structures and power relations is still to be determined and could yet take on novel forms or incline to earlier ones.

What seems highly likely, however, is that relative stability is due in part to the hegemony of post-communist assumptions against which the transition's economic losers could launch no effective challenge. For losers there have been, with a universally acknowledged growth of inequality within a general context (until the late 1990s) of depleted living standards. Hungary provides the clearest figures. According to Kolosi the average income of the top tenth of the population was 5.8 times greater than that of those in the bottom tenth in 1988 and eight times greater in 1999. Moreover, public opinion greatly exaggerated these shifts, so that whereas the great bulk of Hungarians in 1987 saw social stratification as bulging in the middle with few at the lower end, by 1999 61 per cent saw a society with a few at the top, very few in the middle and the great bulk lower down.[8] The worst affected, their position consistently poor throughout the transition period, were the working class, reflecting the collapse of the old state industries in 'rustbelt' areas like Silesia or textile towns like Łódź. Poland's 200 000 steel-workers had shrunk to 60 000. Only 1 per cent of Hungarian graduates were unemployed, but a quarter of the unskilled, and the higher educated were both more likely to attempt private business and more likely to succeed.[9] The new society was no place if you were thick, said one Polish youth despondently. But while unemployment correlated with educational levels, skilled workers were hit alongside unskilled, with Hungarian figures showing that the depression of the 1990s targeted the wide swaths of previously not so badly off as hard as the low-paid levels. Neither group shared in the recovery of living standards by upper-middle-class elements towards the end of the decade. This rather gloomy social balance both explains the left's swift comeback in the region and points to possible problems for it if in the longer term it cannot deliver for its traditional constituents.

The primary base for strong parties of the left has been the expansion of the urban population at the expense of the rural. Despite some advocacy of a redirection of investment to agriculture as a source of relative advantage and signs of repeasantization in some Balkan milieux, the move away from the countryside has continued since 1989. The numbers gaining a livelihood predominantly from the land have roughly halved in the Czech Republic, Poland and Hungary; an *Economist* report claimed that the Bosnian civil war speeded up urbanization by two generations. Less than a tenth of those who engaged in some agriculture in Hungary did so as their major occupation; half Poland's two million farmers were part-timers and only half the rest relied wholly on the land. Yet in the blunt words of the *Financial Times* in 1995, 'large areas of rural Poland remain a sort of living museum'.[10] Agriculture made up from 20.5 per cent (Romania) to 3.7 per cent (the Czech Republic) of the five largest east European countries' GNP in 1996, as against only 2.1 per cent of the EU average. Here the theme of flawed modernization already voiced (see Chapter 2) remains relevant. Eastern Europe emerged from communism's industrialization drive relatively speaking as backward vis-à-vis the west as before. Agriculture has proved one of communism's worst legacies, though its problems were greatly compounded by becoming an Aunt Sally of post-communist squabbles over collectivism and by the impact of ill-considered Big Bang liberalization. While younger generations lost the wide range of skills and the mentality that underpin independent farming and now head for unemployment in the towns, elderly peasants have been left on the farms whose disgruntlement has supported a variety of distinctly populist movements, like the Hungarian Smallholders and Polish PSL. With the breakdown of the collectives' commercial nexus, many increasingly isolated rural folk, in a Romanian anthropological case-study, have turned to the occult, attributing their misfortunes to the ill-will of their ancestors; indeed, one deceased grandmother terrorized her descendants from the top of the family TV and had to be removed with the help of the parish priest.[11] Such phenomena bode ill for the integration of the post-communist countryside into the European Union.

Communism was a gigantic experiment in social engineering by a purportedly all-provident state, the most extreme form of the reaction to laissez-faire ideas mounting from the later nineteenth century. How has its fall affected those groups traditionally discriminated against and for whom it claimed to work? The number of women MPs fell from about a fifth under communism to a tenth, and far lower in post-communist Romania and Albania, while women party leaders were all but unknown. In most countries – Hungary was an exception – a somewhat higher proportion of women than men were unemployed, partly because new employers shirked taking on maternity leave payments, which states also scaled down. Exposed most directly to the difficulties of household management in recession, more women tended to see their post-1989 circumstances as a change for the worse than did men, and their retrospective view of communism was not so harsh. The association of women's rights with communism had a negative effect, particularly in Romania because of Elena Ceauşescu's unpopularity, while the return of 'traditional values' meant controversy over abortion. In Poland a 1993 law imposed prison terms for medical staff involved in abortion except in very exceptional circumstances. But because communist paternalism had inclined women to passivity, there was little organized protest against the cutbacks in rights to maternity benefits and the like, which had come to be taken for granted; outright feminism had little hold and the popular mood favoured notions of collective patriotism against which women's causes were seen as sectional and divisive. That said, it is possible to exaggerate the setbacks women suffered after 1989. In a longer term the shifts in employment patterns, from heavy industry to service industries, were in their favour. Opinion polls showed that those who thought women's place was exclusively in the home were far from a majority and there was some tendency for them to become more favourably disposed towards women's rights to work as the decade went on. Benefit cuts were far from total and in Hungary the number of women taking advantage of child leave, pre-retirement benefits and nursing aids rose steeply until the mid-1990s.[12]

Among other groups communism claimed to favour, its dispensation has no doubt unravelled more. Youth were everywhere among the highest unemployed and their framework of sports clubs and institutions was decimated, contributing to rising crime and drug levels. The Serbian terrorist Arkan's thugs were largely recruited from supporters of the Red Star Belgrade football team; ironically sport, which in the communist vision was to have united people, had played a role through games fraught with tension between leading Serb and Croat clubs in pulling them apart. One of Tuđman's most ridiculed acts was faking his chosen football team's victory in the Croatian league. Roma (Gypsies) who had at least had lowly jobs as cleaners, caretakers and the like under the communists were dramatically hit by the dismissals of unqualified labour. Roma infant mortality rates were nearly five times the average in Hungary, their children were many times more likely to be sent to remedial schools throughout the region and 43 per cent of Romanian Roma families in the early 1990s had no income from official sources at all.[13] Prejudice against them was such that the Czech towns Ústi nad Labem and Plžen debated building barriers to enclose Gypsy residents.

In the case of communities that communism had discriminated against, the uplift after 1989 fell below expectations. The churches often found their energies exhausted in the fight to recover their expropriated properties and to maintain them insofar as they recovered them. Moreover, this preoccupation and the bid to reassert lost influence risked undermining the goodwill they had enjoyed at the end of communist rule. An extreme case was the Bulgarian Orthodox Church, where an embarrassing schism developed between the allegedly collaborationist octogenarian Patriarch and an anti-communist Synod led by a rival Patriarch in his nineties. Even the popularity of the Polish Catholic Church, which issued guidance on voting in the 1991 election and campaigned vigourously on family values, reportedly fell from 90 per cent to just over 50 per cent by 1994.[14] While 42 per cent of Czechoslovaks had called themselves Catholics in the census of 1990, membership was estimated at a fifth of the Czech population in 2000, and church spokespeople bemoaned the loss of the 'middle generation' and the 'communist categories' in which 'liberal politicians' still thought.[15] Widespread divorce, abortion, unmarried mothers and a secularized outlook were significant social outcomes of communist rule, in that the breach was not only with formal belief but to a fair extent with the social automaticity of religious affiliation such as still existed in Orthodox Greece, as opposed to its Balkan Orthodox neighbours. One feature of communist religious policy curiously survived. Many descendants of Romanian and Ukrainian Uniates forcibly converted to Orthodoxy under Stalinism did not revert to their ancestral allegiance when opportunity offered and undignified conflicts developed over ownership of church buildings in western Ukraine.

One important social group epitomized the ambiguities both of the communist era and its successor. This was the intelligentsia. Given state-subsidized culture and confirmation of their self-image as the guardians of the people's values by the communists, many of them had rebelled against the straitjacket of authoritarian rule and played leading roles in its over-throw. Since the early days of system change, however, intellectuals have largely withdrawn from political prominence. The break-up of Solidarity and Civic Forum, pitting Michnik against Wałęsa and Havel against Klaus, initiated this process; the successor fraction of Civic Forum closest to Václav Havel failed to enter parliament in its first electoral test. The Hungarian Democratic Forum and the Free Democrats, creations of the intelligentsia which led the way in the 1990 Hungarian elections, both declined into near insignificance by 1998. Of individuals, the Czech Jan Kavan and the Romanian Gabriel Plescu became foreign ministers in the late 1990s and Jacek Kuroń, having been minister of labour, stood for the Polish presidency in 1995 – winning 10 per cent of the vote – but only Havel became a political fixture, albeit in a largely ceremonial post.

What lies behind this apparent retreat? In the positive perspective, the 'critical intellectuals' of 1989 have become the 'democratic intellectuals' that the region now needs and remain as relevant as ever.[16] In a more jaun-diced view it is precisely a demotion of intellectuals' sense of importance and mission which is required, as outmoded baggage in a world of global expertise to which the region should aspire. Certainly, as intellectuals with-drew from the public stage it became commonplace to mock the creative intelligentsia of writers and artists for the discomfiture of finding that in a freer society people preferred translations of Jeffrey Archer and Hollywood blockbusters to their own products, though native imitations eventually took on. The most profitable Polish film ever made was an action-comedy called (in Anglo-Polish) *Kiler*. Dominant market share in Czech television was held by the extremely downmarket private channel Nova, whose founders engaged in ruthless struggles over its murky finances. Faced with the near-collapse of once-prestigious state film studios it was little consola-tion that locations like Prague were becoming popular with western film-makers because of the cheapness of labour. The reduced funding and low salaries of academics led to a sharp fall in the number of research scientists – in Poland by over a sixth from 1989. Economic malaise struck in the most varied ways at the institutions of a modern civilized society; in Albania the state zookeepers fed weaker animals to the carnivores and appropriated the lions' rations for themselves.[17]

Criticism of intellectuals was directed both at their alleged remoteness from the people (their elitism and greater than average pro-westernism) and the difficulty of making operative generalized terms like 'civil society'. It was particularly the intellectuals' idea of mission which was attacked. 'Until the intelligentsia imbued with a . . . mission . . . disappears com-pletely, . . . Poland [doesn't stand a chance]' was one summary of purported Polish opinion.[18] The force behind such an observation can be seen from the disastrous role of the Serbian Academy of Sciences's 1986 Memoran-dum in spurring Serbian nationalism. Indeed, there is some tragedy in the fate of the Serbian dissident novelist Dobrica Ćosić, whose historical novels did so much to inspire the pseudo-heroic vein among the Serb public and who ended up as a puppet Yugoslav president under Milošević, overseeing events radically counter to his inflated but not malign sense of Serbia's destiny.

However, most intellectuals have not been grandiloquently nationalist since 1989. The bi-centenary of the birth of the Polish national poet Mickiewicz in 1998 was celebrated with hardly a reference to his roots in 'historic' Polish lands since incorporated into neighbouring states. The willingness of Czech historians to question their national tradition extended to the fraught relation with the Germans and the expulsion of the latter after the Second World War. Intellectuals have taken up the cudgels for liberal tolerance against nationalistic tendencies, like Hungarian writers orchestrating criticism of the ruling party's right-wing trend in the early 1990s or Adam Michnik opposing clerical nationalism as editor of the best-selling Polish newspaper, *Gazeta Wyborczy*. This kind of stance has not made intellectuals popular in conservative quarters but does not seem too different from that of the left-leaning intellectual community in the west. The downside is that intellectual issues or debate no longer seem so central in communities where matters of cultural and national tradition have always enjoyed high prestige. The past simply did not exist for her 20-year-old son and his friends, a Czech mother was reported as saying,[19] an observation echoed in other lands. This posed something of a dilemma for idealists. Discredited old nationalisms were not yielding to a modern historiography for a plural Europe, but to indifference and the glossier chains of American-orientated consumer culture. Thus the collapse of communism has arguably put east European intellectuals in something of a bind: in commendably throwing off the communist invitation to be 'engineers of human souls' and calling for their national cultures to develop 'normally', they risk being sidelined as mere 'chattering classes', like their counterparts in the west.

Two rather different figures show the still considerable role intellectuals can play in post-communist society. Václav Havel was a leader in the rejection of communist utopianism and its distorting results; as Czechoslovak and then Czech president he set himself the modest political goal of fostering good 'public manners': politeness in negotiation, tact and an awareness of the moral aspect in all transactions. True, there is a utopian sub-text in his distaste for the hurly-burly of party politics, even an almost hysterical note in his comments on 'the criminality and the familiar sewage' welling up from 'the nether regions of the collective psyche . . . fanaticism of every conceivable kind, the unprecedented varieties of robbery, the rise of different maffias, and the prevailing lack of tolerance, understanding, taste, moderation and reason'.[20] But critics surprised at his 'naïve' persistence in lecturing his people on these themes have not appreciated that someone who spent half his life being told the pointlessness of banging his head against the wall of communist autocracy and public apathy is not likely to stop at the behest of 'condescending' commentators. In place of the rather superficial view which coloured much economic policy after 1989, that communism had been a surface episode and it sufficed to put correct institutions and policies in its place for all to be well, Havel stressed the moral weaknesses of a society corrupted by totalitarianism. Problems of morale are regularly a factor in emergence from trauma, but unlike the communists after the Second World War or Robespierre chafing at the legacy of absolutism, Havel did not propose eradicating those weaknesses by violence or compulsion. The fact that he became far more popular abroad than in his own country shows the limitations of post-communist success in eastern Europe and no doubt of his own rather high-minded creed, but does not negate the fundamental value of his analysis or his prescription.

By contrast to Havel, Adam Michnik appears to embrace the new society, warts and all. As a successful journalist, he has called himself a businessman rather than a politician and taken his anti-utopianism to the point of hymning the charms of the colour grey. Much of his writing aims at reconciliation with people he has opposed but whom he sees as important figures in modern Polish history: the mercurial Wałęsa, even the enigmatic Jaruzelski. There is a confidence in such evaluations, as of a pluralist liberalism which felt quasi-hegemonic enough to accept the contribution of non-liberals to the national life. Michnik represents the man of parts who under conditions of freedom has spread wings and done things he could never have done under communism. He must be set alongside those whose fortunes have withered or stagnated under the new dispensation. The post-socialist project promised variety in place of communist uniformity and this it has delivered.

Assessment

It is the sheer variety of post-communist experience that makes a balance sheet hard to draw. Commentators have repeatedly noted that places like Warsaw and Prague have become 'normal' cities inhabited by people going through the full gamut of activities of a modern western capital. Yet few scholars would dream of attempting to sum up the quality of life of an entire western country, or would seriously try to rank different societies in these terms. Generalizations about the changes between the pre- and post-1989 experience of eastern Europe are therefore rather banal. On the whole, the educated, talented and well connected have done better from the transition than the less educated, less enterprising and less well connected, as liberal capitalist ideology would lead one to expect.

Banal as this generalization is, it indicates at least that events have followed neither of two opposed scenarios widely touted in 1989–90. The gloomy prognostications of political instability and authoritarianism which quickly followed the initial euphoria have not been borne out. Indeed, in recording this fact adherents of the intellectual project of 1989 have half re-echoed some of the old euphoria, like Michnik in 1999 describing his conscience-troubled support for Balcerowicz's 'shock therapy' in Poland: '[a]long this path – though littered with mistakes, inconsistencies, and scandals – Poland experienced an economic boom and social progress never encountered before',[21] or Haraszti's talk of 'miraculous achievements', consensualism's 'historic handshake' and the 'founding fathers' of a successful transformation.[22] If political development was accompanied by growing inegalitarianism, this need be no criticism in itself. An artificial levelling was one of the prime features of the immobilism to which the communist state succumbed.

On the other hand, events also confounded the social engineering implicit in the dominant liberal capitalist prescriptions of the early 1990s, which would make eastern Europe a showplace for the view that economic success is directly proportionate to the degree of liberalization and privatization. Any major process of transition, even towards laissez-faire, requires the major exercise of state power. The relations between public and private proved too intricate, the very definition of property too uncertain, the chain of unintended consequences too long and the presumptions – public equals bad; private equals good – too dogmatic to yield outcomes as swift and sustained as reformers expected. The tangled history of privatization and decollectivization or rural policy in general (shades of non-collectivized Poland) bear particular witness to this. Though many reformers were in reality highly dogmatic, the assumption behind their theory of transition can be put more generally, namely that the gains of the economic winners would draw up the relative economic losers too in a post-communist system operating at a qualitatively higher level than the old one. All but a handful of observers would wish to embrace this view, since it goes to the heart of the system in which all Europeans now live, but the post-1989 evidence to date falls short of complete reassurance, particularly if matters like the decline in health and welfare services and the growth in crime are factored in. The experience of the Balkans may suggest that not only individuals can find themselves at the bottom of a pile from which it is structurally very hard to rise, but even whole societies. While the popular mood in 1989 was primarily a reaction against communism's bankruptcy and claustrophobic constraints rather than for a little-known capitalism, there was also a feeling that at least under capitalism people's success or failure depended on their own efforts. Yet the global capitalist model of the 1990s was nothing if not a system highly dependent on interlinked informational and bureaucratic structures, and educational and cultural codes. Its individualism was highly organized.

Indeed, reservations about the success of post-communist eastern Europe start from an awareness that the codes underlying a functioning democracy are subtler than was assumed in 1989. It is now clear that restoring property rights is less important than restoring the legal and financial framework in which they are embedded, and the habits of trust which should inform this framework. Ironically, the great Hungarian reformer István Széchenyi preached the same message about the transition from feudalism to capitalism, when, in his most famous book *Credit* (1830), he emphasized that this key capitalist concept had a moral as well as an economic connotation. Credit and trust are again at a discount in the region today. George Schöpflin has pinpointed unfamiliarity with the tacit conventions of western civic society as a reason for east Europeans' resort to ethnic nationalism; nationalism is to be the glue holding together societies which lack the cohesion provided by civic solidarity.[23] Vladimir Tismaneanu, a Romanian-American champion of the civic ideals of 1989, has echoed the disillusionment of many, particularly of Balkan background, at the failure of these ideals to make headway against what he calls the 'ambiguous Leninist legacy of distorted modernity' and the pre-Leninist legacy of 'ethnic-oriented cultural forms' in eastern Europe. In calling on observers to give up the 'neo-Hegelian' game of 'ultimate liberal triumph', he even casts doubt on the central assumption of the 'transition to democracy' approach to the region, namely that democratization is taking place.[24]

Undermining attempts to assess the success of transition are thus doubts about the concept itself. By definition transition presupposes a passage from one state to another, success being defined as arrival at an end point which in the case of eastern Europe was defined in advance by the western model. There is a natural tendency in this perspective to see the all-important goal as justifying the means: János Kornai and Adam Michnik have argued persuasively that compared to the historic dimension of democratic system change the bumps on the way weigh little in the long run. Yet those also have a case who argue that the process of transition creates its own scenarios which then develop a significant life of their own. A snowball of change rolled from the top of the hill A is unlikely to end up exactly in B seen below, but depending on the exact lie of the slope will develop its own trajectories. In this perspective, what happens as the ball rolls down the slope does not become irrelevant when it reaches the bottom, since it may have markedly influenced its destination. It then becomes potentially relevant to set alongside the successful political transition in the Visegrád lands the question as to whether the traumatic economic transition might not yet hinder the catching up with the west which was the ultimate goal of system change. To pose this question is not to presuppose a pessimistic answer. Future historians may well conclude that the existence of a clear-cut economic model à la Sachs at the outset of transition provided both the necessary confidence and the necessary space for politicians to concentrate on refining the consensus-orientated model which has worked well. Deep differences over economic strategy were a key factor in frustrating attempts to construct democracy in eastern Europe after 1918, though critics of Sachs *et al.*, to be fair, never challenged the premise of conversion to a market economy, only the methods.

There is a further reason why the idea of transition as a clearly defined process, with a clearly measurable end goal, has been so influential. It is the hope for the region's integration into an expanded European Union. The EU has appeared as a deus ex machina whose favour will both define transition's successful conclusion and render irrelevant all previous trials. At the time of writing, accession in 2004 has been offered to five of the states discussed in this book (Poland, the Czech Republic, Slovakia, Hungary and Slovenia) and held in prospect for two more in 2007. Referendums having succeeded in all the named states, it remains to be seen whether EU enlargement will be as successful for the Union and the acceding countries as in the cases of Greece, Portugal and Spain in the 1980s.

While such important indicators of east-central Europe's fate remain in the future, the historian can also draw some clues from the past. This is not the first time a liberal project has been essayed there: 1848, 1918 and in the ex-Habsburg lands 1867 had already seen attempts to implement the trinity of individual rights, parliamentary government and liberal economics. The post-communist situation has parallels with all these previous attempts: with 1848 because both were preceded by stultifying authoritarianism; and with 1918 because both espoused universal suffrage democracy. In some ways the comparison with 1867 is the most suggestive because both show elements of liberal elite hegemony after the defeat of more radical hopes. In 1867 the Austrian upper bourgeoisie and Magyar gentry on the one side and the imperial bureaucracy on the other reached accord after the defeat of the 1848 revolutionaries. The consensuses of the 1990s – between ex-communists, intellectual dissidents and technocrats – followed the erosion of reform communist, syndicalist or 'third way' alternatives, and were accompanied by an economic haemorrhage of the working class. Will the successors to the communist nomenklatura prove yet another edition of the elite with too shallow roots or will Szelényi's intelligentsia, the modern equivalent of the 1867 central European *Bildungsbürgertum* (cultured bourgeoisie), finally succeed in establishing a distinctive class rule? Or is a western-style middle class presiding over an alteration of moderate left and right to be the communist legatee? On the basis of this study of the communist regime and its fall it seems possible to say that the post-1989 elites have a better chance than their predecessors. Growing inequalities of wealth are not reinforced to the same extent by differences of mentality: a vast peasant reservoir mobilizable on lines of traditional religious values and/or minority ethnic status no longer exists. Poverty compared to pre-communist times is relative rather than absolute. But while the power structures emerging since 1989 are broader based than a reconstructed nomenklatura or an educated intelligentsia alone, it is unclear how far they will develop along lines of equality with their western counterparts. The possibility remains that they will continue to be largely junior partners and facilitators in the running of their own economies, as adjuncts to a global hegemony of the pre-1989 west.

Thus a historical perspective only confirms the crucial importance of the EU dimension referred to above. The east European transition from communism will not be over until the region is successfully integrated with the European Union. The international dimension was crucial in the failure of the liberal experiments of 1848 and 1918. By contrast the Habsburg quasi-liberalism of 1867–1918 flourished initially on the apparent resolution or suspension of the international tensions which had rocked mid-nineteenth-century Europe: the German, Polish, Hungarian, Italian and Balkan questions. The attraction of EU status for east-central Europe is that it seems to offer membership of a club where democracy, prosperity and peace are indefinitely assured within a new world order. Such, at least, was the prospect which opened up after 1989 and in large measure because of 1989. The international dimension of the fall of communism is therefore the subject of the concluding chapter of this book.

9

1989 in the international context

The events of 1989 were an international sensation. The 'autumn of the peoples', unlike the crises in the region of 1914 and 1939, seemed to open altogether benign perspectives, a fresh start for an embattled planet. There was to be an end of cold war and division; ideas of a global world with all their social, economic and cultural implications advanced powerfully; the whole balance of intellectual preoccupation shifted as themes of class yielded to themes of ethnicity and identity. A previously unknown American political analyst, Francis Fukuyama, rocketed to fame by suggesting that with the fall of communism the 'end of history' itself had come about, in the sense of a world driven by competing ideologies, for 1989 had demonstrated that there was only one contestant in the field: liberal democracy.[1] The possible ramifications of that year have been wide; too wide perhaps for the region's own good. For the danger exists that it could become a surrogate battleground for rival philosophies set out with little regard for the nuances of the region itself. This has happened before, in debates on the origins of the cold war, for example, which turned east Europeans into democratic victims of Stalinist aggression or fascistic nationalists overdue a dose of modernization according to distant writers' persuasions. How far has 1989 created a framework favourable to the region's aspirations for integration into a free, prosperous Europe? This is the question which links the demise of communism most pertinently with the wider span of eastern Europe's modern history.

1989 and international politics

Though it was a conventional wisdom of western life in the second half of the twentieth century that westerners lived in an age of unprecedented change, for most of the time this was simply not true. It was only towards the end of the period that the eclipse of socialism and the cold war, the onmarch of globalization and IT, the replacement of class by ethnicity and Europe as staples of debate, not to speak of the successive wars in the Persian Gulf, Kosovo, Afghanistan and Iraq, shook up the stable patterns which had existed in Britain at least from the aftermath of the Second World War. Of course, the events of 1989 did not simply cause these modern phenomena. As we have seen, in many ways they were the result of them. The shift away from Keynesian economics and social democratic assumptions in the 1970s had gathered pace in the Reagan–Thatcher years of the 1980s, spawning the free market doctrines embraced by east European economists; the IT and global communications boom had already begun and helped further undermine communist legitimacy in eastern Europe – the so-called demonstration effect. But while being spurred by economic and ideological shifts already taking place, 1989 sharply accelerated them. By destroying the socialist bloc and thereby helping to precipitate the collapse of the Soviet Union itself, it largely brought about the single greatest fact in the modern world, the barely challenged hegemony of a country committed to the identification of democracy and the global marketplace. This process is the main theme of the post-communist era.

Central in the chain of events following 1989 were the unification of Germany and the break-up of the Soviet Union. The East German movement reopened the German question locked in amber for 40 years. Chancellor Kohl's quick footwork turned the German socialist state into five *Länder* of a reunited Germany inside NATO by October 1990, to the dismay of Mikhail Gorbachev, whose successive retreats on the unification terms exposed the weakness of his hand. Mrs Thatcher and the French president François Mitterand were almost equally dismayed, fearing a shift in the balance of power in the European Community. It was in order to tie the enlarged Germany back into partnership that Mitterand sponsored the Maastricht treaty's commitment to EC monetary union in 1991, muzzling the mighty power of the Deutschmark, while Kohl saw the deepening of European unity as a way of dispersing non-German fears about resurgent German power. The course towards ever-greater European integration, with the continued side-lining of Eurosceptic Britain by a Franco-German axis, was thus set early after the events of 1989. It led on to the introduction of the Euro currency in 12 of the Union's 15 states in January 2002, while the theme of defence and foreign policy coordination broached at Maastricht moved from the wings to assume the next leading role in the European debate. The concern about a united Germany's potential for hegemony in Europe, which Maastricht was designed to conjure away, proved to be premature, however, as the huge sums Germany spent on integration of its eastern territories contributed to the halting growth and high unemployment which seems finally to have brought the postwar German economic miracle to an end; another contributory cause, by the tenets of the free market philosophy given such a boost by the collapse of communism, is the heavily regulated German welfare state model itself. As it has become increasingly apparent that the aftermath of 1989 would privilege only one hegemony, that of the communist world's ideological antipole, the United States, so European resistance to this prospect has deepened, leading to the deadlock in the UN Security Council over Iraq in early 2003.

Just as the speed of German unification took many contemporaries by surprise, so too did the break-up of the Soviet Union. Gorbachev's refusal to rescue the Soviet empire in eastern Europe gained him the goodwill of President Bush for his bid to transform the USSR into a Union of Soviet Sovereign Republics. But the USSR could not be saved, any more than reform communism elsewhere. Besides incurring the odium of having 'lost' the Soviet empire, Gorbachev found himself hoist on the petard of economic reform, shilly-shallying over implementation of the '500 Days Programme', the Soviet version of the Big Bang. The transformation of a monopolistic communist party to a post-communist institution operating in a pluralist framework eluded Gorbachev as it had Pozsgay. For all his remarkable skill in taking it so far down the road, it has been suggested he might have engineered a clear split between reformers and unreconciled communists when it perhaps still could have worked, in 1990.[2] The catalytic factor in the Soviet case was as in eastern Europe nationhood. But whereas in eastern Europe it had reinforced the sense of solidarity among the demonstrating masses, in the multinational Soviet Union it destroyed solidarity. The USSR lacked the precondition for successful state democratization, which is that its citizens accept the state and oppose only the regime. The Baltic peoples did not accept inclusion in the USSR. In trying to square the circle between separatists and centralists Gorbachev devised his decentralist Union Treaty, whose imminent passage into law provoked the coup of August 1991, by hard-liners fearing the loss of the Soviet homeland after the loss of its empire. Despite the coup's failure Gorbachev, the USSR and reform communism were quickly history. Boris Yeltsin presided over an ex-nomenklatura grab for power by endorsing the credo of Russia's arch-economic liberalizers and their western backers. The ex-Soviet states thus reproduced with exaggeration tendencies in eastern Europe, combining Visegrád deregulation with Balkan nomenklatura corruption until the economic crash of 1998, which completed the discomfiture of a former superpower. Russia's arsenals rusted because of an inability to fund them, while in its traditional Balkan sphere of influence its role was tolerated as long as it smoothed the path of western policy towards Milošević's Serbia, but rebuffed thereafter.

With the retreat of its historic enemy, did NATO have a rationale after 1989 and the formal disbanding of the Warsaw Pact which followed? Would Europe now play a smaller role in American calculations, as the Asian Pacific rim flexed its economic muscle, and even the demography of

America tilted in an Asian and Chicano direction? Certainly a 'peace dividend' was expected from 1989, with cuts in conventional forces and in military budgets; in the process the relative contribution of NATO's European members might well increase, which would strengthen the case they had been making for more influence in the alliance's decision-making process. In the event, NATO leaders had no intention of dispensing with an organization that might play a role in anchoring the new situation, with regard to both Germany and the old Soviet bloc; stable reduction of forces in both halves of the continent also implied that there would still be US troops in Europe to act as a balance. But NATO's role would change, with more emphasis on peace-keeping, crisis management and arms agreement verification. The Clinton presidency which took office in 1993 did indeed believe that Europe was now capable of playing a bigger role in its own security. Bodies like the European Union (so named from 1993), the Western European Union, created for west European military coordination from 1955, and the Conference on Security and Cooperation in Europe (CSCE) set up at Helsinki (1975) were available to supervise a bedding down of the continent's new structures. Something closer to a partnership between the European and North American wings of NATO seemed in the offing, with Combined Joint Task Forces permitting the Europeans to use NATO facilities in operations undertaken without US participation. Thus NATO remained, and as the completeness of the west's victory in the cold war sank in and fears of annoying the Russians slackened, even questions of its expansion into former Warsaw Pact territories (not just East Germany) came on the agenda. To try to conciliate an indignant Russia and also the east Europeans who were impatient for immediate entry into NATO, Partnerships for Peace were offered to non-NATO countries (1994). Twenty-seven of these were soon formed, though some critics saw them as merely fobbing off east Europeans, 'little more than a mechanism for postponing decisions on difficult issues which require urgent attention'.[3]

Yet things did not work out according to plan. Europe's limited capacity for partnership was exposed by the Yugoslav crisis of 1991–95, which the Americans had originally left largely to the Europeans to sort out. The ambitious goal of a common European foreign policy was revealed as a step too far. The EC response to the crisis was first slow, then riven by internal differences and contradictions. Germany pressed successfully for recognition of Croatia for both moral and historic/pragmatic reasons; repugnance for Serbian actions reinforced closer historic ties of central Europe with the Croats. The greater Anglo-French emollience towards the Serbs sprang from a more traditional Realpolitik sense that Serbia would be the key to any ultimate Balkan settlement. The ensuing recognition of a Bosnian state lacking means of defence against its own Serbs put the international community in the invidious position of sending in lightly armed peacekeeping forces for humanitarian purposes before peace had been made, so that they could not resist blackmailing pressure tactics from the combatants, particularly Serbs. A gulf opened up between the Europeans and the Americans when the latter advocated bombing the Serbs, which the former rejected for fear of Serb reprisals against their peacekeepers on the ground. The international community appeared discredited by its dithering policy in the face of ethnic cleansing. The Bosnian war was finally brought to a close when the Americans stepped in, engineered and armed an anti-Serb coalition, bombed the Serbs and arm-twisted the parties into a settlement.[4]

The course and conclusion of the Yugoslav wars have had huge consequences. Theoretically speaking, they have been pored over by students of United Nations peacekeeping, who have drawn the lesson that peacekeeping must never be confused with peace enforcing. They have stirred arcane but in implication highly significant debates among international lawyers about the respective claims of state sovereignty, the right of national self-determination and the rights of national minorities. Upholding the territorial integrity of existing states had been a major postulate of international postwar politics, conditioned partly by memories of Hitler's prewar use of ethnic claims against his neighbours and Soviet desire for recognition of its post-1945 borders. Now international approval of Croat and Slovene secession from Yugoslavia extended the right of self-determination. Yet how far should it go? Croats, Slovenes and the Baltic peoples were nations, but were Croatian Serbs, a section of a nation, entitled to reject the authority of the new Croatia as Croats had done that of Yugoslavia? The EC-sponsored Badinter Commission of 1991–92 inclined to the view that they were entitled only to minority rights, but its full elaboration of these rights was itself a step forward, in keeping with the democratizing spirit of the post-1989 era. Indeed, the increasing linkage of self-determination and human rights in the 1990s opened the way for innovative lawyers to push further, arguing for international monitoring of minority grievances, where concepts of 'good governance' and state 'dissolution' could be relevant. 'The function of the international lawyer is to change the course of human history' was one bold claim.[5] Theoretical speculation became germane in the case of the Kosovo Albanians who were patently subject to bad governance in Serbia. Suggestions were heard that the Kosovars might merit self-determination because unlike the Croatian and Bosnian Serbs, they already enjoyed autonomy in their republic (Serbia) before 1991. Though Kosovan secession was not formally endorsed by the powers either before or after NATO's war with Serbia over Kosovo in 1999, NATO's attack on a sovereign state for its mistreatment of its own citizens would hardly have been thinkable before 1989. Thus the general loosening of cold war rigidities after 1989 and the specific Yugoslav crisis have set on foot a process potentially subversive of previous doctrines of inviolable state sovereignty, in the name of fundamental principles of the new world order. An international tribunal at The Hague, with Milošević the first ex-head of state to be tried by it, is to be institutionalized as an international criminal court. The vision justifying such perspectives is of a democratic world, quite different from the ideals of the post-1815 Holy Alliance or the Brezhnev Doctrine. But the structural parallels with these earlier experiments is what aroused some of the anxiety felt by opponents of intervention in Iraq, which took the form of a pre-emptive strike.

What gives both the Kosovo and the Iraq issues their relevance for this book is that military action in each case claims legitimacy – certainly rhetorically – from a discourse of human rights and moral universalism which has received a tremendous fillip from the collapse of the bipolar world after 1989. The conception of international politics in terms of standards of governance relativizing state sovereignty, while not absent before, required the cumulative experience of 1989 and its aftermath to feed into a doctrine of action. The ideals of the new world order have taken on flesh and few with a sense of history could fail to be struck by this bid to expand the bounds of the moral dimension in a sphere where Realpolitik has traditionally dominated. True, many advocates of action against Iraq would ground it in the most traditional of rights, those of self-defence and reprisal, but clearly appeal is also being made to the illegitimacy of countenancing evil and the need to aspire to something better. This is the sense in which Tony Blair calls on the British people not to look askance at America and its ideals. Here we catch the authentic accents of 1989 as it was understood by its liberal progenitors and it is no accident that the strongest advocates of interventionism in the war against terror are America and Britain, the countries most committed to the free-market liberal democracy which became the model for the east European transitions.

The difficulty for observers is to know where to draw the line between high ideals and the human frailties of partiality and self-interest. The widespread suspicions of the United States reflect fear that it is moving towards a hegemony which, however benign, is open to abuse. The legacy of 1989 has legitimized one project, to which others must conform or suffer disadvantage. Here the support for American policy of east European countries admitted to NATO in 1999 (Poland, Hungary, the Czech Republic, Slovakia), or aspiring to membership, while no doubt heartfelt, shows a keen sense of where power is located in the post-communist world. It is an attempt to reap maximum benefit from association with the events which brought the present balance of forces about. This symbolic importance of eastern Europe for the new order is thus a potential strength but it is not without its danger. The region may be subsumed into broader debates which no longer consider it in its own terms or with much real knowledge. This is often the fate of regions seen as peripheral or exotic. How has the western world actually handled the challenge of integrating the countries of central and eastern Europe into the liberal democratic order? Usually in human affairs the devil is in the detail.

1989 and European unity

Historically the liberal democratic ideal for eastern Europe has been the acceptance of its peoples into the European comity of nations on equal terms, in peace and prosperity. In the latest period this has come to be defined as acceptance into the European Union. President Mitterand's words at a heads of governments summit in November 1989 inevitably fed contemporary optimism that existing Community members were as committed to its speedy consummation as east Europeans: the summit, he said, had been about 'solidarity and unity: unity . . . tomorrow why not with those who feel able to integrally associate themselves with the disciplines which we impose on ourselves'.[6] The aftermath has been more equivocal.

To be fair to the western world, the criticism that the same urgency was not shown in lifting up eastern Europe as was shown by the Marshall Plan in the recovery of western Europe after 1945, overlooks the differences. Schemes and dreams of postwar reconstruction had occupied minds for years before the chance of realization came; the eastern Europe issue arose out of the blue. Marshall Aid came from one country; the body foreshadowed in G7 discussions of Paris in July 1989, the G24, consisting of 24 states with corresponding problems of coordination, in Europe, North America, Australasia and Japan. Its concerns quickly extended from Poland and Hungary to include other east European states. The $86 billion it had pledged by 1995 were, at constant prices, some way under the $13 billions of Marshall Aid and much of this went in debt reorganization, emergency aid and export credits or to fund technical assistance of variable quality from donor countries. Some 29 per cent took the forms of grants as opposed to 80 per cent under the Marshall Plan. Just over half came from the European Community. The EU's main contribution was through the PHARE programme of grant aid, first aimed at budget stabilization, then increasingly available for investment. By the end of 1996, 6.6 billion ecus (c.£4.5 billion) had been committed, a sum equivalent, however, to a mere 0.02 per cent of the Union's GNP. Whereas France had received from 10 per cent to 11.5 per cent of its GNP from Marshall aid in 1949, PHARE funding made up only 0.5 per cent of Hungary's budget in 1995. The EU was spending about 25 times less per head on eastern Europe than on the Structural Funds aimed at building up its own backward regions (Mayhew 1998: 135–42).

East European illusions about western intentions were deflated by the Europe Agreements concluded between the EC and most of the region's states between 1991 and 1996. The Agreements were intended to bring the east into conformity with western practice in matters of anti-subsidy rules and pro-competitive policies in the interest of establishing efficient market economies. It was particularly EC refusal to specify that the Agreements entailed commitment to eventual east European membership, however, which hurt. Indeed, the agreement negotiations were characterized by hard-nosed trade bargaining on the EC's part. While there was some asymmetry of treatment favouring the new boys – their own companies had immediate access to the EC but they could delay establishment of EC members' companies – on agriculture, one of their strongest suits, they gained virtually nothing in the teeth of the EC protectionism and ample room was left for the EC to undermine trade liberalization in industrial matters. The most invidious issue was EC invoking of anti-dumping clauses, which had an effect beyond the numerical incidence because the threat of such action intimidated east European companies. The bureaucratic nature of the EC meant that complaints by individual western firms could lead to bans on eastern exports without overall account being taken of the breach of the ostensible spirit of intra-continental collaboration. Alleged dumping was hardly ever 'predatory', using cheap prices to win a predominant market share in the west, since east European businesses had no prospect of this, nor was the Agreements' reference to damage to 'Community interests' taken into account, which would have prevented complaints being upheld that often involved little more than a western company's desire to maintain a previous monopoly position. There was a distinct tendency for EC authorities to hold their new partners to standards which expressed EC theory rather than actual practice. The Agreements also contained 'safeguards' which enabled western resort to protection against Czech steel. In the wake of the Agreements a previous positive balance in east European trade with the west quickly turned into a very large deficit, sparking protectionist pressure. After the tariff liberalization of 1990 east European countries in part reaction raised duties and became more protectionist than they had been before 1989, particularly in relation to non-EC markets.

Yet for all disappointment in detail the trajectory opened up by 1989 held. The German foreign minister Genscher first spoke out for the accession of the Visegrád countries into the EC as soon as possible, and the Copenhagen summit of January 1993 confirmed this as the goal. In a laborious process applications for membership arrived from ten east-central European and Baltic countries (1993–96), the EU Commission presented a 1200-page document, *Agenda 2000*, negotiations with a first tier of applicants (Poland, the Czech Republic, Hungary, Slovenia and Cyprus) began in March 1998 and with a second tier including Romania and Bulgaria in February 2000. The hurdles involved in turning the European destiny into reality have proved formidable. Forty thousand pages of EU regulations (the *acquis*) had to be incorporated into applicants' law and practice, including environmental overhaul at an estimated cost of 120 billion euros. Accession costs are likely to be over 6 per cent of applicants' GNP. Bringing roads up to scratch alone was estimated by *The Economist* in 1999 at $48 billion. Overhauling or decommissioning nuclear power stations – a particular Austrian concern – will be problematic for countries heavily dependent on them for energy. East European countries also become liable to maintain the outer border of the EU against illegal immigration, which entails not only costs and vexation, but a clamping down on fruitful cross-border trade which has been a life-line to impoverished Ukrainians and Russians beyond. For all this effort the pre-accession funds promised have been modest; *Agenda 2000* proposed 500 million ecus for agricultural restructuring for 2000–6, 'a relatively small sum considering' in an expert view,[7] and 45 billion of the 275 billion of the EU Structural Fund envisaged for this period, increasing proportionally to amount to some one-third of the Fund by the end year. The bottom line is that east European farmers are deemed too numerous and would bankrupt the existing CAP (Common Agricultural Policy) scheme, which already swallows nearly half the EU budget.

Thus there has been a duality in the east–west relationship since 1989. The hopes then felt for an integrated Europe have not been disavowed but the path to the goal has been more dispiriting than was anticipated. The outside world can hardly be said to have abandoned the region when so many organizations have concerned themselves with its fate: CSCE, UNHCR, IFOR, in the Yugoslav imbroglio alone; the EU, the IMF, the World Bank, the EBRD, the EIB, the G24 on the economic side. In 1996 a third of the Albanian budget came from foreign funds. The flip side of this has been the know-all tendency to hold the apron strings. East European applicants to the EU were not even consulted on the accession partnership documents setting out their obligations during the accession process. The Commission has engaged itself in all sorts of issues, from a plan for the river Bug area shared by Poland, Belarus and Ukraine, to a Vienna-based transport infrastructure needs-assessment body for central and eastern Europe. The IMF and World Bank have made their loans conditional on the most specific terms, stating for example, the percentage of Bulgarian state industry that must be divested by a given time, detailing the companies that the Romanians must privatize, specifying maximum permitted budget deficits. The number of structural requirements attached to IMF programmes rose from two or three in the mid-1980s to a dozen or so by the later 1990s, reflecting a hubristic would-be precision which its director has since publicly regretted.[8] Indeed, unwillingness to let slip the appearance of total control of complex situations where its rigidly controlled agents on the ground often sympathized with the benighted 'clients' helped make for the lack of transparency of these high forums' decision-making processes.[9]

One reason for western bossiness has been awareness that east Europeans desperate for acceptance are hardly in a position to complain. Bulgaria claimed to have lost $6 billion and Romania $7 billion through observing international sanctions against their Yugoslav neighbour; a western think-tank estimated a 2 per cent Bulgarian loss in GNP from NATO's Kosovo war alone. But the Bulgarian foreign minister put a positive spin on

this sacrifice: 'We've proved that we can be a serious and trustworthy partner.'[10] The reward was pats on the back like the American Secretary of State
Madeleine Albright's statement after Kosovo that Romania was part of the
NATO family. Leszek Miller, the socialist Polish prime minister, has nailed
his colours to the mast of EU entry as the essential motor of Poland's much-
needed modernization. His all too obvious angling for papal approval of
this project during Pope John Paul II's summer 2002 visit to his homeland
highlighted the irony which has made former communists the strongest
Europeanists in modern eastern Europe, while the patriotic right now
inveigh against the 'civilization of death' in an abortion-ridden, materialis-
tic EU. Generally, enthusiasm for the European Union waned, from around
four-fifths in the early 1990s to less than half at times in Poland and the
Czech lands, though the eventual referendums showed solid majorities on
lowish turn-outs. Surveys have shown most Poles seeing themselves as
likely second-class citizens for the foreseeable future even if they 'entered
Europe'. Czechs fear pressure to repeal the 'Beneš decrees' expropriating
Sudeten Germans in 1945; they and the Poles are calling for lengthy transitions before other, now much wealthier EU citizens have the right to buy
land which might lead to the recreation of the German minority. At times
anti-western sentiment boiled over. The EU General Secretary Prodi was
pelted with eggs on a visit to Warsaw in 2001. More insidious is cumulative irritation at the west's know-all assumptions; everything westerners
suggested to solve the Gypsy problem had already been tried 20 years ago,
sighed one Slovak official.[11]

Yet the EU offer of accession to Poland, the Czech Republic, Slovakia,
Hungary and Slovenia, made in December 2002, must be seen as an epo-
chal moment. The terms on which these countries' electorates have now
voted are tough. A special clause has had to be inserted to ensure that the
vastly poorer accessor countries will not be net contributors to the EU's
budget in the entry year, a bizarre prospect reflecting a process in which
new members pay their dues initially and reap full benefits only later. Thus
east European farmers will receive only a quarter the level of subsidy of
existing members, to be gradually raised to equality by the time the projected reduction of the agricultural budget is achieved in 2013. Through
such sleights of hand the EU Commission has sought to balance the need
to finance the entry of states whose average GNP per capita at purchasing
power parity is a mere third of the existing Union with the ever stronger
opposition of net EU budget contributors like Germany and the
Netherlands to increased expenditure. The underlying issue is that the
strains on the 15-member Union, budgetary and organizational, are already
severe and further expansion requires structural overhaul. Matters like
each member state's right to at least one Commissioner and the relative representation of large and small states in the European Council will become
vastly more problematic in a body of 25 members. The necessity of reform

is recognized but the nettle has not yet been grasped. Thus east Europeans have voted on a Union whose precise shape remains to be determined. If such vital matters have been postponed to later negotiation, it is because of their sheer complexity and sensitivity but also because of the pressures driving the negotiators to some kind of conclusion, however immediately imperfect. These pressures are testimony to the significance ascribed to the negotiations on all sides. Nevertheless, they have been conducted on the basis of substantially different assumptions: whereas east Europeans have seen them as essentially a political/moral/strategic process aimed at recognizing and consolidating their achievement of 1989 in opting for western freedoms, the EU has been engaged in a tough bargaining exercise with a view to creating a viable and efficient economic entity.[12] The process has been a recognition of the fact of 1989 but not of what was once seen as its spirit.

The demise of communism and the history of eastern Europe

It was the spirit of 1989 which more than anything stirred observers. It seemed to teach something about the indomitable human desire for freedom. It was a dramatic step in the process towards a democratic world of equal nations. These final pages seek to relate these high-flown sentiments to what actually happened in eastern Europe. Where should the demise of communism be situated in the region's struggle for social and national emancipation? What has it meant for the terms of its relationship with the wider world?

The justification for casting the debate so broadly is given by widespread views that the events of 1989 have marked a caesura in modern history. The common stance on the right is that the caesura is positive. Autumn 1989 meant the defeat of communism, the end of the relentless advance of egalitarian ideas since the French Revolution and the definitive victory of liberal capitalism as motor of a new world order. In an east European version, it meant the eclipse of an alien, unnatural regime. The ex-Marxist Tony Judt's comments reflect a less bland perspective, the sense of ground shifting beneath one's feet, felt by many of left-wing background. The year 1989 ended the revolutionary discourse of 1789 and the dominion of the nation state, wrote Judt in 1994; it highlighted the crisis of the Enlightenment by marginalizing (in what followed) the intellectuals who had set society's agendas since its day: 'the implications are startling'.[13] The argument that will be developed below is that the east European revolutions do not fit easily into such overarching schema; it remains the region's fate that its experience is interpreted by the 'first world' it seeks to join according to that world's preoccupations. What east-central Europeans sought by the overthrow of communism is explicable in the light of their own history and aspirations. These aspirations, however, do have something to tell us about 'the human spirit' in both its more elevated and its humdrum forms.

East European communism fell because from the start it was a utopian experiment, which has nowhere achieved satisfactory political and economic results. Its loss of legitimacy was cumulative, as even supporters attracted by its developmental and egalitarian goals came to see that the claim to a new, higher kind of human being had brought violations of basic norms of legality and decency; that attempts to reform the system clashed with the single party's claim to a fullness of the truth; and that economic inefficiencies could not be cured by injecting elements of the market but only by generalizing the market principle itself. With the human instinct to clarify and systematize at work, these apprehensions fused into an over-arching perception: that communism's extreme rejection of the liberal model had brought the disadvantages of the Enlightenment project without its advantages – a mechanistic impersonal world geared to material production without the solace of individual liberty and creativity. Many who had at first embraced the Marxist project were drawn by this process of logical recognition to endorse the liberal opposite of their former beliefs. The process was gradual. Even after the reform Marxism of the Prague Spring had been abandoned, the Solidarity movement retained socialist features not always acknowledged as such, particularly because its working-class base had a concrete interest in social welfarism. The final fusion of intellectual and economic wings of what would become a purely liberal project only came at the end of the 1980s and then for select numbers of Hungarians, Poles and maybe Slovenes and Czechs, in the first instance. The great bulk of those who demonstrated in 1989 were not yet up to date with these processes and were motivated by Solidarity-style proto-socialism or by national, religious or simply human responses that communism had not touched: hence, in fair measure, the confusions in the working out of communism's demise. The communist regimes of the 1980s were far from the totalitarian model of theory. They were a patchwork of improvisations that had come into being to keep the unwieldy system functioning, weak in their capacity to mobilize unwilling populations and reliant on pervasive use of arbitrary power and fear.

Contrary to views of communism as a mere carapace imposed on the national life, however, the fact that it proved utopian does not mean that it had little real effect. Communism's utopianism lay in its means: the belief it could achieve its modernizing goals through a single-party system of dedicated revolutionaries and an economy divorced from the disciplines of the market. The modernizing goals themselves went back to the national revivals in the nineteenth century, which had also had a strong vein of egalitarianism. Communism was undoubtedly more successful than the interwar regimes in creating an industrial infrastructure and an educated population. Its story was one of flawed modernization but modernization all the same, over most of the region. Only in the Czech lands were the lineaments of an urban-orientated industrial society already present in 1945; by 1989 this was true of all but Albania. Of course, such a shift might well have occurred without communism, and on better terms, as the advance of Portugal and Greece from about the 1970s implies. Use of the term 'flawed modernization' simply denotes the fact that the communist phase marked too important a stage in the region's evolution to be dismissed as a mere blip in its history. Not all aspects of the communist experiment went against the grain of east European history. People hated the lack of liberty, the propaganda and the economic lag vis-à-vis the west rather than an egalitarian, materialist society. This duality between unpopular means but more acceptable goals helps explain why some communist leaders like Gorbachev and Pozsgay, by the late 1980s, thought they could abandon old ideological shibboleths and still survive, adding a final component in the process that led to dissolution. Yet they were not alone in misconception. Neither western statesmen and academics, nor the region's dissidents, surmised that the end was nigh. Like Havel, they took it for a strength of the regime that it could function even when its functionaries did not believe in it; in hindsight this was to look through the wrong end of the telescope.

The suddenness of collapse was crucial. It is hard to recall now that in the 1960s it had seemed the west that was ideologically challenged by the New Left and the student movement, that in the 1970s Soviet power was extending almost throughout the 'third world', that the high point of Honecker's relations with West Germany came in the mid-1980s. While opposition networks multiplied from 1987, they included a tiny proportion of the population; dissidents were caught without a programme for an alternative order in 1989, as their reliance on Round Table partnership tactics in the final dénouement indicated. The vacuum was filled by a west which had gone on the offensive in the Reagan–Thatcher years: the privatization programme central to the east European transition was undreamt of a decade earlier. Thus 1989 was not just a victory of western ideas, but of very specific ones: a package in which free trade economics joined forces with onmarching managerialism and the explosion of media outlets. Triumphant capitalism stereotyped its fallen foe into a totalitarianism which did not correspond to the messy late communist reality, with its profusion of new enterprise forms attempting to rejuvenate a failed centralism.

The post-1989 dismissal of the communist experience as a kind of black hole, understandable as it is, had two negative consequences: it helped exacerbate the unavoidable pain of the transition, and it rooted the region's image in existential victimhood. The pain of transition was exacerbated because reforms went too far in assuming: state is bad, private is good. The sense of being history's victims made east Europeans, for all that they threw off the yoke of communism, the objects rather than the subjects of the historical process, not truly free agents but dependencies of the wider world they have now joined. It is this attribution of victimhood which made the region seem suitable terrain for almost a reverse experiment of the communist one. Just as the abolition of capitalism, communists thought, would cleanse all ills, so the removal of statist shackles would see withered societies regenerate like limbs from which fetters are removed. Though east European governments in practice could not and did not close down the state sector and the extensive social welfare net all at once, the fact is that east Europeans were guinea pigs. Of the several extant varieties of liberal democracy, it was the American identification of the market and democracy that they underwent, rather than the German–Scandinavian welfarist model or East Asian etatism; and much of the advice they received reflected more a liberal utopia than western liberal practice. The economic downturn of the early 1990s undermined free-market liberalism's talismanic credentials and helped restore ex-communist governments to power.

Of course, these governments too accepted the basic post-communist premise, that the pain of transition was a price worth paying for ultimate incorporation into the European Union. For the Visegrád states Mayhew's words on this process are not untypical: '[w]hile today there is much criticism of detail, the achievements have been remarkable overall'.[14] The truth behind this statement is that if EU accession is successfully accomplished in 2004, the travails of the interregnum between systems will quite likely be swiftly forgotten, as the area is caught up in an upward spiral like Spain and Portugal after their accession in 1986. Thus it can be argued that, difficult as the path has been, the goal of European democratic integration at which 1989 aimed has been steadily pursued all the while. On this reading 2004 will be the apotheosis of 1989 and a sign that its idealistic impulse, which people deemed lost, will have triumphed after all, if in workaday clothes rather than gala dress.

Some reservations must be entered against this desirable consummation. The new entrants are unlikely to enjoy the upward drafts which bore Spain, Portugal and Greece out of relative poverty. Eastern enlargement at this or further stages might yet prove bridges too far for a Union facing huge economic and organizational challenges, and a big fall in prestige and self-confidence since the high point at the end of the 1980s. Spain and Portugal entered as states already in economic upswing. The background to accession in eastern Europe will be over a decade in which the region has struggled to regain its GNP of 1989. In the circumstances, polls suggest that East Europeans fear they will remain second-class members of 'Europe'; the loss of 20 per cent of income resentfully noted by commentators in the mid-1990s may not prove a temporary blip but a permanent drag on the looked-for march to continental equality. This is where Mayhew's 'criticism of detail' comes in. Could what may have been no more than inevitable errors in the complex process of post-communist reconstruction come back to haunt a resentful region? Even in the Visegrád lands, the discourse of transition from communism feeds western perceptions of these countries as objects rather than partners in the European body politic, emphasizing the backwardness of the Polish countryside, Czech and Slovak susceptibility to racism (which has tarnished received ideas of Czech civic superiority) and, in general, the relative poverty which induces patronage and superciliousness – witness West German contempt for the 'Ossies' of former East Germany. The region's people became sardonically aware of how their countries succeeded each other as flavour of the season for western agencies keen to spot the green shoots of progress that would justify their advice: initially Hungary, then Balcerowicz's Poland, then Klaus's Czechoslovakia, then Poland again played this role, only to be dropped when the shoots withered.

Certainly, the reader of a western journal like *The Economist* may be taken aback by the way the chirpy style reflects the bullish contents: east Europeans are adjured to open up to foreign investment as the key to efficiency, then the malversations of foreign firms are described, but the brisk exhortations continue; successive apostles of the free market set up as models against the bad guys are revealed as having feet of clay, yet the confident prescriptions never cease nor is there a backward glance. The pattern of discourse is loaded. However well intentioned, pressure to conform to western values of ethno-cultural pluralism is another example. The Canadian scholar Will Kymlicka's urging that east Europeans should note the patterns of territorial autonomy granted to Quebec, Scotland and Catalonia, for example, and prioritize minority rights rather than state unity, is directed against the perceived paranoia of east European nationalism.[15] Not just traditionalists, though, might doubt how far the western model, whose outcome is anyway not yet clear, parallels their own circumstances. The terms of the east–west relationship bespeak a western superiority complex hard to square with the equality to which eastern Europeans have always aspired.

How much more is this so for south-eastern Europe. One consequence of the demise of communism has been to reopen the divide between the central European states of the northern tier and the Balkan lands, symbolized in the latter's relegation in the process of European union: to 2007 for Romania and Bulgaria, still indefinitely for others. The Croatian writer Slavenka Drakulić commented in 1996 that in the post-communist era the east European was even more a creature apart than before, the object of heightened surveillance by western frontier authorities guarding their wealthy citizens from putative economic migrants, still obliged, if they were intellectuals, to explain themselves and their strange fate to uncomprehending westerners, locked uncomprehending in a 'democracy' they experienced as a 'kind of natural calamity' and a capitalism they saw as mere absence of rules – in short: 'Europe is a divided continent, and only those who could not travel to see it for themselves believed that Easterners and Westerners could become equal'.[16] With no doubt double-edged irony, Drakulić describes the surly, if English-fluent, receptionist in an expensive international hotel in Sofia who preserves her self-respect in her off-handedness, not having yet learnt that money gives those who have it the right to demand courtesy. Another master of wry perception, the Russian–Ukrainian humourist Vitali Vitaliev, notes a Bulgarian's sense of counting for nothing in contemporary Europe.[17] In the Balkans the fall of communism has brought neither west European standards, nor prospects or understanding.

Unsurprisingly, western stereotypes of the Balkans as 'other' were re-inforced by the Yugoslav wars, which provided ample ammunition for views of the region as hopelessly patriarchal, ethnocentric and barren soil for western values. But the opposition of liberal western intellectuals to the idea of Balkan ancient hatreds, which they felt legitimized the west's failure to intervene against Serbian ethnic cleansing, was also defective. It presupposed a view of Bosnia as a model multi-cultural society disrupted by Serb invasion, which overlooked centuries of communal tension and saw the Balkans through the prism of western multi-culturalism. The problem for the region, however, was much more than summoning up the ethnic tolerance expected – if not necessarily found – in western cities. It was multi-nationalism, accommodating separate national claims to the same territory. As a state of recognized Muslim, Croat and Serb nations, each demanding recognition for its distinctive language, Bosnia's problems in the 1990s were closer to those Americans would have if required to integrate a United States containing white, black and Chicano nations, with English, Spanish and Ebonics (the term for black speech) as their official languages and each claiming mutually hostile histories and destinies. Not all references to such difficulties should be dismissed as 'moral equivalence' in favour of Milošević's plainly disastrous role. The categories of goodies and baddies, to which some western observers reduced the immensely complex historical legacy, raise the suspicion that Balkan politics could become a battlefield in which western agendas were being played out by proxy. Thus Brendan Simms' much praised indictment of British foreign policy over Bosnia, *Unfinest Hour*, shows only perfunctory knowledge of Bosnia, however justified it might be in its purpose of attacking British criticism of the United States.[18] The evidence of the 1990s suggests that communist isolation had only strengthened the western tendency to see the Balkans as a land apart, to be forced into western categories in view of incomprehension of its own. The Bulgarian historian Maria Todorova's *Imagining the Balkans* (1997) is a protest against this perception, arguing that the age of political correctness has passed the Balkans by. Edward Said's *Orientalism* has set out a critique of stereotyping of the Islamic world, but the Balkans remain fair game, while central European writers (the Hungarian Szücs, the Czechs Havel and Rupnik) are busy dissociating their own region from the benighted Balkanites. The difficulty is that Todorova's book is written in the vein of up-to-the-minute western academic discourse. It seems the Balkans can produce the traditional images of authoritarian leaders and nationalist zealots, and also sophisticated intellectuals, but not the businessmen and civic-minded professionals of mainstream modernity.

The sanguine perspective for the Balkans is that the shocks of the 1990s, in particular the catastrophic failures of Serbian policy, may have finally undermined the appeal of the national romanticism of the nineteenth century, in other words that a corner is about to be turned. Meanwhile, as High Representatives in the virtual UN protectorates in Bosnia and Kosovo regularly abrogate the election of nationalist leaders, in a curious inversion of the democracy which is being taught,[19] and one by one the ultra-nationalists are being hauled before the War Crimes Court in The Hague, the perspective is that in this war of attrition the forces of moderation and ethnic cooperation will eventually be enabled to gain the upper hand. The change of regimes in Serbia and Croatia lends some hope to this perspective, but to believe it wholeheartedly requires a fair dose of optimism. It is not just that there have been points in the past when, as with a man climbing a mountain, the goal seemed to be equally in sight. Even if Serb and Croat nationalism is finally sated, that of Bosniaks (the preferred name of Bosnian Muslims), Albanians and Macedonians is fresher and under less opprobrium. The issue of nationalism in former Yugoslavia is not just about goodwill or even commitment to pluralism. There are territorial conflicts in Bosnia and Macedonia even if the multi-ethnic cause in Kosovo is lost. The problem goes back to the fact that the principle at stake is not the multi-cultural but the multi-national state and this principle was dealt a heavy blow with the fall of the old Yugoslavia. It is a problem which is unlikely to find a full solution without more upheavals. Even if the old Adam of ethnic intolerance and macho illusion is leached out of Balkan peoples, the psychological scars inflicted are not the best basis from which to tackle the reality of humiliatingly weak and, in the case of Kosovo and Bosnia, destroyed economies.

The Kosovan case may yet prove the most significant legacy of the fall of communism for global politics. The politics of armed intervention in failed states to replace violent regimes by democratic ones, now being pursued in Afghanistan and Iraq, had its original inspiration in Kosovo. It is not altogether a comforting observation. Thirty thousand troops and a plethora of international agencies in a province just over half the size of Wales have not succeeded over four years so far in securing a multi-ethnic community or a half way satisfactory economy. Liberal interventionism Anglo-American style has not generated formulae for solving the kind of developmental and ethnic problems which communism tackled with equal hubris after 1945. Eastern Europe has proved problematic terrain for a democratic world order as for a communist utopia.

The nations of eastern Europe in modern times have mostly had to hitch their fortunes to the agendas of more powerful peoples. For 40 years they were part of the 'socialist world', following Soviet-derived models of the party state, central planning and Leninist nationality policy. With the demise of communism they entered another discourse, much closer to their choice but still regulated elsewhere, of free-market liberalism, multi-culturalism and good governance legitimizing limitations on national sovereignty. How far does it correspond to the aspirations which found expression in 1989?

The most striking feature of the overthrow of communism was the defiance of massive state power by unarmed demonstrators. It was the proof that dictatorship had not eroded moral sensibility or inured populations to apathetic opportunism, as dissidents had often feared. The masses showed they could not be conned. They preferred the dissidents' view of reality and individual opportunity to official propaganda. To an extent communism dug its own grave insofar as the social and educational changes it brought put more people in a position to think as individuals about their own destinies. The year 1989 was part of a wider European retreat from collectivist values as the great classes which had broken into the continent's history since the late nineteenth century, the peasantry and unskilled industrial workers, lost their massivity of nuimbers and communal experience, while the attendant radical intellectuals lost their faith. But 1989 also had roots in the history of the region, in the demonstrators of spring 1848 and autumn 1918 in Prague, Berlin, Budapest and elsewhere. These were all movements for political liberty against authoritarian orthodoxies.

Yet the crowds of 1989 were not demonstrating for radical individualism. The demonstrations themselves had a communal aspect. There was a place for theatre and the solidarity of crowds, for the anonymous many to cock a snook at the authority of the few. One might also conjecture that for some participants the communists were unpopular because they had been around too long rather than for anything much profounder, like the Conservatives for many British people celebrating the Labour victory in 1997. People are readily susceptible to an appeal for change on the lines that 'things can only get better'. There is no evidence that demonstrators wanted or expected the slashing cuts in state industry and welfare or the increase of wealth disparities which followed. A generalized predisposition in favour of the market was due to its association with the success of the west and the benefits of small-scale private business filling gaps in state provision in the 1980s; but that this mood was potentially fickle was assumed by free marketeers themselves, who advocated a 'big bang' to seize a moment of opportunity when people were biddable. Opinion polls in the early 1990s showing near majorities preferring the communist days, then the actual polls bringing ex-communists to power, suggested what the liberal Tocqueville had noted regretfully about the French Revolution, that after the first flush of revolutionary fervour most people seemed to prefer equality to liberty.

There was undoubtedly a nationalist aspect to the collective mood of 1989 and its aftermath. Subordination to Moscow and the curtailing of western links was the most widely resented aspect of the communist system, and replacement of communist by national symbols was one of the most common acts of the movements of 1989. Nationality helped cement the solidarity which gave 1989 its festive and buoyant character. The East German chant, 'we are one nation', the symbolism of the Prague student demonstration of 17 November on the fiftieth anniversary of the death of Jan Opletál at the hands of Nazi occupiers, the echoes of 1848 in Hungary, are scarcely surprising given the centrality of national struggles in the region. People's refusal to be conned appeared also in Milošević's crowds, and their rejection of the stale official slogans of inter-ethnic brotherhood, which contradicted Serbs' lively dislike of Albanians and others. Their solidarity was less amiable than that of the cheerful, teasing crowds of Prague in November 1989. Although liberals are reluctant to acknowledge it, democracy arose in the nineteenth century in close conjunction with nationalism, and the association of civic sentiment with patriotic solidarity remains strong in the most developed countries. It is its national aspect that is most out of line with western progressives' view of 1989, with their suspicion of ethnicity. Some on the left, however, have taken up the challenge to try to reconcile national and international motifs along lines recalling the Austro-Marxist Bauer's synthesis of socialism and nationalism before 1914, another would-be global age.[20] Thus Mary Kaldor foresees a future world with a multiplicity of 'cultural homelands' subsisting alongside transnational networks like Greenpeace and Amnesty International.[21] It is unlikely that this vision will do justice to east Europeans' sense of nationhood.

This brief review demonstrates how the events of 1989 repeated themes in the region's history. They were movements against another flawed system which frustrated the fulfilment of democratic and national goals, rather than the birth point of new, original ideas. Their chief intellectual achievement was the relegitimation of ideas of non-violence, civic values and dialogue against the communist rhetoric of revolution and relentless struggle. This synthesis, informing the work of people like Michnik, Kuroń and Havel, was quarried from many sources: the bases of liberal philosophy, the region's own civic nation-building process under the pre-1914 empires and the use they made of this as (mainly) ex-Marxists operating under a new empire. Its originality lay in the journey, negotiating the troubled waters of their own national pasts, rather than the goal, which was a western haven. It did not have an economic dimension: hence the ease with which free-market liberal ideas took over the stage after the fall of communism, and the intellectuals were pushed aside. Their work was not in vain, however. The liberal spirit of compromise rather than confrontation helped ensure the 'normal' political functioning of the Visegrád states, whose relative stability is the chief achievement of the post-communist era.

If the above analysis is correct, the fall of communism in eastern Europe has interesting wider implications but not on the apocalyptic lines of commentators like Judt (see above, p. 185). It clarified the 1789 legacy, rather than repudiating it. Liberty, equality and fraternity (shorthand for patriotic solidarity) were its themes, as they were for the French two centuries previously. What 1989 and its aftermath did challenge were partisan glosses on the relative importance of these themes: the Marxist assumption that the key goal was 'equality', as communists presented it in the march to a collectivist future of banner-waving, slogan-shouting 'masses'; and the modern right-wing assumption that 'liberty' alone was the key. Here it repeated Tocqueville's lesson. As to fraternity, the nation-state principle was extended, not challenged. The emergence of separate Slovak, Croat, Slovene and other states after 1989 has been the latest in the line of dates starting with Italian and German unification, whereby waves of ever smaller groups have claimed the right to a political identity: 1878 (the Balkans), 1918 (east-central Europe) and 1945 (Czechoslovak and Yugoslav federalism) went before. Fraternity seems able to unite people who disagree on the relative weight of the other two principles.

Thus in many ways 1989 has confirmed the reality as opposed to the image of 1789. It sought the balance between the liberty of representative government, the equality of civil rights and life opportunities, and the solidarity of cultural identity which has largely been achieved in the west of the continent in the last two centuries, but has so far eluded the east. It was thus a manifestation of the human spirit in that it sought what most ordinary human beings want rather than the schema of ideologues. Of course, this benign picture is truer of the northern states than the Balkans, where the demise of communism came about later and by a more troubled process. Ironically, too, as this chapter has suggested, communism's overthrow has been sucked into an ideological discourse justifying dogmatic views of free-market globalization and liberal interventionism in 'terrorist' states: an unprecedented situation of a world order with a single superpower has been created. Whether this development or the successful incorporation of east European states in the European Union will appear as the more significant outcome of the fall of communism in the region remains to be seen.

Notes

Preface

1 P.S. Roeder, 'Precision and the Social Sciences', *Slavic Review* 58 (1999), p. 750.

1 A flawed legacy

1 E. Beneš, 'Postwar Czechoslovakia', *Foreign Affairs* (April 1946), p. 407.
2 T. Aczel and T. Meray, *The Revolt of the Mind* (London, 1960), p. 37.
3 C. Miłosz (ed.), *Postwar Polish Poetry. An Anthology*, 3rd edn (Berkeley and London, 1983), p. 86.
4 W. Gomułka, *Z kart naszej historii* (Warsaw, 1982), p. 192 (article of 22 July 1947).
5 A. Polonsky and B. Drukier (eds), *The Beginnings of Communist Rule in Poland* (London, 1980), p. 314 (speech of 10 October 1944).
6 *Josip Broz Tito. Selected Speeches and Articles 1941–1961* (Zagreb, 1963), p. 75 (speech of September 1946).
7 *Košický vládní program* (Prague, 1984), p. 11.
8 B. Kovrig, *Communism in Hungary: from Kun to Kádár* (Stanford, 1979), p. 184.
9 See the testimony of old Stalinists in T. Torańska (ed.), *Oni. Stalin's Polish Puppets* (London, 1987), pp. 22–3 (Minc); 206–7 (Berman).
10 J. Connelly, 'Students, Workers and Social Change: the Limits of Czech Stalinism', *Slavic Review* 56 (1997), p. 310.
11 G. Paloczi-Horvath, *In Darkest Hungary* (London, 1964), p. 152.
12 S. Kopacsi, *In the Name of the Working Class* (London, 1989), pp. 112–13.

13 P.S. Wandycz, *The Price of Freedom* (London, 1992), p. 247.

14 J. Rothschild, *Return to Diversity. A Political History of East Central Europe Since World War II*, 2nd edn (New York, 1993), p. 122.

15 N. Swain, *The Rise and Fall of Feasible Socialism* (London, 1992), p. 71.

16 M. Pittaway, 'Industrial Workers, Socialist Industrialisation and the State in Hungary, 1948–1958' (Liverpool PhD, 1998), p. 240, citing James C. Scott, *Domination and the Arts of Resistance: Hidden Transcripts* (New Haven and London, 1990).

17 Kopacsi, *In the Name*, p. 72.

18 *Imre Nagy on Communism. In Defence of the New Course* (London, 1957), pp. 43, 46.

19 Z. Mlynář, *Night Frost in Prague* (London, 1980), p. 66.

20 M. Djilas, 'Anatomy of a Moral' in A. Rothenberg (ed.), *The Political Essays of Milovan Djilas* (London, 1959), pp. 145–76.

21 Paloczi-Horvath, *In Darkest Hungary*, p. 159.

22 J. Gunther, *Inside Russia Today* (London, 1958), pp. 525–6.

23 See particularly, L. Kołakowski, *Marxism and Beyond* (London, 1968).

24 R.A. Remington (ed.), *Winter in Prague. Documents on Czechoslovak Communism in Crisis* (London, 1969), p. 98.

25 Mlynář, *Night Frost*, p. 146.

26 See J. Navrátil (chief ed.), *The Prague Spring 1968: a National Security Archive Documents Reader* (Budapest, 1998), partic. pp. 345–56.

27 'Lessons of Prague. A Conversation with Eduard Goldstücker', *Encounter* (August 1971), p. 82.

28 E.P. Thompson, 'An Open Letter to Leszek Kołakowski', *Socialist Register* (1973), pp. 1–100; L. Kołakowski, 'My Correct Views on Everything. A Rejoinder to Edward Thompson's "Open Letter to Leszek Kołakowski"', *Socialist Register* (1974), pp. 1–20.

29 W. Mackiewicz, 'The Transformation of Polish Consciousness', *Polish Perspectives* 22 (1979), p. 24.

30 See, for example, the works of G. Ionescu: *The Break-up of the Soviet Empire in Eastern Europe* (London, 1965); *The Politics of the East European Communist States* (London, 1967).

31 S. Huntington, 'Social and Political Dynamics of One-Party Systems' in S. Huntington and C. Moore (eds), *Authoritarian Politics in Modern Society* (New York and London, 1970), pp. 3–47. On efficiency, S. Huntington, *Political Order in Changing Societies* (New Haven, 1968), p. 1.

32 A. Korbonski, 'Reply', *Slavic Review* 33 (1974), p. 253; see also, A. Korbonski, 'The "Change to Change" in Eastern Europe' in J. Triska and P.M. Cocks (eds), *Political Development in Eastern Europe* (New York and London, 1977), pp. 145–76.

33 P.M. Johnson, 'Modernisation as an Explanation of Political Change in

East European States' in J. Triska and P. Cocks (eds), *Political Development in Eastern Europe* (New York, London, 1977), pp. 30–50 (p. 34).

34 M.E. Fischer, 'Participatory Reforms and Political Development in Romania' in Triska and Cocks, *Political Development*, p. 217.

35 L. Kołakowski, 'Reply', *Slavic Review* 29 (1970), p. 202.

36 G. Konrád and I. Szelényi, *The Intellectuals on the Road to Class Power* (London, 1979).

37 W. Connor, 'Social Change and Stability in Eastern Europe', *Problems of Communism* (November–December 1977), pp. 16–32.

2   The 1980s: a flawed society

1 Y. Glückstein, *Stalin's Satellites in Eastern Europe* (London, 1951), pp. 51–2.

2 Statistics in this chapter are taken largely from B.R. Mitchell (ed.), *International Historical Statistics. Europe 1750–1993* (London, 1998), and the statistical yearbooks published by east European countries.

3 J. Lovenduski and J. Woodall, *Politics and Society in Eastern Europe* (London, 1987), pp. 369–72; H.W. Morton, 'Housing Problems and Policies of Eastern Europe and the Soviet Union', *Studies in Comparative Communism* 12 (1979), pp. 300–21; H.-G. Heinrich, *Hungary. Politics, Economics and Society* (London, 1986), p. 107.

4 Lovenduski and Woodall, *Politics and Society*, p. 84.

5 For these details and references, see R. Okey, 'East European Peasants and National Integration: the Communist Impact' in S. Minamizuka (ed.), *The Transformation of the Systems of East-Central Europe. Rural Societies before and after 1989* (Kecskemét, 1996), pp. 109–24; H. Slabek, 'The Peasants in Polish Society, 1949–70', *Acta Poloniae Historica* 59 (1989), p. 152.

6 J. Krejči, *Social Change and Social Stratification in Post-War Czechoslovakia* (London, 1972), p. 63.

7 S.L. Wolchik, *Czechoslovakia in Transition* (London, 1991), p. 180.

8 V. Kostka, 'Czechoslovakia' in J. Riordan (ed.), *Sport under Communism*, 2nd edn (London, 1981), p. 62.

9 See particularly H. Scott, *Women and Socialism: Experiences from Eastern Europe* (London, 1976); C. Corrin (ed.), *Superwomen and the Double Burden* (London, 1992).

10 J. Szczepański, *Polish Society* (New York, 1970), Ch. 6; Zs. Ferge, *A Society in the Making. Hungarian Social and Societal Policy 1945–75* (London, 1979), pp. 41–2.

11 W. Connor, *Socialism, Politics and Equality. Hierarchy and Change in Eastern Europe and the USSR* (New York, 1979), pp. 289–90, for these examples.

12 D.S. Mason, *Public Opinion and Political Change in Poland, 1980–1982* (Cambridge, 1985), p. 74; H.G. Skilling, *Czechoslovakia's Interrupted Revolution* (Princeton, 1976), p. 450; B. Denitch, *The Legitimation of a Revolution: The Yugoslav Case* (New Haven, 1976), pp. 168, 174.

13 P. Ramet (ed.), *Yugoslavia in the 1980s* (Boulder and London, 1985), pp. 98–9.

14 D. Ost, *Solidarity and the Politics of Anti-Politics. Opposition and Reform in Poland since 1968* (Philadelphia, 1990), Chs 2–4.

15 R. Laba, 'Worker Roots of Solidarity', *Problems of Communism*, July–August (1986), pp. 47–67.

16 Mason, *Public Opinion*, p. 118.

17 Krejči, *Social Change*, p. 104.

18 T. Garton Ash, *The Polish Revolution: Solidarity 1980–1982* (London, 1983), p. 286.

19 L. Tyrmand, 'The Hair-Styles of Miecysław Rakowski', *Survey* 116 (1982), pp. 165–81 (p. 174).

20 Figures in M.C. Kaser (ed.) *The Economic History of Eastern Europe 1919–75*. Vol. 3 (Oxford, 1986), p. 150.

21 A. Zaubermann, 'The East European Economies', *Problems of Communism*, April (1978), pp. 55–70 (p. 56).

22 Krejči, *Social Change*, p. 176.

23 This paragraph is based on Z Fallenbuchl, in D. Kemme (ed.), *Economic Reform in Poland: the Aftermath of Martial Law, 1981–88* (London, 1991), pp. 17–38; M. Myant, *The Czechoslovak Economy 1948–88* (Cambridge, 1989); N. Swain, *Hungary: the Rise and Fall of Feasible Socialism* (London, 1992); H. Lydall, *Yugoslavia in Crisis* (Oxford, 1989); J. Rupnik, *The Other Europe* (London, 1988).

24 E. Noam, *Telecommunications in Europe* (Oxford, 1992), pp. 78, 99, 274–9.

25 I. Szelényi, *Urban Inequalities under State Socialism* (Oxford, 1983).

26 C. Gati, *The Bloc That Failed. Soviet–East European Relations in Transition* (London, 1990), p. 150.

27 G. Konrád and I. Szelényi, *The Intellectuals on the Road to Class Power* (Brighton, 1979); S. Brucan, *Pluralism and Social Conflict. A Social Analysis of the Communist World* (Westport, 1990); S. Brucan, *Social Change in Russia and Eastern Europe* (Westport, 1998), see p. 20 for rural mechanics.

28 J. Szczepański, 'Societal Developments', *Polish Perspectives* 27 (1985), pp. 5–13.

29 I. Szelényi, *Embourgeoisement in Rural Hungary* (London, 1988), pp. 5, 211.

30 Z. Mynař, *Night Frost in Prague* (London, 1980), p. 125.

31 V. Dedijer, *Novi prilozi za biografiju Josipa Broza Tita*. Vol. 2 (1984), p. 581.
32 M. Tatur, 'Catholicism and Modernization in Poland', *Journal of Communist Studies* 7 (1991), pp. 335–49 (pp. 347–8).
33 P. Ramet, *Cross and Commissar* (Bloomington, 1987), p. 99.
34 L. Tőkés, *With God, for the People* (London, 1990), pp. 26–30.
35 P. Matvejević, *Jugoslavenstvo danas* (Zagreb, 1982), p. 13.
36 V. Đuretić, *Saveznici i jugoslovenska ratna drama*, 5th edn (Belgrade, 1992), Foreword to 1st edition and p. 14.

3   The centre cannot hold

1 W. Ullmann, *The United States in Prague, 1945–1948* (Boulder, 1978), p. 22.
2 See, for example, G. Schöpflin and N. Wood (eds), *In Search of Central Europe* (London, 1989); F. Herteich and E. Semler (eds), *Dazwischen: Ostmitteleuropäische Reflexionen* (Frankfurt, 1989).
3 G.R. Chafetz, *Gorbachev, Reform and the Brezhnev Doctrine: Soviet Policy Toward Eastern Europe, 1985–90* (Westport, 1992), pp. 80, 95, 100.
4 M. Checinski, 'Warsaw Pact/CMEA Military–Economic Trends', *Problems of Communism* (March–April 1987), pp. 15–28 (p. 18).
5 C. Gati, *The Bloc That Failed. Soviet–East European Relations in Transition* (London, 1990), p. 119.
6 J. Staniszkis, *Post-Communism: The Emerging Enigma* (Warsaw, 1999), Ch. 7.
7 K. Dawisha, *Eastern Europe, Gorbachev and Reform*, 2nd edn (Cambridge, 1990), p. 88.
8 Institute of the Economics of the World Socialist System, 'East–West Relations and Eastern Europe. The Soviet Perspective', *Problems of Communism* 37: 3–4 (1988), pp. 60–7.
9 A.G.V. Hyde-Price, 'Perestroika or Umgestaltung: East Germany and the Gorbachev Revolution', *Journal of Communist Studies* 5 (1989), pp. 185–210 (p. 188).
10 D. Doder, *Gorbachev. Heretic in the Kremlin* (London, 1990), p. 229.
11 For example, M. Myant, 'Poland – The Permanent Crisis', in R.A. Clarke (ed.), *Poland: The Economy in the 1980s* (London, 1989), pp. 1–28.
12 J. Kornai, *Vision and Reality, Market and State* (New York, 1990), p. 99.
13 Figures in N. Swain, *Hungary: the Rise and Fall of Feasible Socialism* (London, 1992), p. 20.
14 K. Brandys, *Warsaw Diary 1978–81* (London, 1981), p. 164.
15 V. Havel, 'The Power of the Powerless' in V. Havel *et al.*, *The Power of the Powerless* (London, 1985), p. 70.

16 Brandys, *Warsaw Diary*, p. 115.

17 Havel *et al.*, *Power of the Powerless*, p. 42.

18 A. Michnik, *Letters from Prison and Other Essays* (Berkeley, 1987), p. 284.

19 Havel *et al.*, *Power of the Powerless*, p. 65.

20 G. Konrád, *Antipolitics. An Essay* (London, 1984), p. 231.

21 R. Bahro, *The Alternative in Eastern Europe* (London, 1978), pp. 362, 409.

22 Brandys, *Warsaw Diary*, p. 37.

23 Havel, *Power,* pp. 27–39.

24 Konrád, *Antipolitics*, pp. 58–61.

25 P. Kenney, *A Carnival of Revolution. Central Europe 1989* (Princeton, 2002), p.87.

26 M. Haraszti, 'The Beginnings of Civil Society: The Independent Peace Movement and the Danube Movement in Hungary', in V. Tismaneanu (ed.), *In Search of Civil Society. Independent Peace Movements in the Soviet Bloc* (New York, London, 1990), p. 73.

27 M. Fulbrook, *Anatomy of a Dictatorship. Inside the GDR 1949–89* (Oxford, 1995), p. 239.

28 M. Waller, 'The Ecology Issue in Eastern Europe', *Journal of Communist Studies* 5 (1989), pp. 303–28 (p. 317).

29 J. Staniszkis, *The Ontology of Socialism* (Oxford, 1992), p. 154. Staniszkis emphasizes the postmodernist aspect of much late 1980s protest.

30 P. Campeanu, 'Romanian Television. From Image to History', in P. Drummond, R. Paterson and J. Willis (eds), *National Identity and Contemporary Europe. The Television Revolution* (Bury St Edmunds, 1993), pp. 110–16.

31 Staniszkis, *Ontology of Socialism*, pp. 6–12.

32 J. Kornai, *Vision and Reality*, p. 155.

33 A. Dragičević, *Suton socijalizma. Kraj masovnog društva* (Zagreb, 1988).

34 T. Garton Ash, 'The Empire in Decay', *New York Review of Books*, 29 September 1988, pp. 53–60.

35 E. Hankiss, *East European Alternatives* (Oxford, 1990), p. 224. Hankiss offers a detailed account of the variety of views at this time.

36 Ibid., p. 217, for what seemed to be a vicious stalemate in Hungary and Poland in mid-1988. One Hungarian reformer told Garton Ash his country had only a 30 to 40 per cent chance of success: T. Garton Ash, 'Reform or Revolution?' *New York Review of Books*, 27 October 1988, pp. 47–56.

4   The demise of communism: breach and balance sheet

1 D. Ost, *Solidarity and the Politics of Anti-Politics, Opposition and Reform in Poland since 1968* (Philadelphia, 1990), p. 200 (Wałęsa); E. Hankiss, *East European Alternatives* (Oxford, 1990), p. 150 (Kuroń).

2 Ciosek's comments in 'Communism's Negotiated Collapse. Polish Round Table, Ten Years Later. Conference held at the University of Michigan, April 7–10, 1999' in *Negotiating Radical Change: Understanding and Extending the Lessons of the Polish Round Table,* project directed by M.D. Kennedy and B. Porter, http://www// umich.edu//~iinet/PolishRoundTable/negotiatingradicalchange/ panels 2 and 6.

3 Ibid., panels 4 (dog) and 5 (Goethe).

4 For example, C. Lucas, 'Nobles, Bourgeois and the Origins of the French Revolution', *Past and Present* 60 (1973), pp. 84–126.

5 K.Z. Poznanski, *Poland's Protracted Revolution. Internal Change and Economic Growth 1970–1994* (Cambridge, 1996), pp. 215–24.

6 L. Kolarska-Bobińska, 'The Myth of the Market and the Reality of Reform', in S. Gomułka and A. Polonsky (eds), *Polish Paradoxes* (London, 1990), pp. 160–79.

7 I. Pozsgay, 'Life and Politics', reprinted from *The New Hungarian Quarterly* 29 (Winter 1988), pp. 4, 5, 7.

8 R.L. Tőkés, *Hungary's Negotiated Revolution* (Cambridge, 1996), p. 301.

9 As noted by P. Frentzel-Zagorska, 'Civil Society in Poland and Hungary', *Soviet Studies* 42 (1990), pp. 759–77 (p. 775).

10 For example, A. Przeworski, *Democracy and the Market. Political and Economic Reforms in Eastern Europe and Latin America* (Cambridge, 1991).

11 M. Fulbrook, *Anatomy of a Dictatorship. Inside the GDR 1949–89* (Oxford, 1995), p. 238.

12 T. Torańska. *Oni. Stalin's Polish puppets* (London, 1987), pp. 257, 272.

13 J. Szczepański, 'Societal developments', *Polish Perspectives* 27 (1985), pp. 5–13.

14 T. Garton Ash, *In Europe's Name. Germany and a Divided Continent* (London, 1993), p. 120. On this theme see also J. Dumbrell, *American Foreign Policy. Carter to Clinton* (London, 1997), Ch. 6; and M. Bowker, 'Soviet Foreign Policy in the 1980s' in M. Bowker and R. Brown (eds), *From Cold War to Collapse* (Cambridge, 1993), pp. 103–6.

15 Dumbrell, *American Foreign Policy*, p. 114.

16 G. Eyal, I. Szelényi and E. Townsley, *Making Capitalism without Capitalists* (London, 2000), p. 180.

17 J. Kornai, *Vision and Reality, Market and State* (New York, 1990), pp. 166, 143 (1986); p. 215 (1988).

18 J. Kornai, *The Road to a Free Economy* (New York, 1990), p. 58.

19 W. Brus and K. Laski, *From Marx to the Market. Socialism in Search of an Economic System* (Oxford, 1989), partic. Chs 1, 5.

20 P. Kenney, A *Carnival of Revolution. Central Europe 1989* (Princeton, 2002), pp. 33, 163–4.

21 J. Szacki, *Liberalism after Communism* (Budapest, 1995), pp. 121–2, 126–7.

22 Ost, *Solidarity*, p. 166.

5 Autumn 1989

1 K. Dawisha, *Eastern Europe, Gorbachev, and Reform*, 2nd edn (Cambridge, 1990), p. 95.

2 G. Halmai, 'The Protection of Human Rights in Poland and Hungary', in I. Pogány (ed.), *Human Rights in Eastern Europe* (Aldershot, 1995), p. 160.

3 T. Garton Ash, *In Europe's Name. Germany and a Divided Continent* (London, 1993), p 371. For background, H.-H. Hertle, *Der Fall der Mauer. Die unbeabsichtigte Selbstauflösung des SED-Staates*, 2nd edn (Wiesbaden, 1999), pp. 91–109.

4 For a full discussion of the failed decision-making process: Hertl, *Fall der Mauer*, pp. 164–80, 202–40.

5 H. Modrow, *Aufbruch und Ende* (Hamburg, 1991), pp. 10, 118.

6 For this point by a member of the opposition, see E. Neubert, *Geschichte der Opposition in der DDR 1949–1990*, 2nd, extended, edn (Berlin, 1998), p. 845.

7 Neubert, *Geschichte der Opposition*, p. 886.

8 C. Wolf, *Parting from Phantoms. Selected Writings, 1990–94* (Chicago, 1997), p. 10.

9 J.F.N. Bradley, *Czechoslovakia's Velvet Revolution: A Political Analysis* (Boulder, 1992), p. 88.

10 M. Otáhal, *Opozice, moc, společnost 1969–1989* (Prague, 1994), p. 110.

11 B. Wheaton and Z. Kavan, *The Velvet Revolution: Czechoslovakia, 1988–1991* (Boulder, 1992), Ch. 5.

12 H. Schwermer, *The Velvet Revolution. Czechoslovakia, November–December 1989* (Staffordshire Polytechnic, 1990), p. 42.

13 Slogans from Appendix A in Wheaton and Kavan, *Velvet Revolution*, pp. 188–94.

14 Otáhal, *Opozice*, p. 95.

15 For this argument, J. Krapfl, 'The Rhetoric of the Velvet Revolution', paper given at the School of Slavonic Studies, London, 18 November 2001.

16 Wheaton and Kavan, *Velvet Revolution*, p. 102.

17 L. Tőkés, *With God, for the People* (London, 1990), p. 144.

18 D. Deletant, *Ceauşescu and the Securitate. Coercion and Dissent in Romania, 1965–1989* (London, 1995), p. 347.

19 Ibid., pp. 342–67.

20 T. Garton Ash, 'Eastern Europe: The Year of Truth', *New York Review of Books*, 15 February 1990, pp. 17–22.

21 W.R. Roberts, 'A New Status for Eastern Europe', *World Today* (October 1989), pp. 165–6; D. Armour, 'East Germany after Honecker', ibid. (December 1989), p. 203.

22 Fukuyama's journalistic themes later appeared in book form as *The End of History and the Last Man* (New York, 1992).

23 M. Šimečka, *The Restoration of Order. The Normalization of Czechoslovakia, 1969–1976* (London, 1984), p. 150.

24 M. Lötsch, 'From Stagnation to Transformation: the Sociology of the GDR Revolution', in G.-J. Glaessner and I. Wallace (eds), *The German Revolution of 1989. Causes and Consequences* (Oxford, 1992), p. 52. The statement is made of the East German exodus.

25 Lord Macaulay, *The History of England*, edited and abridged by H. Trevor-Roper (London, 1979; this statement first published in 1848), p. 51.

26 L. Kołakowski, 'Amidst Moving Ruins', *Daedalus* (Spring 1992), p. 45.

27 G. Partos, 'Hungarian–Soviet Relations', in A. Pravda (ed.) *The End of the Outer Empire. Soviet–East European Relations in Transition 1985–90* (London, 1992), pp. 120–50 (p. 145).

28 R.L. Garthoff, *The Great Transition. American–Soviet Relations and the End of the Cold War* (Washington, 1994), p. 601 (January); Garton Ash, *In Europe's Name*, p. 124 (June).

29 Garthoff, *Great Transition*, p. 400; J. Dumbrell, *American Foreign Policy. Carter to Clinton* (London, 1997), p. 140.

30 G.R. Chafetz, *Gorbachev, Reform and the Brezhnev Doctrine* (Westport, 1992), p. 118.

31 For example, M. Bowker, 'Soviet Foreign Policy in the 1980s', in M. Bowker and R. Brown (eds), *From Cold War to Collapse* (Cambridge, 1993), p. 108.

32 For a convenient insight into these debates, see P.C. Schmitter and T.L. Karl, 'The Conceptual Travels of Transitologists and Consolidologists. How Far to the East Should They Attempt to Go?' in *Slavic Review 53* (1994), pp. 173–85; V. Bunce, 'Should Transitologists Be Grounded?' *Slavic Review 54* (1995), pp. 111–27; and their further exchange in ibid., pp. 965–87.

6   System change: the liberal moment in east-central Europe

1 R. Kilroy-Silk, 'Why History will say Gorbachev was a Fool', *The Times*, 9 February 1990.
2 O. Figes, *Guardian*, 17 February 1990.
3 J. Eyal, 'Giving up Illusions and Unravelling Ties', in A. Pravda (ed.) *The End of the Outer Empire. Soviet–East European Relations in Transition, 1985–1990* (London, 1992), pp. 205–31.
4 C.G.A. Bryant, 'Economic Utopianism and Sociological Realism. Strategies for Transformation in East-Central Europe', in C.G.A. Bryant and E. Mokrzycki (eds), *The New Great Transformation? Change and Continuity in East-Central Europe* (London, 1994), p. 71. The figure for Britain and the Low Countries was 88–90 per cent.
5 J. Sachs, *Poland's Jump to the Market Economy* (Cambridge, Mass., 1994), p. 2; based on 1991 lectures.
6 V. Havel, 'Politics and Conscience', in J. Vladislav (ed.) *Václav Havel. Living in Truth* (London, 1987), pp. 141–6.
7 J. Kornai, *The Road to a Free Economy* (New York, 1990), pp. 58, 71.
8 R. Dahrendorf, *Reflections on the Revolution in Europe* (London, 1990), pp. 54–7.
9 J. Szacki, *Liberalism after Communism* (Budapest, London, 1995), p. 151
10 For example, J. Křen, *Bílá místa v našich dějinách?* (Prague, 1990), pp. 95, 98.
11 B. Lomax, 'Obstacles to the Development of Democratic Politics', *Journal of Communist Studies* 10: 3 (Sept. 1994), pp. 81–100 (p. 82).
12 T.A. Bayliss, 'Presidents versus Prime Ministers: Shaping Executive Authority in Eastern Europe', *World Politics* 48 (1995), pp. 297–323 (p. 313).
13 See A. Körösényi, *Government and Politics in Hungary* (Budapest, 1999), partic. ch. 13 for this theme.
14 See notes 5 and 7.
15 'No Third Way Out. Creating a Capitalist Czechoslovakia. Václav Klaus interview by John H. Fund', Reasononline, June 1990, http://reason.com/klausint.shtml (April 2002).
16 Kornai, *Road to a Free Economy*, p. 101.
17 J. Kornai, 'Transformational Recession: The Example of Hungary', in C.T. Saunders (ed.), *Eastern Europe in Crisis and the Way Out* (Basingstoke, 1995), pp. 29–77 (p. 30).
18 H. Aage, 'Transition and Transplantation of Economic Systems', in A. Lorentzen and M. Rostgard (eds), *The Aftermath of 'Real Existing Socialism' in Eastern Europe*. Vol. 2 (London, 1997), p. 23.
19 J.R. Wedel, *Collision and Collusion. The Strange Case of Western Aid to Eastern Europe, 1989–1998* (London, 1998), p. 58.

20 P.A. Messerlin, 'Trade Relations of the Eastern European Countries', in Saunders, *Eastern Europe in Crisis*, pp. 201–28; F. Levčik, 'Economic Transformation in the East', in ibid, pp. 13–28 (p. 22 – mockery).

21 J.M. van Brabant, *Industrial Policy in Eastern Europe* (London, 1993), particularly Chs 6–7.

22 For example, S. Zecchini, 'Transition Approaches in Retrospect', in S. Zecchini (ed.), *Lessons from the Economic Transition. Central and Eastern Europe in the 1990s* (London, 1997), pp. 1–34.

23 *Privatization in the Transition Process: Recent Experiences in Eastern Europe* (United Nations, Geneva, 1994), pp. 99, 371.

24 F.L. Pryor, *A Guidebook to the Comparative Study of Economic Systems*, cited in Lorentzen and Rostgard, *Aftermath of 'Real Existing Socialism'*, p. 21.

25 Dahrendorf, *Reflections*, p. 20.

26 Sachs, *Poland's Jump*, p. 10.

27 D. Gros and A. Steinherr, *Winds of Change. Economic Transition in Central and Eastern Europe* (London, 1995), p. 86.

28 Levčik, 'Economic Transformation', in Saunders (ed.), *Eastern Europe in Crisis*, p. 26.

29 M. Ksierzopolski, 'The Prospects for Social Policy Development in Poland', in B. Deacon (ed.), *Social Policy, Social Justice and Citizenship in Eastern Europe* (Avebury, 1992), p. 235; S. Ringen, 'How People Live in Eastern Europe', in S. Ringer and C. Wallace (eds), *Societies in Transition. East-Central Europe Today.* Vol. 1 (Avebury, 1994), p. 7.

30 F. Millard, 'Developments in Polish Health Care', in Ringen and Wallace (eds), *Societies in Transition*, pp. 73–89.

31 Zs. Ferge, 'Social Security Systems in the New Democracies of Central and Eastern Europe', in G.A. Cornia and S. Sipos (eds), *Children and the Transition to the Market Economy* (Aldershot, 1991), p. 83.

32 Zs. Szeman, 'New Policy for the Old?', in Deacon (ed.), *Social Policy*, p. 154.

33 K. Müller, *The Political Economy of Pension Reform in Central-Eastern Europe* (Cheltenham, 1999), for these comparisons.

34 Cornia and Sipos (eds), *Children and the Transition*, p. 221.

35 R. Hettlage and K. Lenz, *Deutschland nach der Wende* (Munich, 1995), pp. 53–9. For a vivid case study, see T. Garton Ash, *The File: a Personal History* (London, 1997).

36 M. Łoś and A. Zybertowicz, *Privatizing the Police-state: The Case of Poland* (London, 2000), pp. 145–53.

37 See E. Mokrzycki, 'The Legacy of Real Socialism and Western Democracy' for this argument, in *Studies in Comparative Communism* 24 (1991), pp. 211–17.

38 See S. Zbierski-Salamek, 'Responses to Postsocialist Reforms' in M. Burawoy and K. Verdery (eds), *Uncertain Transition: Ethnographies of*

Change in the Postsocialist World (London, 1999), pp. 189–222, for the reversal of favourable late-communist trends for peasants under post-1989 circumstances.

39 I. Varga, 'Churches, Politics, and Society in Postcommunist East Central Europe', in W.H. Swatos Jnr, *Politics and Religion in Central and Eastern Europe* (Westport, 1994), p. 108.

7 Balkan vicissitudes

1 M. Rady, *Romania in Turmoil* (London, 1992), pp. 137, 165.

2 T. Gallagher, *Romania after Ceauşescu: the Politics of Intolerance* (Edinburgh, 1995), p. 88.

3 *Daily Telegraph*, 27 December 1989, cited in Rady, *Romania in Turmoil*, p. 134.

4 For example, D. Grindea, *Shock Therapy and Privatization. An Analysis of Romania's Economic Reform* (New York, 1997), pp. 60–79.

5 BBC, Summary of World Broadcasts (SWB), 63rd series. Part 2, Central Europe, the Balkans, 17 December 1994.

6 All figures from D. Grindea, *Shock Therapy and Privatization. An Analysis of Romania's Economic Reform* (New York, 1997), pp. 108, 111, 116.

7 SWB, 63rd series. Part 2, 6 October 1994.

8 Rady, *Romania*, p. 194.

9 G. Fotev, in J. Coenen-Huther (ed.), *Bulgaria at the Crossroads* (New York, 1996), p. 29.

10 A.C. Janos, 'Continuity and Change in Eastern Europe', *East European Politics and Societies*, 8, 1994, pp. 3–4, cited in Coenen-Huther (ed.), *Bulgaria*, p. 116.

11 J.D. Bell (ed.), *Bulgaria in Transition* (Boulder, Colorado, 1998), p. 45.

12 Coenen-Huther (ed.), *Bulgaria*, p. 92

13 C.A. Moser, *Theory and History of the Bulgarian Transition* (Sofia, 1994), pp. 197, 167, 137.

14 G.W. Creed, 'The Deconstruction of Socialism in Bulgaria', in M. Burawoy and K. Verdery (eds), *Uncertain Transition: Ethnographies of Change in the Postsocialist World* (London, New York, 1999), pp. 223–44.

15 M. Keluya, 'The Transformation of Agriculture', in Coenen-Huther (ed.), *Bulgaria*, p. 243.

16 Bell (ed.), *Bulgaria in Transition*, p. 317.

17 N. Genov (ed.), *Sociology in a Society in Transition* (Sofia, 1994), pp. 113–14.

18 O. Sjöberg and M.L.Wygan (eds), *Economic Change in the Balkan States: Albania, Bulgaria, Romania and Yugoslavia* (London, 1991), p. 143.

19 M. Bléjer *et al.*, *Albania: From Isolation Toward Reform*. Occasional paper: IMF 98 (Washington, 1992), p. 55.

20 M. Vickers and J. Pettifor, *Albania. From Anarchy to a Balkan Identity* (London, 1997), pp. 268, 269.

21 Ibid., p. 4.

22 M. Omladinović, 'The Ruling Party', in N. Popov (ed.), *The Road to War in Serbia* (Budapest, 1996), p. 429; R. Thomas, *Serbia under Milošević* (London, 1999), p. 77.

23 Popov (ed.), *Road to War*, p. 117.

24 L.J. Cohen, *Broken Bonds. The Disintegration of Yugoslavia* (Boulder, 1993), p. 82.

25 See R. Okey, 'The Legacy of Massacre: The "Jasenovac Myth" and the Breakdown of Communist Yugoslavia', in M. Levene and P. Roberts (eds), *The Massacre in History* (Oxford, 1999), pp. 263–83, partic. 271–6.

26 For these themes: B. Magaš, *The Destruction of Yugoslavia. Tracking the Break-Up, 1980–1992* (London, 1993); S.P. Ramet, 'Slovenia's Road to Democracy', *Europe–Asia Studies* 45 (1993), pp. 869–86; L.C. Cohen, *Broken Bonds: the Disintegration of Yugoslavia* (Boulder, 1993).

27 The most useful of many studies of the Bosnian crisis is S. Burg and P. Shoup, *The War in Bosnia-Herzegovina* (New York, 1999).

28 M. Uvalić, *Privatization in Disintegrating East European States: the Case of Former Yugoslavia*, EUI Working Paper. RSC No. 1994/11 (Florence, 1994), p. 21.

29 Thomas, *Serbia under Milošević*, p. 165.

30 R.M. Hayden, 'Muslims as "Others" in Serbian and Croatian Politics', in J.L. Halpern and D.A. Kideckel (eds), *Neighbors at War: Anthropological Perspectives on Yugoslav Ethnicity, Culture and History* (Pennsylvania State U.P., 2000), p. 118.

31 J.D. Bell, 'Bulgaria's Search for Security', in Bell (ed.), *Bulgaria in Transition*, p. 312.

32 R. Daskalov, 'Democracy Born in Pain. Bulgarian Politics, 1989–97', in Bell (ed.), *Bulgaria in Transition*, p. 9.

33 P.S. Roeder, 'The Revolutions of 1989: Precision and the Social Sciences', *Slavic Review* 58 (1999), p. 750. See also the articles by Valerie Bunce and M. Steven Fish in the 'Special Issue' entitled 'Ten Years after 1989: What Have We Learned' in this number. As an example of the kind of generalization sought, Bunce claimed that success in democratization correlated best with the victory of non-communists in the first post-communist elections.

34 S. Huntington, *The Clash of Civilizations and the Remaking of World Order* (New York, 1996).

35 C. Sudetic, *Blood and Vengeance: One Family's Story of the War in*

Bosnia (New York and London, 1998). Mart Bax's article on how inter-clan slaughter in the pilgrimage village of Medjugorje in 1992 related to earlier insecurities and ethnic tensions is also illuminating for the 'little wars' that accompanied the main Bosnian conflicts: 'Barbarization in a Bosnian Pilgrimage Centre', in Halpern and Kideckel (eds), *Neighbors at War*, pp. 187–202.

36 E. Dunn, '"Slick Salesmen and Simple People." Negotiated Capitalism in a Privatized Polish Firm', in Burawoy and Verdery (eds), *Uncertain Transition*, pp. 125–50.

8   The internal dimension: an end to transition?

1 *The Economist*, 16 December 2000, p. 52.
2 Ibid., 21 April 2001, p. 54.
3 Ibid., 29 March 1997, p. 54.
4 T. Garton Ash, 'Conclusions', in S. Antohi and V. Tismaneanu (eds), *Between Past and Future. The Revolutions of 1989 and their Aftermath* (Budapest, 2000), p. 399.
5 G. Eyal, I. Szelényi and E. Townsley, *Making Capitalism without Capitalists. Class Formation and Elite Struggles in Post-Communist Eastern Europe* (London, 2000), p. 164.
6 Eyal *et al.*, *Capitalism without Capitalists*, pp. 154–5.
7 K.Z. Poznanski, 'The Morals of Transition', in Antohi and Tismaneanu (eds), *Between Past and Future*, p. 235.
8 T. Kolosi, *A terhes babapiskóta* (Budapest 2000), pp. 108, 124
9 Ibid., pp. 85, 102–3.
10 *The Financial Times*, 28 May 1995.
11 L. Chelcea, *The Pragmatics of Post-socialist Society. Magic Practices: Transition and Popular Culture in Romania*, paper given at the School of Slavonic Studies, London, 18 November 2001.
12 See J.S. Jaquette and S.L. Wolchik (eds), *Women and Democracy in Latin America and Central and Eastern Europe* (Baltimore, 1998); M. Rueschemeyer (ed.), *Women in the Politics of Postcommunist Eastern Europe* (New York, 1994).
13 Z. Barany, *The East European Gypsies, Regime Change, Marginality and Ethnopolitics* (Cambridge 2002), pp. 167, 176, 179.
14 *The Economist*, 16 April 1994: 'Survey on Poland', p. 22.
15 J. Luxmore, 'Czech Monasteries Struggle', *Christianity Today*, 5 October 2000, http://www.christianitytoday.com/ct/2000/119/36/0.html.
16 V. Tismaneanu, 'Fighting for the Public Sphere: Democratic Intellectuals under Postcommunism', in Antohi and Tismaneanu (eds), *Between Past and Future*, pp. 154–5.
17 *The Economist*, 16 February 2001, p. 59.
18 M. Kemny, 'Between Tradition and Politics: Intellectuals after Commu-

nism', in A. Bozóki (ed.), *Intellectuals and Politics in Central Europe* (Budapest, 1999), pp. 151–66 (pp. 160–1).

19 *The Economist*, 20 February 1999, p. 43.

20 V. Havel, *Summer Meditations on Politics, Morality and Civility in a Time of Transition* (London, 1992), pp. 2–3.

21 A. Michnik, 'Independence Reborn and the Demons of the Velvet Revolution', in Antohi and Tismaneanu (eds), *Between Past and Future*, pp. 88–9.

22 M. Haraszti, 'The Handshake Tradition: A Decade of Consensus Politics Bears Liberal Fruit in Hungary – But What Next?', in Antohi and Tismaneanu (eds), *Between Past and Future*, pp. 272–9.

23 This is the central theme of G. Schöpflin, *Nation, Identity, Power. The New Politics of Europe* (London, 2000).

24 V. Tismaneanu, *Discomforts of Victory: Democracy, Liberal Values, and Nationalism in Post-Communist Europe*. EUI Working Paper. RSC No. 2002/4 (Fiesole, 2002), pp. 10, 23.

9   1989 in the international context

1 F. Fukuyama, *The End of History and the Last Man* (New York, 1992). But Fukuyama's controversial views first hit the headlines through an article on this theme in the autumn of 1989.

2 A. Brown, *The Gorbachev Factor* (Oxford, 1997), p. 272.

3 A view recorded in R. Latter, *European Security and Defence* (Wilton Park Paper, no. 90: HMSO, 1994), p. 21. Latter's contributions to the Wilton Park Papers series, nos 24, 31, 77, 90, 94, 98 (HMSO, 1990–95) underlie much of this paragraph.

4 S. Burg and P. Shoup, *The War in Bosnia-Herzegovina* (New York, 1999), is the most rounded of many accounts. For other views, B. Simms, *Unfinest Hour. Britain and the Destruction of Bosnia* (London, 2002); D. Owen, *Balkan Odyssey* (London, 1995).

5 P. Allott, 'The New International Law', in P. Allott *et al.*, *Theory and International Law: An Introduction* (London, 1991), p. 116, cited in S. Terrett, *The Dissolution of Yugoslavia and the Badinter Arbitration Commission* (Aldershot, 2000), p. 11.

6 A. Mayhew, *Recreating Europe. The European Union's Policy towards Central and Eastern Europe* (Cambridge, 1998), pp. 15–16.

7 M.J. Baun, *A Wider Europe. The Principles and Politics of European Union Enlargement* (New York, 2000), p. 145.

8 *The Economist*, 16 June 2001, pp. 89–90.

9 P. Blurtan, *The Chastening. Inside the the Crisis that Rocked the Global Financial System and Humbled the IMF* (New York, 2001), p. 27.

10 *The Economist*, 28 October 2000, p. 48.

11 *The Economist*, 12 May 2001, p. 32.

12 Baun, *Wider Europe*, p. 229.

13 T. Judt, 'Nineteen Eighty-Nine, The End of *Which* European Era?' *Daedalus* 123: 3 (Summer 1994), pp. 1–19 (p. 10).

14 Mayhew, *Recreating Europe*, p. 203.

15 W. Kymlicka, 'Western Political Theory and Ethnic Relations in Eastern Europe' and 'Reply and Conclusion', in W. Kymlicka and M. Opalski (eds), *Can Liberal Pluralism be Exported?* (Oxford, 2001), pp. 13–105 and 347–95.

16 S. Drakulić, Café Europa. *Life after Communism* (London, 1996), pp. 37, 21 for the quotations.

17 V. Vitaliev, *Borders Up! Eastern Europe Through the Bottom of a Glass* (London, 1999), p. 265.

18 Simms, *Unfinest Hour*. Thus Simms accuses British policy of 'reduc[ing] the attraction of the integrationist Bosnian ideal to potentially loyal Croats, and Serbs for that matter' (p. 80). But once the Yugoslav integrationist ideal had failed, most Bosnian Croats' and Serbs' loyalty wholly predictably, however regrettably, reverted to the respective national ideas which had already matured among them by 1914, rather than to a Bosnian state which had not existed since incomparably different medieval circumstances.

19 D. Chandler, *Faking Democracy after Dayton*, 2nd edn (London, 2000).

20 O. Bauer, *Die Nationalitätenfrage und die Sozialdemokratie* (Vienna, 1907).

21 M. Kaldor, 'European Institutions, Nation-States and Nationalism', in D. Archibugi and D. Held (eds), *Cosmopolitan Democracy. An Agenda for a New World Order* (London, 1995), pp. 68–95.

Bibliography

This bibliography does not necessarily contain all items mentioned in references, particularly where works in east European languages are concerned. Internet articles are not included below. However, a valuable source of material on the crises of 1956 (Hungary and Poland), 1968 (Czechoslovakia) and 1980–81 (Poland) can be found on the Cold War International History Project website (http://wwics.si.edu).

Aczel, T. and Meray, T., *The Revolt of the Mind* (London, 1960).

Akhavan, P. (ed.), *Yugoslavia: the Former and Future. Reflections by Scholars from the Region* (Geneva, 1995).

Antohi, S. and Tismaneanu, V. (eds), *Between Past and Future. The Revolutions of 1989 and their Aftermath* (Budapest, 2000).

Archibugi, D. and Held, D. (eds), *Cosmopolitan Democracy. An Agenda for a New World Order* (London, 1995).

Ascherson, N., *The Polish August* (London, 1981).

Azulović, B., *Heavenly Serbia. From Myth to Genocide* (London, 1999).

Babić, A., 'The Emergence of Pluralism in Slovenia', *Communist and Post-Communist Studies* 26 (1993), pp. 367–86.

Bacon, K.G., 'The Prospects for Democracy in Serbia and Croatia', *East European Quarterly* 29 (1995), pp. 509–26.

Bahro, R., *The Alternative in Eastern Europe* (London, 1978).

Barany, Z., *The East European Gypsies. Regime Change, Marginality, and Ethnopolitics* (Cambridge, 2002).

Baun, M.J., *A Wider Europe. The Principles and Politics of European Union Enlargement* (New York, 2000).

Bayliss, T.A., 'Presidents versus Prime Ministers: Shaping Executive Authority in Eastern Europe', *World Politics* 48 (1995), pp. 297–323.

Behr, E., *Kiss the Hand You Cannot Bite. The Rise and Fall of the Ceaușescus* (London, 1992).

Bell, J.D. (ed.), *Bulgaria in Transition* (Boulder, Colorado, 1998).

Berend, I., *Central and Eastern Europe, 1944–1993* (Cambridge, 1996).

Bideleux, R. and Jeffries, I., *A History of Eastern Europe* (London, 1998).

Blanchard, O., *The Economics of Post-Communist Transition* (Oxford, 1998).

Blanchard, O. *et al.*, *Post-Communist Reform. Pain and Progress* (Cambridge, Mass., 1993).

Bléjer, M., *et al.*, *Albania: From Isolation toward Reform*. Occasional paper: IMF 98 (Washington, 1992).

Blurtan, P., *The Chastening. Inside the the Crisis that Rocked the Global Financial System and Humbled the IMF* (New York, 2001).

Bodnár, J., 'Assembling the Square: Social Transformation in the Public Space and the Broken Mirage of the Second Economy in Postsocialist Budapest', *Slavic Review* 57 (1998), pp. 489–515.

Bowker, M. and Brown, R. (eds), *From Cold War to Collapse* (Cambridge, 1993).

Bradley, J.F.N., *Czechoslovakia's Velvet Revolution: A Political Analysis* (Boulder, 1992).

Brandys, K., *Warsaw Diary 1978–81* (London, 1981).

Broekmeyer, M. (ed.), *Yugoslav Workers' Self-Management* (Dordrecht, 1970).

Brown, A., *The Gorbachev Factor* (Oxford, 1997).

Brown, J.F., *Eastern Europe and Communist Rule* (Durham and London, 1988).

Brown, J.F., *Hopes and Shadows. Eastern Europe after Communism* (London, 1994).

Brucan, S., *Pluralism and Social Conflict. A Social Analysis of the Communist World* (Westport, 1990).

Brucan, S., *Social Change in Russia and Eastern Europe* (Westport, 1998).

Brus, W., *The Economics and Politics of Socialism. Collected Essays* (London, 1973).

Brus, W. and Laski, K., *From Marx to the Market. Socialism in Search of an Economic System* (Oxford, 1989).

Brzezinski, Z., *The Soviet Bloc. Unity and Conflict* (Harvard, 1967).

Bunce, V., 'Should Transitologists Be Grounded?', *Slavic Review* 54 (1995), pp. 111–27.

Bunce, V., 'The Political Economy of Postsocialism', *Slavic Review* 58 (1999), pp. 756–93.

Burawoy, M. and Verdery, K. (eds), *Uncertain Transition: Ethnographies of Change in the Postsocialist World* (Lanham, Oxford, 1999).

Burg, S.L., *Conflict and Cohesion in Socialist Yugoslavia. Political Decision Making since 1966* (Princeton, 1983).

Burg, S.L. and Shoup, P., *The War in Bosnia-Herzegovina* (New York, 1999).

Bush, G., *All the Best. My Life in Letters and Other Writings* (New York, 1999).

Chafetz, G.R. *Gorbachev, Reform and the Brezhnev Doctrine: Soviet Policy Toward Eastern Europe, 1985–90* (Westport, 1992).

Chandler, D., *Faking Democracy after Dayton*, 2nd edn (London, 2000).

Checinski, M., 'Warsaw Pact/CMEA Military-Economic Trends', *Problems of Communism* (March–April 1987), pp. 15–28.

Clarke, R.A. (ed.), *Poland: The Economy in the 1980s* (London, 1989).

Coenen-Huther, J. (ed.), *Bulgaria at the Crossroads* (New York, 1996).

Cohen, L.J., *Broken Bonds. The Disintegration of Yugoslavia* (Boulder, 1993).

Connelly, J., 'Students, Workers and Social Change: the Limits of Czech Stalinism', *Slavic Review* 56 (1997), pp. 307–35.

Connor, W.D., 'Social Change and Stability in Eastern Europe', *Problems of Communism* (November–December 1977), pp. 16–32.

Connor, W.D., *Socialism, Politics and Equality. Hierarchy and Change in Eastern Europe and the USSR* (New York, 1979).

Connor, W.D., 'Dissent in Eastern Europe – A New Coalition?', *Problems of Communism* 29 (January–February 1982), pp. 1–17.

Connor, W.D., *Socialism's Dilemmas: State and Society in the Soviet Bloc* (New York, 1988).

Cornia, G.A. and Sipos, S. (eds), *Children and the Transition to the Market Economy* (Aldershot, 1991).

Corrin, C. (ed.), *Superwomen and the Double Burden* (London, 1992).

Crampton, R., *Eastern Europe in the Twentieth Century – and After* (London, 1997).

Creed, G.W., 'The Politics of Agriculture. Identity and Socialist Sentiment in Bulgaria', *Slavic Review* 54 (1995), pp. 843–68.

Curry, J.L. (ed.), *Poland's Permanent Revolution* (New York, 1996).

Dahrendorf, R., *Reflections on the Revolution in Europe* (London, 1990).

Dawisha, K., *Eastern Europe, Gorbachev and Reform*, 2nd edn (Cambridge, 1990).

Dawisha, K. and Hanson, P., *Soviet–East European Dilemmas. Coercion, Competition and Consent* (London, 1981).

Dawisha, K. and Valdez, J., 'Socialist Internationalism in Eastern Europe', *Problems of Communism* (March–April 1987), pp. 1–14.

De Palma, G. 'Legitimacy from the Top to Civil Society: Politico-Cultural Change in Eastern Europe', *World Politics* 44 (1991), pp. 49–80.

Deacon, B. (ed.), *Social Policy, Social Justice and Citizenship in Eastern Europe* (Avebury, 1992).

Deacon, B. (ed.), *The New Eastern Europe. Social Policies, Past, Present and Future* (London, 1992).

Dedijer, V., *Novi prilozi za biografiju Josipa Broza Tita*. Vol. 2 (1984).

Deletant, D., 'Myth-Making and the Romanian Revolution', *Slavonic and East European Review* 72 (1994), pp. 483–91.

Deletant, D., *Ceauşescu and the 'Securitate'. Coercion and Dissent in Romania, 1965–1989* (London, 1995).

Denitch, B., 'Sociology in Eastern Europe. Trends and Prospects', *Slavic Review* 30 (1971), pp. 317–39.

Denitch, B., *The Legitimation of a Revolution: The Yugoslav Case* (New Haven, 1976).

Djilas, M., *The New Class* (London, 1957).

Djilas, M., *Anatomy of a Moral. The Political Essays of Milovan Djilas* (London, 1959).

Doder, D., *The Yugoslavs* (London, 1979).

Doder, D., *Gorbachev. Heretic in the Kremlin* (London, 1990).

Dragičević, A., *Suton socijalizma. Kraj masovnog društva* (Zagreb, 1988).

Drakulić, S., *Café Europa. Life after Communism* (London, 1996).

Drummond, P., Paterson, R. and Willis, J. (eds), *National Identity and Contemporary Europe. The Television Revolution* (Bury St Edmunds, 1993).

Dumbrell, J., *American Foreign Policy. Carter to Clinton* (London, 1997).

Earle, J.S. and Sapatoru, D., *Privatization in a Hypercentralized Economy: the Case of Romania*. Working paper no. 15, Centre for Economic Reconstruction, Faculty of Social Studies, Charles University of Prague (Prague, 1992).

East, D., *Revolutions in Eastern Europe* (London, 1992).

Eyal, G., Szelényi, I. and Townsley, E., *Making Capitalism without Capitalists* (London, 2000).

Falk, R., *On Humane Governance. Toward a New Global Politics* (London, 1995).

Fejtö, F., *History of the People's Democracies* (London, 1971).

Ferge, Z., *A Society in the Making. Hungarian Social and Societal Policy 1945–75* (London, 1979).

Fischer, M.E., *Nicolae Ceauşescu. A Study in Political Leadership* (Boulder, 1989).

Fischer-Galati, S., *Twentieth-Century Rumania* (New York, 1970).

Frankland, M., *The Patriots' Revolution. How East Europe Won its Freedom* (London, 1990).

French, R.A. and Hamilton, F.E. Ian (eds), *The Socialist City. Spatial Structure and Urban Planning* (Toronto, 1979).

Frentzel-Zagorska, J. and Zagorski, K., 'Polish Public Opinion on Privatisation and State Intervention', *Europe–Asia Studies* 45 (1993), pp. 705–28.

Frentzel-Zagorska, J. 'Civil Society in Poland and Hungary', *Soviet Studies* 42 (1990), pp. 759–77.

Fukuyama, F., *The End of History and the Last Man* (New York, 1992).

Fulbrook, M., *Anatomy of a Dictatorship. Inside the GDR 1949–89* (Oxford, 1995).

Gallagher, T., *Romania after Ceauşescu: the Politics of Intolerance* (Edinburgh, 1995).

Garthoff, R.L., *The Great Transition. American–Soviet Relations and the End of the Cold War* (Washington, 1994).

Garton Ash, T., *The Polish Revolution: Solidarity 1980–1982* (London, 1983).

Garton Ash, T., *The Uses of Adversity: Essays on the Fate of Central Europe* (Cambridge, 1989).

Garton Ash, T., *We, the People: the Revolution of 1989* (London, 1990).

Garton Ash, T., *In Europe's Name. Germany and a Divided Continent* (London, 1993).

Garton Ash, T., *The File: a Personal History* (London, 1997).

Garton Ash, T., *History of the Present: Essays, Sketches and Despatches from Europe in the 1990s* (London, 2000).

Gati, C., 'Imre Nagy and Moscow, 1953–56', *Problems of Communism* 3 (1986).

Gati, C., *The Bloc That Failed. Soviet–East European Relations in Transition* (London, 1990).

Gella, A., 'The Fate of Eastern Europe under Marxism', *Slavic Review* 29 (1970), pp. 187–202.

Genov, N. (ed.), *Sociology in a Society in Transition* (Sofia, 1994).

Gilberg, T., *Nationalism and Communism in Romnania. The Rise and Fall of Ceauşescu's Personal Dictatorship* (Boulder, 1990).

Glaessner, G.-J. and Wallace, I. (eds), *The German Revolution of 1989. Causes and Consequences* (Oxford, 1992).

Glenny, M., *The Rebirth of History. Eastern Europe in the Age of Democracy* (London, 1990).

Glenny, M., *The Fall of Yugoslavia: the Third Balkan War* (London, 1992).

Gluckstein, Y., *Stalin's Satellites in Eastern Europe* (London, 1951).

Golan, B., *Reform Rule in Czechoslovakia. The Dubček Era 1968–1969* (Cambridge, 1971).

Golan, G., *The Czechoslovak Reform Movement. Communism in Crisis, 1962–68* (Cambridge, 1971).

Gomułka, S. and Polonsky, A. (eds), *Polish Paradoxes* (London, 1990).

Gow, J., *Legitimacy and the Military. The Yugoslav Case* (London, 1992).

Gow, J, *Triumph of the Lack of Will. International Diplomacy and the Yugoslav War* (London, 1997).

Gow, J., *The Serbian Project and its Adversaries. A Strategy of War Crimes* (London, 2003).

Graham, L.S. and Ciechocińska, M. (eds), *The Polish Dilemma. Views from Within* (Boulder, 1987).

Grindea, D., *Shock Therapy and Privatization. An Analysis of Romania's Economic Reform* (New York, 1997).

Gros, D, and Steinherr, A., *Winds of Change. Economic Transition in Central and Eastern Europe* (London, 1995).

Gruenwald, O., 'Yugoslav Camp Literature', *Slavic Review* 46 (1987), pp. 513–28.

Halpern, J.L. and Kideckel, D.A. (eds), *Neighbors at War: Anthropological Perspectives on Yugoslav Ethnicity, Culture and History* (Pennsylvania State U.P., 2000).

Hankiss, E., *East European Alternatives*, (Oxford, 1990).

Hann, C.M., Postsocialist Nationalism: Rediscovering the Past in Southeast Poland', *Slavic Review* 57 (1998), pp. 840–63.

Hann, C.M. (ed.), Special Issue on Market Economy and Civil Society in Hungary, *Journal of Communist Studies* 6: 2 (June 1990).

Havel, V., *Summer Meditations on Politics, Morality and Civility in a Time of Transition* (London, 1992).

Havel, V. et al., *The Power of the Powerless* (London, 1985).

Hawkes, N. (ed.), *Tearing Down the Curtain. The People's Revolution in Eastern Europe by a Team from 'The Observer'* (London, 1990).

Hayden, R.M., 'Nationalism in the Formerly Yugoslav Republics', *Slavic Review* 54 (1992), pp. 654–73.

Hayden, R.M., 'Muslims as "Others" in Serbian and Croatian Politics', in J.L. Halpern and D.A. Kideckel (eds), *Neighbors at War: Anthropological Perspectives on Yugoslav Ethnicity, Culture and History* (Pennsylvania State U.P., 2000).

Heinrich, H.-G. *Hungary. Politics, Economics and Society* (London, 1986).

Heller, A., *The Theory of Need in Marx* (London, 1974).

Hersh, J. and Schmidt, J.D., *The Aftermath of 'Real Existing Socialism' in Eastern Europe. Vol. 1. Between Western Europe and East Asia* (London, 1996).

Herteich, F. and Semler, E. (eds), *Dazwischen: Ostmitteleuropäische Reflexionen* (Frankfurt, 1989).

Hertle, H.-H., *Der Fall der Mauer. Die unbeabsichtigte Selbstauflösung des SED-Staates*, 2nd edn (Wiesbaden, 1999).

Hettlage, R. and Lenz, K., *Deutschland nach der Wende* (Munich, 1995).

Huntington, S., 'Social and Political Dynamics of One-Party Systems', in S. Huntington and C. Moore (eds), *Authoritarian Politics in Modern Society* (New York, London, 1970), pp. 3–47.

Huntington, S., *The Third Wave: Democratization in the Late Twentieth Century* (Norma, Okla.; London, 1991).

Huntington, S., *The Clash of Civilizations and the Remaking of World Order* (New York, 1996).

Hyde-Price, A.G.V. 'Perestroika or Umgestaltung: East Germany and the Gorbachev Revolution', *Journal of Communist Studies* 5 (1989).

Institute of the Economics of the World Socialist System, 'East–West Relations and Eastern Europe. The Soviet Perspective', *Problems of Communism* 37: 3–4 (1988), pp. 60–7.

Ionescu, G., *The Break-up of the Soviet Empire in Eastern Europe* (London, 1965).

Ionescu, G., *The Politics of the East European Communist States* (London, 1967).

Jaquette, J.S. and Wolchik, S.L. (eds), *Women and Democracy in Latin America and Central and Eastern Europe* (Baltimore, 1998).

Judah, T., *Kosovo. War and Revenge* (New York, 2000).

Judt, T., 'Nineteen Eighty-Nine. The End of *Which* European Era?', *Daedalus* 123 (Summer 1994), pp. 1–19.

Kaplan, R.B., *Balkan Ghosts: a Journey Through History* (New York, 1993).

Kaser, M.C. (ed.) *The Economic History of Eastern Europe 1919–75*. Vol. 3 (Oxford, 1986).

Kavan, J., 'Czechoslovakia 1968. Workers and Students', *Critique 2*, pp. 61–70.

Kawecka-Wyrzykowska, E. (ed.), *Stosunki Polski z unia europejska* (Warsaw, 2002).

Keane, J., *Václav Havel: a Political Tragedy in Six Acts* (London, 1999).

Kemme, D. (ed.), *Economic Reform in Poland: the Aftermath of Martial Law, 1981–88* (London, 1991).

Kenney, P., *A Carnival of Revolution. Central Europe 1989* (Princeton, 2002).

Király, B.K. and Jonas, P. (eds), *The Hungarian Revolution in Retrospect* (Boulder, 1977).

Klatt, W., 'The Politics of Economic Reforms', *Survey* 70 (1969), pp. 154–65.

Kołakowski, L., *Marxism and Beyond* (London, 1968).

Kołakowski, L, 'The Fate of Marxism in Eastern Europe', *Slavic Review* 29 (1970), pp. 175–81.

Kołakowski, L., 'My Correct Views on Everything. A Rejoinder to Edward Thompson's "Open Letter to Leszek Kołakowski"', *Socialist Register* (1974), pp. 1–20.

Kołakowski, L., 'Amidst Moving Ruins', *Daedalus* (Spring 1992), pp. 43–56.

Kolosi, T., *A terhes babapiskóta* (Budapest, 2000).

Kolosi, T. and Wnuk-Lipiński, E., *Equality and Inequality under Socialism: Poland and Hungary Compared* (London, 1983).

Konrád, G., *Antipolitics. An Essay* (London, 1984).

Konrád, G. and Szelényi, I., *The Intellectuals on the Road to Class Power* (London, 1979).

Kopacsi, S. *In the Name of the Working Class* (London, 1989).

Korbonski, A., 'The Prospects for Change in Eastern Europe', *Slavic Review* 31 (1974), pp. 219–39.

Kornai, J., *The Road to a Free Economy* (New York, 1990).

Kornai, J., *Vision and Reality, Market and State* (New York, 1990).

Kornai, J., *From Socialism to Capitalism* (London, 1998).

Körösényi, A., *Government and Politics in Hungary* (Budapest, 1999).

Kosík, K., *The Crisis of Modernity. Essays and Observations from the 1968 Era*, ed. J.H. Satterwhite (Lanham, MD, 1995).

Kovrig, B., *Communism in Hungary: from Kun to Kádár* (Stanford, 1979).

Kramer, J.M., 'Drug Abuse in Eastern Europe', *Slavic Review* 49 (1990), pp. 18–31.

Kramer, J.M., 'Eastern Europe and the "Energy Shock", 1990–91', *Problems of Communism* 3 (1991), pp. 85–96.

Kramer, M. 'Polish workers and the post-communist tradition, 1989–93', *Communist and Post-Communist Studies* 28 (1995), pp. 71–114.

Krastev, I., 'Party Structure and Party Perspectives in Bulgaria', *Journal of Communist Studies and Transition Politics* 13 (1997), pp. 91–106.

Krejči, J., *Social Change and Social Stratification in Post-War Czechoslovakia* (London, 1972).

Křen, J., *Bíla místa v našib dějinách?* (Prague, 1990).

Kurti, L., 'Hierarchy and Workers' Power in a Csepel Factory', *Journal of Communist Studies* 6 (1990), pp. 61–84.

Kusin, V., 'Overview of East European Reformism', *Soviet Studies* 28 (1976), pp. 338–61.

Kusin, V., *From Dubček to Charter 1977. A Study of 'Normalisation' in Czechoslovakia, 1968–78* (Edinburgh, 1978).

Kusin, W. *Political Grouping in the Czechoslovak Reform Movement* (London, 1972).

Laba, R., 'Worker Roots of Solidarity', *Problems of Communism* (July–August 1986), pp. 47–67.

Laba, R., *The Roots of Solidarity: The Political Sociology of Poland's Working Class Democratization* (Princeton, 1991).

Landis, Z. and Tomaszewski, J., *The Polish Economy in the Twentieth Century* (London, 1985).

Lane, D. and Kolankiewicz, G., *Social Groups in Polish Society* (London, 1973).

Latter, R., *European Security and Defence*. Wilton Park Paper, no. 90 (HMSO, 1994).

Lewis, D. and McKenzie, J.R.P. (eds), *The New Germany: Social, Political and Cultural Challenges of Unification* (Exeter, 1995).

Lewis, P.G., *Central Europe since 1945* (London, 1991).

Lewis, P.G., *Political Parties in Post-Communist Eastern Europe* (London, 2000).

Lilley, C.S., *Power and Persuasion. Ideology and Rhetoric in Communist Yugoslavia 1944–53* (Boulder, 2001).

Litván, G., *The Hungarian Revolution of 1956* (London, 1996).

Lomax, B., *Hungary 1956* (London, 1976).

Lomax, B., 'Obstacles to the Development of Democratic Politics', *Journal of Communist Studies* 10: 3 (September 1994), pp. 81–100.

Lomax, B., 'The Strange Death of "Civil Society" in Post-Communist Hungary', *Journal of Communist Studies and Transition Politics* 13 (1997), pp. 41–63.

Lorentzen, A. and Rostgard, M. (eds), *The Aftermath of 'Real Existing Socialism' in Eastern Europe*. Vol. 2 (London, 1997).

Łoś, M. and Zybertowicz, A., *Privatizing the Police-state: the Case of Poland* (London, 2000).

Lovenduski, J. and Woodall, J., *Politics and Society in Eastern Europe* (London, 1987).

Lydall, H., *Yugoslav Socialism. Theory and Practice* (Oxford, 1984).

Lydall, H., *Yugoslavia in Crisis* (Oxford, 1989).

McAdams, A. James, *Judging the Past in Unified Germany* (Cambridge, 2001).

Magaš, B., *The Destruction of Yugoslavia. Tracking the Break-Up, 1980–1992* (London, 1993)

Malcolm, N., *Kosovo. A Short History* (London, 1998).

Marković, M. and Cohen, R., *Yugoslavia. The Rise and Fall of Socialist Humanism, a History of the 'Praxis' Group* (Nottingham, 1975).

Mason, D.S., *Public Opinion and Political Change in Poland, 1980–1982* (Cambridge, 1985).

Mayhew, A., *Recreating Europe. The European Union's Policy Towards Central and Eastern Europe* (Cambridge, 1998).

Meier, V., 'Yugoslavia's National Question', *Problems of Communism* (March–April 1983), pp. 47–60.

Merta, V., *Songs for a Velvet Revolution* (Prague, 1994).

Mervin, D., *George Bush and the Guardianship Presidency* (Basingstoke, 1996).

Mešić, S., *Kako smo srušili Jugoslaviju. Politički memoari* (Zagreb, 1992).

Michnik, A., *Letters from Prison and Other Essays* (Berkeley, 1987).

Michnik, A., *Letters from Freedom: Post-Cold War Realities and Perspectives* (Berkeley, 1998).

Milenkovitch, M. and Milenkovitch, D. (eds), *Milovan Djilas. Parts of a Lifetime* (New York, 1975).

Miller, N.J. 'Nonconformists: Dobrica Ćosić and Mićo Popović Envision Serbia', *Slavic Review* 58 (1999), pp. 518–36.

Minamizuka, S. (ed.), *The Transformation of the Systems of East-Central Europe. Rural Societies Before and After 1989* (Kecskemét, 1996).

Mitchell, B.R. (ed.), *International Historical Statistics. Europe 1750–1993* (London, 1998).

Mlynář, Z., *Night Frost in Prague* (London, 1980).

Modrow, H., *Aufbruch und Ende* (Hamburg, 1991).

Mokrzycki, E., 'The Legacy of Real Socialism and Western Democracy', *Studies in Comparative Communism* 24 (1991), pp. 211–17.

Morris, L.P., *Eastern Europe Since 1945* (London, 1984).

Morton, H.W., 'Housing Problems and Policies of Eastern Europe and the Soviet Union', *Studies in Comparative Communism* 12 (1979), pp. 300–21.

Moser, C.A., *Theory and History of the Bulgarian Transition* (Sofia, 1994).

Müller, K., *The Political Economy of Pension Reform in Central-Eastern Europe* (Cheltenham, 1999).

Müller, R., *Die Rolle des Fernsehens während des politischen Umbruchs in Bulgarien 1989–91* (Hamburg, 1992).

Munck, G., 'Bringing Postcommunist Studies into Democratization Studies', *Slavic Review* 56 (1997), pp. 542–50.

Myant, M., *Poland: A Crisis for Socialism* (London, 1982).

Myant, M., *The Czechoslovak Economy 1948–88* (Cambridge, 1989).

Nagy, I., *Imre Nagy on Communism. In Defence of the New Course* (London, 1957).

Naimark, N. and Gibianski, L. *Establishing Communist Regimes in Eastern Europe 1944–49* (Westview Press, 1997).

Navrátil, J. (chief ed.), *The Prague Spring 1968: a National Security Archive Documents Reader* (Budapest, 1998).

Neubert, E., *Geschichte der Opposition in der DDR 1949–1990*, 2nd extended edn (Berlin, 1998).

Noam, E., *Telecommunications in Europe* (Oxford, 1992).

Nowak, S., 'Value Systems and Social Change in Contemporary Poland', *The Polish Sociological Bulletin* 14 (1982, published 1986), pp. 119–32.

Okey, R., 'The Legacy of Massacre: The "Jasenovac Myth" and the Breakdown of Communist Yugoslavia', in M. Levene and P. Roberts (eds), *The Massacre in History* (Oxford, 1999), pp. 263–83.

Ost, D., *Solidarity and the Politics of Anti-Politics, Opposition and Reform in Poland Since 1968* (Philadelphia, 1990).

Otáhal, M., *Opozice, moc, společnost 1969–1989* (Prague, 1994).

Owen, D., *Balkan Odyssey*, (London, 1995).

Paloczi-Horvath, G., *In Darkest Hungary* (London, 1964).

Partos, G., 'Hungarian–Soviet Relations', in A. Pravda (ed.) *The End of the Outer Empire. Soviet–East European Relations in Transition 1985–90* (London, 1992), pp. 120–50.

Pavković, A., 'The Serb National Idea: A Revival 1986–92', *Slavic Review and East European Review* 72 (1994), pp. 440–55.

Pehe, J. (ed.), *The Prague Spring: A Mixed Legacy* (New York, 1988).

Pelikán, J (ed.), *The Czechoslovak Political Trials, 1950–54* (London, 1971).

Pittaway, M., 'Industrial Workers, Socialist Industrialisation and the State in Hungary, 1948–1958' (Liverpool PhD, 1998).

Pogany, I. (ed.), *Human Rights in Eastern Europe* (Aldershot, 1995).

Pogany, I., *Righting Wrongs in Eastern Europe* (Manchester, 1997).

Poland: the State of the Republic. Two reports by the Experience and the Future Discussion Group (DiP) Warsaw (London, 1981).

Polonsky, A. and Drukier, B. (eds), *The Beginnings of Communist Rule in Poland* (London, 1980).

Popov, N. (ed.), *The Road to War in Serbia* (Budapest, 1996).

Porket, J.L., 'Czechoslovak Women under Soviet-style Socialism', *Slavonic and East European Review* 59 (1981), pp. 241–63.

Power and Opposition in Post-Revolutionary Societies (London, 1979).

Poznanski, K.Z., *Poland's Protracted Revolution. Internal Change and Economic Growth 1970–1994* (Cambridge, 1996).

Pozsgay, I., 'Life and Politics', reprinted from *The Hungarian Quarterly* 39: 112 (Winter 1988).

Pravda, A. (ed.) *The End of the Outer Empire. Soviet–East European Relations in Transition 1985–90* (London, 1992).

Privatization in the Transition Process: Recent Experiences in Eastern Europe (Geneva, 1994).

Przeworski, A., *Democracy and the Market. Political and Economic Reforms in Eastern Europe and Latin America* (Cambridge, 1991).

Rady, M., *Romania in Turmoil* (London, 1992).

Rady, M., 'Minority Rights and Self-Determination in Contemporary Eastern Europe. Review Article', *Slavonic and East European Review* 71 (1993), pp. 717–28.

Rai, S., Pilkington, H. and Phizaklea, A. (eds), *Women in the Face of Change. The Soviet Union, Eastern Europe and China* (London, 1992).

Raina, P., *Political Opposition in Poland 1954–77* (London, 1978).

Rakovski, M. (pseud.), *Towards an East European Marxism* (London, 1978).

Ramet, P., *Nationalism and Federalism in Yugoslavia 1963–1983* (Bloomington, 1984).

Ramet, P., 'Religious Ferment in Eastern Europe', *Survey* 123 (1984), pp. 87–116.

Ramet, P. (ed.), *Yugoslavia in the 1980s* (Boulder, 1985).

Ramet, P., *Cross and Commissar* (Bloomington, 1987).

Ramet, P. (ed.), *Religion and Nationalism in Soviet and East European Politics* (Durham and London, 1989).

Ramet, S.P., Slovenia's Road to Democracy, *Europe–Asia Studies* 45 (1993), pp. 869–86.

Ramet, S.P., *Balkan Babel. The Disintegration of Yugoslavia* (Boulder, 1992).

Reisinger, W., 'The International Regime of Soviet–East European Economic Relations', *Slavic Review* 49 (1990), pp. 554–67.

Remington, R.A. (ed.), *Winter in Prague. Documents on Czechoslovak Communism in Crisis* (London, 1969).

Ringen, S. and Wallace, C. (eds), *Societies in Transition. East–Central Europe Today.* Vol. 1 (Avebury, 1994).

Riordan, J. (ed.), *Sport under Communism*, 2nd edn (London, 1981).

Robinson, W.R., *Patterns of Reform in Hungary* (New York, 1971).

Roeder, P.S., 'Ten Years After 1989', *Slavic Review* 58 (1999), pp. 743–81.

Rothschild, J., *Return to Diversity. A Political History of East Central Europe Since World War II*, 2nd edn (New York, 1993).

Rueschemeyer, M. (ed.), *Women in the Politics of Postcommunist Eastern Europe* (New York, 1994).

Rupnik, J., *The Other Europe* (London, 1988).

Rusinow, D., *The Yugoslav Experiment 1948–1974* (London, 1977).

Sachs, J., *Poland's Jump to the Market Economy* (Cambridge, Mass., 1994).

Sanford, G., 'The Polish Communist Leadership and the Onset of the State of War', *Soviet Studies* 36 (1984), pp. 494–512.

Saunders, C.T. (ed.), *Eastern Europe in Crisis and the Way Out* (Basingstoke, 1995).

Schmitter, P.C. and Karl, T.L., 'The Conceptual Travels of Transitologists and Consolidologists. How Far to the East Should They Attempt to Go?', *Slavic Review* 53 (1994), pp. 173–85.

Schöpflin, G., 'The Stalinist Experience in Eastern Europe', *Survey* 30: 3 (1988), pp. 124–47.

Schöpflin, G., *Politics in Eastern Europe: 1945–92* (Oxford, 1993).

Schöpflin, G., *Nations, Identity, Power. The New Politics of Europe* (London, 2000).

Schöpflin, G. and Woods, N. (eds), *In Search of Central Europe* (London, 1989).

Schwermer, H., *The Velvet Revolution. Czechoslovakia, November–December 1989* (Staffordshire Polytechnic, 1990).

Scott, H., *Women and Socialism. Experiences from Eastern Europe* (London, 1976).

Seroka, J., 'Economic Stabilization and Communal Politics in Yugoslavia', *Journal of Communist Studies* 5 (1989), pp. 131–47.

Shawcross, W., *Crime and Compromise. János Kádár and the Politics of Hungary since the Revolution* (London, 1974).

Shawcross, W., *Dubček* (London, 1990).

Shepherd, R.H., *Czechoslovakia. The Velvet Revolution and Beyond* (Basingstoke, 2000).

Shoup, P., *Communism and the Yugoslav National Question* (New York, 1968).

Šik, O., *The Bureaucratic Economy* (New York, 1972).

Silber, L., *The Death of Yugoslavia* (London, 1995).

Šimečka, M., *The Restoration of Order. The Normalization of Czechoslovakia, 1969–1976* (London, 1984).

Simmons, M., *The Reluctant President. The Political Life of Václav Havel* (London, 1991).

Simms, B., *Unfinest Hour. Britain and the Destruction of Bosnia* (London, 2002).

Sinanian, S., Deak, J. and Ludz, P. (eds), *Eastern Europe in the 1970s* (New York, 1972).

Singleton, F., *Twentieth-Century Yugoslavia* (London, 1976).

Singleton, T. and Carter, B., *The Economy of Yugoslavia* (London, 1982).

Sirc, L., *The Yugoslav Economy under Self-Management* (London, 1979).

Sjöberg, Ö. and Wygan, M.L. (eds), *Economic Change in the Balkan States: Albania, Bulgaria, Romania and Yugoslavia* (London, 1991).

Skilling, H.G., *Czechoslovakia's Interrupted Revolution* (New York, 1976).

Skilling, H.G., *Charter 77 and Human Rights in Czechoslovakia* (London, 1981).

Skilling, H.G., 'Independent Historiography in Czechoslovakia', *Canadian Slavonic Papers* 25 (1983), pp. 518–35.

Skilling, H.G., 'Independent Currents in Czechoslovakia', *Problems of Communism* (January–February 1985), pp. 32–49.

Slabek, H., 'The Peasants in Polish Society, 1949–70', *Acta Poloniae Historica* 59 (1989).

Spring, D.W. (ed.), *The Impact of Gorbachev. The First Phase, 1985–90* (London, 1991).

Staniszkis, J., *Poland's Self-Limiting Revolution* (Princeton, 1984).

Staniszkis, J., *The Ontology of Socialism* (Oxford, 1992).

Staniszkis, J., *Post-Communism: the Emerging Enigma* (Warsaw, 1999).

Stern, J.P., 'Soviet Energy Prospects in the 1980s', *The World Today* (May 1980), pp. 188–94.

Stokes, G., Lampe, J. and Rusinow, D., 'Instant History; Understanding the Wars of Yugoslav Secession', *Slavic Review* 55 (1996), pp. 136–60.

Sudetic, C., *Blood and Vengeance: One Family's Story of the War in Bosnia* (New York, 1998).

Sugar, P.F. (ed.), *Ethnic Diversity and Conflict in Eastern Europe* (Santa Barbara, 1980).

Swain, G. and Swain, N., *Eastern Europe Since 1945* (London, 1993).

Swain, N., *Hungary: the Rise and Fall of Feasible Socialism* (London, 1992).

Swatos, W.H. Jnr, *Politics and Religion in Central and Eastern Europe* (Westport, 1994).

Szacki, J., *Liberalism after Communism* (Budapest, 1995).

Szalai, E., 'Political and Social Conflict Arising from the Transformation of

Property Relations in Hungary', *Journal of Communist Studies* 10 (1994), pp. 56–77.

Szczepański, J., *Polish Society* (New York, 1970).

Szczepański, J., 'Societal developments', *Polish Perspectives* 27 (1985), pp. 5–13.

Szelényi, I., 'The Position of the Intelligentsia in the Class Structure of State Socialist Societies', *Critique* 10–11 (Winter–Spring, 1978–79).

Szelényi, I., *Urban Inequalities under State Socialism* (Oxford, 1983).

Szelényi, I., *Embourgeoisement in Rural Hungary* (London, 1988).

Tarkowski, J., 'Old and New Forms of Corruption in Poland and the USSR', *Telos* 80 (Summer 1989), pp. 51–62.

Tatur, M., 'Catholicism and Modernization in Poland', *Journal of Communist Studies* 7 (1991), pp. 335–49.

Teichova, A., *The Czechoslovak Economy 1918–1980* (London, 1988).

Terrett, S., *The Dissolution of Yugoslavia and the Badinter Arbitration Commission* (Aldershot, 2000).

Thomas, R., *Serbia under Milošević* (London, 1999).

Thompson, E.P., 'An Open Letter to Leszek Kołakowski', *Socialist Register* 1973, pp. 1–100.

Tighe, C., *The Politics of Literature: Poland 1945–89* (Cardiff, 1999).

Tismaneanu, V., 'Ceausescu's Socialism', *Problems of Communism* (January–February 1985), pp. 50–66.

Tismaneanu, V., (ed.), *In Search of Civil Society. Independent Peace Movements in the Soviet Bloc* (New York and London, 1990).

Tismaneanu, V., (ed.) *The Revolutions of 1989* (London, 2000).

Todorova, M., *Imagining the Balkans* (Oxford, 1997).

Tőkés, L., *With God, for the People* (London, 1990).

Tőkés, R.L. (ed.), *Opposition in Eastern Europe* (Baltimore, 1979).

Tőkés, R.L., *Hungary's Negotiated Revolution* (Cambridge, 1996).

Torańska, T. (ed.), *Oni. Stalin's Polish puppets* (London, 1987).

Touraine, A. (ed.), *Solidarity. The Analysis of a Social Movement. Poland 1980–82* (Cambridge, 1983).

Triska, J. (ed.), *Blue Collar Workers in Eastern Europe* (London, 1981).

Triska, J. and Cocks, P. (eds), *Political Development in Eastern Europe* (New York and London, 1977).

Tyrmand, L., 'The Hair-Styles of Miecysław Rakowski', *Survey* 116 (1982), pp. 165–81.

Uvalić, M., *Investment and Property Rights in Yugoslavia* (Cambridge, 1992).

Uvalić, M., *Privatization in Disintegrating East European States: the Case of Former Yugoslavia*, EUI Working Paper. RSC No. 1994/11 (Florence, 1994).

Valenta, J., *Soviet Intervention in Czechoslovakia, 1968* (Baltimore, 1979).

van Brabant, J.M., *Industrial Policy in Eastern Europe* (London, 1993).

van Brabant, J.M., *The Political Economy of Transition* (London, 1998).

Verdery, K., 'Nationalism and National Sentiment in Post-Socialist Romania', *Slavic Review* 52 (1993), pp. 179–203.

Verdery, K., *What was Socialism, and What Comes Next?* (Princeton, 1996).

Vickers, M., *The Albanians. A Modern History* (London, 1995).

Vickers, M. and Pettifor, J., *Albania. From Anarchy to a Balkan Identity* (London, 1997).

Vladislav, J. (ed.), *Václav Havel. Living in Truth* (London, 1987).

Wachtel, A.B., *Making a Nation, Breaking a Nation. Literature and Cultural Politics in Yugoslavia* (Stanford, 1998).

Wachtel, H.L., *Workers' Management and Workers' Wages in Yugoslavia. The Theory and Practice of Participatory Socialism* (Ithaca, 1978).

Waller, M., 'The Ecology Issue in Eastern Europe', *Journal of Communist Studies* 5, (1989), pp. 303–28.

Wandycz, P.S., *The Price of Freedom* (London, 1992).

Wedel, J.R., *Collision and Collusion. The Strange Case of Western Aid to Eastern Europe, 1989–1998* (London, 1998).

West, R., *Tito and the Rise and Fall of Yugoslavia* (London, 1994).

Wheaton, B. and Kavan, Z., *The Velvet Revolution: Czechoslovakia, 1988–1991* (Boulder, 1992).

White, S., Batt, J. and Lewis, P.G. (eds), *Developments in East European Politics* (London, 1993).

Williams, K., 'New Sources on Soviet Decision Making during 1968 in Czechoslovakia', *Europe–Asia Studies* 48 (1996), pp. 457–70.

Wolchik, S.L., 'The Status of Women in the Socialist Order in Czechoslovakia, 1948–1978', *Slavic Review* 38 (1979), pp. 583–602.

Wolchik, S.L., *Czechoslovakia in Transition* (London, 1991).

Wolf, C., *Parting from Phantoms. Selected Writings, 1990–94* (Chicago, 1997).

Wolff. R.L., *The Balkans in our Time* (Cambridge, Mass., 1956).

Wydra, H., *Continuity in Poland's Permanent Transition* (London, 2000).

Zaubermann, A., 'The East European Economies', *Problems of Communism* (April 1978), pp. 55–70.

Zecchini, S. (ed.), *Lessons from the Economic Transition. Central and Eastern Europe in the 1990s* (London, 1997).

Zeman, Z.A.B., *The Making and Breaking of Eastern Europe* (Oxford, 1991).

Zubek, W., 'The Phoenix out of the Ashes. The Rising Power of Poland's Post-Communist SdRP', *Communist and Post-Communist Studies* 29 (1995), pp. 273–306.

Zvosec, C., 'Environmental Deterioration in Eastern Europe', *Survey* 123 (1981), pp. 117–41.

Index